OPEN WOUND

My Physical, Psychological and Philosophical Journey through the War in Vietnam

By Robert Richert

pg 175

To Rodney & Rosemary,
I wish you all the
Best!

Robert D. Richert

i

Praise for *Open Wound*

"The literature on the Vietnam War is huge and ever growing as Americans continue to wrestle with the enigma of a conflict that tore apart our social consensus and largely altered the perceptions we held of our national purpose and destiny. What is sometimes missing in this search for meaning is the sense of the personal. What was the human face of this war? Who were the men and women who found themselves embedded in an event of unimaginable complexity? Robert Richert gives us one answer. He offers us a vivid and detailed examination of a young man thrust into the heat of the war. It's an honest and probing look into the events that deeply affected him and how he dealt with the consequences of his experiences. *Open Wound* will help readers understand the depth and intensity of the decade's long conflict that left a lasting wound on the American psyche."

—Craig Hendricks, historian, author

"Robert's memoir includes the good, the bad and the ugly about the Vietnam War. Some moments will shock you, some will surprise you and some are darned right charming. It's a good read and I recommend it."

—Noel Markham, mystery writer

"This book is a must read for anyone who thinks the life of a soldier in war is glamorous. Richert writes of his experiences in Vietnam in detail: The miserable rainy nights sleeping on the ground, the days of drudgery punctuated by sudden moments of horror, and the loss of control over his life. *Open Wound* offers a welcome antidote to the popular, but fictitious Rambo image. Buy it for your son or daughter before he or she enlists!"

—Rachael Lehmberg, author

"Witty and enthralling; Robert takes you inside every aspect of a soldier's life."

—David Silva, Political Activist, Writer

Dedication

I dedicate my book to all who served and sacrificed during the Vietnam War, to their families, and to the Vietnamese people.

Acknowledgements

Special thanks to the therapists at the Long Beach, California VA, and my family and friends, for your encouragement, assistance and advice. Without you, this book would not have been possible.

Robert Richert

Ray
(310) 850-5842 ✓

Preface

From mid-June, 1969 to mid-December, 1969, I served as a rifleman and assistant machine gunner with the US Army's 23rd Infantry Division, called Americal. The Division encompassed the northeastern section of the Republic of South Vietnam. After serving seven months in the Americal, the army disbanded a portion of the division and its soldiers were reassigned to various other units within country. Between late December, 1969 and the end of my tour in early June, 1970, I was stationed first at an artillery base called Landing Zone Gator, and then at another artillery base called Arty Hill. I pulled guard duty throughout the night at both locations.

I saw combat on several occasions during my one year in Vietnam and came close to being killed or wounded by the enemy at least three times—that I know about! That being said, most of our unit's firefights were light compared to those of other infantrymen who served in this war. For example, I never experienced sustained contact with the enemy, battles lasting for hours or days, and I never engaged in hand to hand combat. However, as you shall see, firefights are not the only dangerous situations in a combat zone. Like almost every infantry soldier who served in Vietnam, some of my wartime experiences haunt me to this day. I was diagnosed with Post Traumatic Stress Disorder (PTSD) at the Long Beach, California, VA Hospital in 2012.

I emphasize that this is not a book about a wannabe war hero— far from it! Many works of literature, TV programs, and movies have romanticized war and glorified the adventures of soldiering, but my book is most emphatically not intended to be among their ranks. The Vietnam War I experienced was an arduous, brutal, and ugly affair. Although I had no qualms about firing at the Viet Cong (VC) or North Vietnamese Army (NVA) during an attack, I saw no glory or honor in killing, or in the war effort as a whole. Instead, I choose to direct my feelings of glory and honor toward most—but not all, as you shall see later—of my fellow soldiers who had to endure this unpopular and difficult war.

The Vietnam experience motivated the American public and our leaders to rethink America's place on the world stage, the relationship between military and political decision makers, how and under what circumstances the US should become involved in the internal conflicts of other nations, and how future wars should be conducted. Decades after the war, many of our Vietnam veterans continue to suffer from survival guilt, substance abuse, anger issues, alienation, homelessness, and sadly for some, the finality of suicide. Like an enormous cleaver, the long, costly conflict divided and wounded our nation and the soldiers who served in it like no other since the Civil War. Although some healing has taken place, the war in Vietnam remains an *Open Wound* that lingers to this day.

Writing and Memory

Recalling details accurately about life in the infantry more than 40 years after they occurred presented a daunting task. For example, I remember only a handful of my fellow infantry soldier's names, and then either a first or last. I don't remember the names of most of the places our unit operated, or the dates. While I learned and practiced those things necessary to be prepared for combat, knowledge of detailed geographical information and military tactics was not required of a low ranking grunt like me.

In light of the above information, initially I felt trepidation about relating my experiences so long after they occurred. During the process I often asked myself, *is this how it really happened? Am I taking elements from a memory of one event and attaching it to another?* Fortunately, my mom saved every letter I sent home from Vietnam. Written at the time and place of actual events, they filled in some long forgotten details. Mom also saved a ninety-minute long audio cassette containing several stories from the infantry I recorded at an artillery base during the month of February, 1970. Throughout my book I have included several excerpts from my letters and the audiotape. An added bonus is re-reading my letters and listening to the audiotape helped me to better recall details of other experiences for which my memory had faded. However, so as not to contribute to my family's already high level of anxiety, I avoided writing home about most of my combat episodes. Those are left solely to memory.

In writing this memoir:

- I found it necessary to recreate the dialogue in this book, but in each case I have attempted to capture the gist of the original conversations.
- I researched information about the war on the internet in order to supplement details lost to memory, or due to my lack of knowledge.
- Most books about Vietnam include the names and numerical designations of weapons, units, and locations. I tried to keep these details at a minimum because I think they are of interest only to those who served in Vietnam. I seek a wider audience.
- Out of respect for their privacy and because I did not seek and receive their permission, I changed all my fellow soldier's names and invented names for those I forgot. Inventing names allows for a smoother literary flow.
- Throughout my book I made a stoic effort not to over glorify or hype the substance of a story. My intention is to capture the spirit, essence, and main message to the best of my ability.

I have been writing about my experiences in Vietnam since advised by doctors during therapy sessions at the VA Mental Health Center in 2013, and through creative writing classes I attended at the facility. At first I spewed out a few short essays, but the process kept snowballing. I kept writing and writing and the result is this book. This process has greatly helped to improve my emotional well-being. Now I understand the symptoms associated with PTSD and how to better cope with them. I am wiser, happier, more content, and on the road to healing.

Thank you VA! Thank you America!

Table of Contents

CHAPTER 1

A Face of War

The Trigger

On a spring morning in 2012, I busily brushed acrylic paint on a canvas at my art studio located on the second floor of a commercial building near my home. All of a sudden I heard a loud, crackling *ZAP!* Simultaneously, my computer screen flashed brightly, turned off, and the room lights went out. "Jeez!" I jumped from my chair and scurried to the window. I guessed a car hit a telephone pole causing a power failure. It wouldn't be the first time. At first glance I didn't see anything unusual. Next, I noticed a small stream of white smoke rising from the pavement about 120 feet down the alley, but I didn't see flames. *Weird.* A few seconds later and from under the rising smoke, a strong, but muffled explosion rocked the area. My window rattled and I felt a shock wave. Simultaneously, a six-foot square section of the alley rose about a foot into the air and then crashed down. *What the hell was that?*

I hurried downstairs to obtain a better look and find out what happened. Several of the building occupants began gathering outside, and many expressed curiosity and concern. Someone suggested an underground transformer had exploded, which later

1

turned out to be true. Fortunately, no one was nearby when the blast occurred. An explosion capable of blowing a large section of concrete into the air requires a force similar to that of a hand grenade. I moved forward and noticed a manhole in the middle of the blown off section of pavement. Something about the eerie scene began agitating my nerves. *What's wrong with me? It's just a freak explosion—not such a big deal.* Then, like a punch in the stomach, I made the connection. The muffled sound of the underground explosion and sight of the manhole triggered a flashback from the Vietnam War. Memories of one terrible day 43 years earlier came streaming through my mind like rounds through a machine gun. Just as I was ready to leave, my friend and fellow artist, Robert, who also rented space in the building, drove up and parked.

Spotting me, he came forward and asked, "What's going on?"

I told him about the explosion. He noticed I appeared more upset than the others gathered.

Robert asked, "Are you okay? What's wrong?"

"I'm okay. The power's out, and who knows for how long. There's no sense hanging around, so I'm going home. I'll catch you later."

I offered a reasonable explanation and I think Robert bought it, but it was a half-truth. I couldn't wait to get the hell out of there. I rushed to my van and drove home. For the remainder of the day I couldn't shake the anxiety.

For weeks after the explosion, I had difficulty concentrating on my work and my sleep cycle became erratic. Memories of Vietnam dominated my thoughts, and nightmares occurred at least three times a week. By summer of 2012, I decided I had enough. I sought help at the VA, and they assigned me to individual and group therapy sessions. During treatment I managed to jot down the gist of one recurrent bad dream that haunted me worse than the others.

A Face of War

His demonic face hovers menacingly over my bed. I'm terrified. I want to scream but cannot. I want to strike out, but cannot. I am frozen with fear and cannot twitch a muscle.

Totally helpless, I am at his mercy. I don't see a body at all, just a bizarre, distorted manifestation of his Asian face—like a threatening Samurai mask. The mouth is slightly open in a distorted Mona Lisa half-smile, but it isn't a friendly expression. Perhaps it is gleeful hate. The cheekbones are abnormally wide and protruding, and his large, piercing black eyes slant upward and back. They see right through me. The demon does not speak—he need not. I know who he is and why he torments me night after night. He seeks revenge for my killing him. I wake up in a sweat and my sheets are soaked. I'm shaking like a scared rabbit and my heart is pounding, pounding. In an effort to calm my nerves and regain my composure, I get out of bed and look around my home seeking reassurance that no one is there.

Like a cleaver, the explosion in the alley opened up an emotionally painful wound from Vietnam. For more than forty years I told no one about the following incident—not my parents, not my brother or sister, not my girlfriend, none of my friends, and not even members of my platoon. Now, with the help of three years of therapy, I am finally able to share with you.

One Terrible Day in Vietnam

I'm sure the incident occurred during my first two months in Vietnam, but I don't remember the date and location. Although I recall the traumatic aspect of the following story clearly, my memory of details is hazy because for years I tried suppressing the experience. I have filled in the gaps with what I believe are probable or possible occurrences.

One hot, steamy morning, the 90 men in my infantry company conducted an inspection of a Vietnamese hamlet. Like ninety-percent of their fellow countrymen, the residents eked out a sparse living by growing and harvesting rice. Unless we received fire or possessed accurate intelligence going in, it was nearly impossible to distinguish between friendly, neutral, and hostile villages in rural

3

areas. The Viet Cong dressed in civilian attire and easily blended in with the locals.

My platoon secured the dirt road leading into the village. We saw no signs of the enemy. Meanwhile, two other platoons busily inspected huts, which we called hooches, and searched for tunnel entrances. The Vietnamese people dug like gophers. Many rural villages contained hidden tunnels which led to one or more underground chambers or bunkers. The Viet Cong used them to hide and store arms and supplies.

During an attack, the VC commonly hit our forces then quickly retreated or hid underground until US soldiers left the area. To complicate matters, the bunkers also served to shelter women, children, and the elderly from our napalm bombs, artillery, and firefights. Sometimes men of military age, although not VC, also hid because they feared intense grilling from the South Vietnamese interpreters who often accompanied our forces. Any young men found hiding were handed over to the South Vietnamese Army for further interrogation.

Apparently radio traffic became busy or garbled. Frustrated, my platoon sergeant ordered me to enter the village, gather more information, and report back. Although the entire area had been secured, I carried a full pack along with my weapons the few hundred feet to the village compound.

Our company captain was nowhere in sight, but, I noticed a lieutenant I didn't recognize and approached; "Sir—private Richert, third platoon. My platoon sergeant sent me to find out what is going on."

The lieutenant replied, "Nothing we can't handle. Your platoon will remain guarding the road until we sort things out."

Suddenly, a soldier came forward and announced the discovery of a tunnel entrance that had been hidden under some items stored in a nearby shed. After a brief check of the area, the lieutenant noticed three grenades hanging on my rucksack.

He asked, "How long have you been in country, private?"

"A couple of months, sir."

"Okay, I need a good man to toss a grenade into this tunnel entrance. Are you up for it?"

4

"No problem, sir."

I felt trepidation because although I had tossed grenades during training back in the states, this would be my first attempt within a potential combat situation. While grabbing the grenade from my rucksack strap, apprehension quickly gave way to a feeling of exhilaration—like the adrenaline rush pulsing through my boyhood veins when I set off fireworks. *Hell, I can do this.* Naturally, I was concerned some VC might be down in the bunker ready to attack anyone who peered into the two foot in diameter opening. *No way am I going to stick my head over that hole for a closer look.* In order to boost my confidence, I rationalized—*okay, there's probably no one down there, and if there is, they're likely cowering deep in a corner.*

While the other soldiers took cover nearby, I cautiously approached the tunnel entrance, located near the hut's bamboo wall. I squatted about three feet away, pulled the pin, extended my right hand over the entrance, tossed the grenade into the opening, shouted "Fire in the hole!" and scrambled to take cover with the others. Ten seconds later, the explosion produced a muffled, low frequency boom. *Huh, I'm surprised. I thought it would be loud, like in the movies.* I couldn't have known then that the unusual sound would reverberate in my head forty years later. After checking the immediate area to ensure all was safe, the lieutenant gave me an approving nod, and I returned to my platoon.

Thirty minutes later, word came down that four male bodies had been dug out of a bunker located below the tunnel entrance. It's likely some villagers had been given the unpleasant task of crawling down, searching, and hauling them out. No weapons were recovered. My platoon received orders to join the rest of the company. Although reticent about re-entering the hamlet, I simultaneously felt curious about seeing the results of my grenade toss. My platoon joined the others, and most soldiers stood around waiting for further orders.

From twenty feet away, I gazed upon the bodies. Each man had been laid on the ground side by side and face up. Probably because of intense heat and humidity inside the bunker, each wore only black or cream colored shorts and sandals. Each showed multiple shrapnel wounds, including potato-sized chunks of ripped away flesh, exposing underlying muscle, tissue, and bone. I expected worse. I expected to see bodies torn to pieces.

Are they VC or just civilians who feared our presence and thus, decided to hide? Would it ease my conscience to learn they are enemy soldiers? What went through their minds when they saw my grenade tumble into their bunker? Perhaps it was too dark and they never knew what hit them. I hope so. One thought stood out. These four men were the first I knew for sure died because of my actions in Vietnam. Unnerved, I retreated into myself and said little to the soldiers around me.

Moving closer for a better look at the bodies, I noticed, *oh no, that one is only a boy. He can't be more than 14 years old. What was he doing down there?* It felt like a dagger had pierced my heart. Just then I became momentarily distracted by the curious expression on the boy's unmarred face. *Is he smiling? Why is he smiling?* It wasn't a wide grin, more like the subtle twist in Da Vinci's famous painting of the Mona Lisa. *Was it a last minute grimace, a reflex action to terror that only mimicked a smile, or was he in the act of smiling just as the unanticipated grenade exploded?* I would never know, but his face became etched into my memory.

He's so young. He must belong to a family. I've taken his future away. I... A range of emotions, including guilt, remorse, and frustration, bounced around the inside of my head like a pinball. *STOP! Get a grip.* I looked at the soldiers around me and my demeanor suddenly shifted into soldier mode. I visualized one of the basic training drill sergeants scowling in my face, "Suck it up, Private Richert!" It's hard to describe accurately, but I detached my emotions from my actions. *It was the grenade, not me, that killed those men. I'll be okay.* My remedy for distress and guilt was to become emotionally numb. This feeling, or should I say lack of feeling, allowed me to carry on throughout the rest of the day, and for much of my tour.

When the mind distances itself from traumatic experiences, psychologists call it, *Dissociative Disorder.* I'm told this is a common reaction among soldiers who have harmed or killed their fellow human beings in combat situations. A detached mindset better enables a soldier to suppress the extreme emotional anxiety caused by his actions.

In time and to varying degrees, a soldier's psyche adjusts to the death and destruction of war. For me, not to the point where it became acceptable, but yes, tolerable to some degree. In order to maintain sanity, a soldier must harden his heart to this bitter reality. However, when a soldier leaves the battlefield for the comfort and security of home, his actions in combat inevitably clash with the moral norms of civil society. These contrasting conditions eventually become too much to bear and something has to give way. Guilt, anger, bitterness, and nightmares emerge and fester. Many years after the Vietnam War, this affliction came to be known as Post Traumatic Stress Disorder, PTSD.

For greater perspective, one more element of my story must be shared. The values I learned growing up influenced my beliefs about the ethics of war. During childhood I learned that games and life have rules and laws, and these are to be followed. My parents, coaches, and teachers taught me good sportsmanship—to accept losing gracefully, and to play fair. I was also taught to take responsibility for my actions.

Like most adolescent boys, I engaged in my share of fist fights, and sometimes they had to be postponed until after school. My adversary and I agreed where to meet, fought, and settled our dispute on the spot. I saw honor in this ritual and afterward, win or lose, I usually felt a degree of respect toward my opponent. Our crude ritual was a scaled down version the classic western showdown between two gunfighters who meet in the street, look each other in the eye, and draw their pistols. This common plot theme conveyed a message—honorable men follow a set of rules, even if they are not written down. On the other hand, men who ambush their adversaries or shoot them in the back are depicted as evil. Fifties and early sixties movies and TV shows typically drew clear moral lines between the good guys and the bad guys.

Echoing the ethics I learned during childhood, I regarded firefights in Vietnam as a more or less fair and honorable form of battle. In a firefight, the enemy shoots at you and you shoot back at them—a somewhat equivocal situation. I held no qualms about firing back when attacked, or about the potential of killing the enemy under such conditions. However, killing the three men and boy by

7

dropping a grenade down a hole is an entirely different matter. I saw it as one-sided and unfair. The men and boy cowering in the dark corners of a bunker never had a chance to fight back. It's not like the classic gunfight in which both parties faced an equal chance of suffering harm. *Tossing a grenade into a hole is no act of bravery. Anyone could do it.* I felt no honor or glory in carrying out the surreptitious act. In fact, I believed my act was cold, callous, and borderline cowardly. I felt like the bad guy in Westerns who shoots a man in the back. My actions on that day violated the ethical ideals of honor and fairness I learned in childhood.

Yes, I knew I was doing my duty. I knew those three men and even the boy may have been VC, and might have previously killed American soldiers. I knew in war terrible things happen and people die, and low ranking grunts like me are mere pawns in the process. All of the above was brought to my attention many years later in group therapy. Nonetheless, the gravity of my act and its ethical implications became so painful that guilt and anxiety eclipsed my reason. The therapy sessions I attended over forty years later motivated me to think deeply about that day in Vietnam, and eventually I found a glimmer of light at the end of this dark tunnel. Now I wish to share the following so that others may gain insight into dealing with horrible situations and moral dilemmas like mine.

I try to draw positive life lessons from adverse experiences. Adversity can be a great character builder. Thus, I chose to place myself in the underground bunker. If I could somehow switch places with the boy I killed on that terrible day, what would I say to him? Would I lash out in anger or hatred like the demon in my nightmares, or express empathy? I like to believe I would choose to ease his pain. I like to believe I would advise my killer; *I cannot place blame on you for your actions. By dropping the grenade into a dark hole, you were performing your duty as a soldier. I cannot fulfill my boyhood dreams, so I ask you to honor my short life by living yours to its fullest potential. Live your dreams and be a good person. This is what I ask of you.*

No, this philosophical switching of places has not cured me of guilt and nightmares, but it has helped to place the incident in the village in a more enlightened perspective, and thus, bring me solace.

Thanks to these insights the demon in my nightmares appeared less frequently.

Now that you have read my story perhaps you, like me, have come to understand the deeper meaning behind the *face of war* in my nightmares. The true meaning has revealed itself late in my life— thanks to the therapy I have received at the VA, along with considerable self-reflection. The horrible demon is *not* an apparition of the Vietnamese boy seeking revenge for my act of terror. No, it is not his ghost haunting me, but my own! The demon is a manifestation of my own deep-seated guilt and remorse. If the price I must pay for killing three men and boy on that terrible day in Vietnam is to suffer with guilt, nightmares, and sleeplessness, then so be it. I accept the responsibility.

CHAPTER 2

Caught in a Draft

"Parents can only give good advice or put them on the right paths, but the final forming of a person's character lies in their own hands."
Anne Frank, Diarist, Holocaust victim

In the previous chapter I shared how western movies and TV shows impacted my beliefs about combat. I believe every young man's upbringing, personality type, and social environment influence his attitude toward and behavior within military service. Thus, I think it important to share some information about my young life.

I grew up along with my older sister Joanne and younger brother Jim in a small three bedroom, one bathroom track home in Long Beach, California. My parents were not religious and the family did not attend church. Instead of founding our ethics on religion, Mom and Dad taught us kids time-tested American values such as honesty, respect for others, and to take responsibility for our actions. They punished us when we misbehaved, but they were not cold-hearted or rigidly authoritarian. They offered support, love, and affection. I compare my family upbringing with fifties and early sixties TV family shows like, *Ozzie and Harriet, Father Knows Best,* and *Leave it to Beaver.*

Dad used to say I was born happy. My personality is outgoing. People admire my sense of humor, and I easily make friends. I like people and they like me. My attitude toward life has been generally positive and optimistic. Passions include art, science, and nature. I've never been excited about macho pursuits like motorcycles and fast cars. In terms of physical challenges, I have never been a risk taker. Sky diving and diamond ski runs are not for me.

Many young men join the military because they feel a sense of duty and seek to serve their country. However, some join the most physically demanding services because they feel the need to assert their manhood. I saw no ego gratification in joining the Marine Corps, Army Airborne School, or Green Berets. I never wanted to be a soldier, and did not believe I was cut out for military life. Soldiering has never been part of my DNA.

Times of Tumult

"You have broader considerations that might follow what you would call the falling domino principle. You have a row of dominoes set up, you knock over the first one, and what will happen to the last one is a certainty that it will go over very quickly."
President Dwight D. Eisenhower; excerpt from a speech about the spread of Communism in Southeast Asia, 1954

Following Eisenhower, presidents Kennedy, Johnson, and Nixon frequently argued we must stop Communism in Vietnam or it would spread country by country like a cancer until it landed on America's doorsteps. During the fifties and into the sixties, most Americans, including me, agreed.

During 1965, the year I graduated from high school, the number of US troops sent to Vietnam increased by 160,000. The law allowed deferments for students seeking higher education. In 1966, I enrolled at my local community college. With the war escalating, the draft lurking in the background, and all of the civil unrest occurring in our

11

country, I had difficulty sustaining focus on my studies. I just wanted to have a good time and distance myself from the nation's problems. However, many of my friends were going off to war and the reality that sooner or later I might be joining them weighed heavily on my mind.

I planned to finish community college in June, 1968. At the beginning of my final year I thought; *will I have the grades to move forward to graduate school? If not, will I be drafted?* My feelings of uncertainty about the future swirled within the dark clouds of one the most turbulent and violent years in recent American history. A review of 1968 is in order:

January 23: Tensions are strained nearly to the breaking point between the US and North Korea. Claiming the American surveillance ship *Pueblo* strayed into their territorial waters, which the US vehemently denied, North Korea captures the ship and its crew. The crew was held prisoner for 11 months and the North Koreans never returned the vessel to the US.

January 30: Marks the beginning of the famous Tet Offensive in which 85,000 North Vietnamese Army and Viet Cong troops target 36 major cities and towns in South Vietnam. Although the US government claimed it a military success, the Tet bloodbath fueled public skepticism about our nation's ability to persevere in Vietnam.

February 1: Cameras capture Saigon Chief of National Police General Nguyen Ngoc Loan firing his pistol into the head of a suspected Viet Cong officer. The widely seen graphic video stuns the American public, causing many to question the legitimacy of the South Vietnamese government.

February 18: The US State Department announces the highest weekly casualty rate of the entire Vietnam War. Between February 10th and 17th, 543 American Soldiers are killed and 2,547 are wounded.

February 27: Popular and trusted CBS Evening News anchorman Walter Cronkite announces his opposition to the war in Vietnam. After hearing this President Johnson is reported to have said, "If I've lost Cronkite, I've lost middle America."

March 16: Although it will not be public knowledge for a year, the infamous My Lai massacre occurs. Between 347 and 504 unarmed civilians, including women and children, are massacred by soldiers of the 23rd Division, US Army.

March 31: With the war in Vietnam mired in a quagmire, and increasing public discontent about the number of US casualties, President Johnson stuns the nation by announcing he will not seek re-election for president of the United States.

April 4: Charismatic Civil Rights leader Martin Luther King, Junior is assassinated in Memphis, Tennessee. Immediately following the incident, six days of race riots occur in Washington D.C.

June 5: While campaigning for President of the United States, Robert F. Kennedy is assassinated at the Ambassador Hotel in Los Angeles, California.

August 20: In order to crush the freedom movement called *Prague Spring*, the Soviet Union invades and occupies Czechoslovakia with 200,000 troops. The US protests vehemently and the Cold War heats up.

August 28: Massive anti-war protests disrupt the Democratic National Convention in Chicago. Violence erupts and the Chicago police use excessive force to subdue protestors. Over 200 civilians and police officers are injured.

October 16: During the medal ceremony at the summer Olympic Games in Mexico City, two African American athletes raise the black power salute in protest of US racial discrimination. Considered one of the most overtly political moments in the history of the games, the incident inflames racial tensions in the US.

November 5: Richard Nixon is elected president of the US. He campaigned with the promise of a secret plan to end the war.

With so many disturbing, violent, and provocative events occurring within a single year, and the Vietnam War possibly looming in my future, it felt like I was about to be swept into the heart of a tornado.

"You're not supposed to be so blind with patriotism that you can't face reality. Wrong is wrong, no matter who says it."

13

Malcolm X, American civil rights activist

As the war dragged on into the late sixties, more and more of our nation's young men shipped off to Vietnam, and more and more of them arrived home in body bags. Graphic combat video from the field appeared almost nightly on the news, and despite the large increase of US troops, the war seemed to be descending further into a quagmire. As a result, increasing numbers of Americans lost faith in the Domino Theory.

Massive anti-war demonstrations took place on college campuses and at public places all across America. Mobs of protesters displayed posters proclaiming—*end the war now, bring our boys home—make love, not war—hell no, I won't go*. Young men burned their draft cards in the street, and demonstrators blocked or occupied government buildings. Police beat up on protestors and some in the anti-war movement resorted to violence. As a result, a backlash emerged. In 1968, film icon John Wayne, a political conservative, starred in a pro-Vietnam War movie called *The Green Berets*. The film earned almost 22 million at the box office, a considerable amount at the time. In addition, you couldn't drive anywhere without seeing a bumper sticker that read, *America: Love it or Leave it*. The phrase implicitly impugned the patriotism of opponents to the war.

The Vietnam conflict polarized our nation like no other event since the civil war. Within all of this political flux I became increasingly skeptical about our government's stated reasons for involvement in Vietnam, including the Domino Theory. It wasn't because I faced immediate conscription, and it wasn't because I believed the rhetoric of the radicals. Rather, I found the arguments of knowledgeable critics of the war more reasonable and convincing than those of the hawks. By the late 1960's, not just college students and hippies had come out against the war. Many prominent intellectuals, politicians, and news people also added their voices of opposition.

Unfortunately, the skepticism some Americans aimed toward US *policy* in Vietnam often transferred into negative feelings about the military and the individual soldiers who served. For many of these critics, to serve in the military meant supporting an illegitimate, immoral war. Although I didn't buy into this misguided thinking or all of the anti-war propaganda, by 1968 I opposed US involvement in Vietnam.

"Older men declare war, but it is youth that must fight and die."
President Herbert Hoover, June, 1944

During my second to last semester at community college, I received an induction notice. Having neglected to notify the Selective Service of my intention to continue into the final semester, I immediately informed the agency of my mistake. They granted me a postponement of the draft. After graduating with an AA degree, I thought about furthering my education, but I waited too long to register at the university and my impending draft could not be reversed.

Knowing my opposition to the war, some friends suggested I join the protest movement and avoid conscription.

Terry said, "Some guys are going to Canada. I know friends there who would take you in."

I replied, "I can't tear up my draft card and run away from my family and friends. Besides being illegal, I find it morally distasteful."

My attitude wasn't based upon simple minded phrases like, *America: Love it or Leave it.* I have never believed patriotism meant blind obedience and submission to everything government says and does. Sometimes patriotism means speaking out and protesting when we sincerely believe our government is leading the nation astray.

Although I opposed US involvement in Vietnam, conflicting thoughts occupied my mind. In addition to my disapproval of illegally avoiding conscription, I felt guilty other young men my age were going off to Vietnam while I enjoyed the comforts of suburban life. *I am only 22 years old, what do I know?* My doubts had roots in my upbringing. Like most kids growing up in the fifties and early sixties, my parents raised me to place trust in higher institutions, including government, and show respect for authority. However, the murky nature of the Vietnam War clouded my feelings about sense of duty and obligation to serve my country.

15

Almost all draftees ended up in the army, and the majority of these were assigned to the infantry and sent off to Vietnam. The army and marines held no appeal, so I decided to investigate entering one of the other services. My first choice was to become an air force pilot, but those hopes would soon be dashed. During 1968, air force, navy, and coast guard recruiting facilities had accrued long waiting lists of young men like me wanting to avoid conscription into the army. At the time of my inquiries, none of these services accepted any more names.

Boxed into a corner with the draft blowing in my face, I contemplated an enticement offered by the army—sign up in late December, 1968, and I wouldn't have to enter for active duty until early January, 1969. In addition, I would be discharged the third week in December, 1970.

I sat down with Mom and Dad to discuss my options; "This incentive shaves two weeks off the active duty commitment of two years. It's not a bad deal—I can spend the upcoming holidays with you and only one in the army."

Mom said, "It's certainly worth considering. Your college education and intelligence might get you out of going into a combat zone."

Dad added, "They would be foolish not to take advantage of your brains and talent. Maybe they'll make you an army artist."

I said, "It would be nice, but that's a long shot. I don't think the army uses many artists, if any."

Dad asked, "So, what are you going to do?"

"Well, it's too late to enroll at Cal-State. I'm out of options, and I think the army's offer isn't bad. It beats the agony of waiting to be drafted. It's driving me crazy."

Putting her hand on my shoulder, Mom said, "Whatever happens, we'll give you our full support."

I made the decision to accept the army's offer. It pleased me to learn that basic training would take place at Fort Ord, near Monterey, California.

You're in the Army Now

Song composed by Isham Jones, 1917; lyrics by Tell Taylor and Ole Olsen

On January 6, 1969, I arrived at Fort Ord. All inductees underwent processing before assignment to a basic training company. We filled out paperwork, had blood drawn, took several tests—including to measure intelligence—and were issued uniforms. At this time I stood 5 foot, 11 inches tall and weighed 142 pounds. I knew the eight weeks of basic training would be physically demanding on my lean body. I also knew the drill sergeants would constantly mess with my head. I decided that I must play the army game as best as I can. This meant follow orders to the letter, never volunteer, and keep big mouth shut.

Hair today, gone tomorrow

Nine months before I entered the army, the rock musical *Hair* became a hit on Broadway. The play celebrated the widely popular style of long hair on men. No self-respecting and socially conscious young man in the late sixties would be caught dead with close cropped hair, especially *white walls*—hair cut down almost to the scalp around the ears and the nape of the neck. For some young men, long hair represented not only a style trend, but a libertine life style, rebellion against authority, contempt for the establishment, and opposition to the war in Vietnam.

The army's first overt act at destroying a young man's cultural identity and individuality is cutting every follicle of hair down to the scalp. Just before assignment to basic training barracks, sergeants marched our motley group to the base barber shop. A centipede-like line entered on one side and another centipede-like line exited on the opposite side. Everyone appeared nervous because we dreaded losing our precious locks. The time to fully submit ourselves to the army was at hand, or should I say scalp? I don't recall seeing a candy cane pole, but otherwise the facility looked similar to its old school counterparts back home. Remember Floyd's barber shop in the Andy Griffith Show? Like that, but larger. Noticeably missing were the pleasant aromas of shampoo, talcum powder, and aftershave—

17

plus the friendly banter between barbers and their neighborhood customers.

While waiting in line, I observed the proceedings for several minutes. The inductees sported a wide range of hair styles—straight, curly, wavy, and belt length to just below the ears. I saw only a handful of short military styles. The white inductee standing next to me pointed to a young black man wearing the new *afro* and whispered, "That guy looks like he's wearing a space helmet." I couldn't help but chuckle in agreement. In sharp contrast, each of the barbers wore tell-tale white walls. If these older men were civilians, their appearances, attitudes, and behaviors shouted from the rafters—*conservative and military!*

From my vantage point in line I could see the activity in all six chairs. Deftly maneuvered clippers buzzed up, down, and across scalps at a frenetic pace. With orderly precision, all outward expressions of civilian individualism literally fell by the wayside. Pound after pound of spaghetti-like tangles dropped unceremoniously to the tile floor. As someone arrived to sweep up the mess, I wondered out loud, "What the hell does the army do with all these masses of hair?" Meanwhile, the barbers made no attempt to hide their eagerness and glee at taunting us nervous inductees— especially while turning long-haired hippy heads into shiny new soldier domes.

Just as one nervous inductee sat in the chair, the barber asked, "Do you want to keep those long sideburns?"

"Yes," the soldier replied.

Wearing a superficial grin, the barber sneered, "Then hold your hands open and catch them before they fall to the floor."

His cronies laughed, but I thought, *I'll bet that joke is one of their golden oldies.*

Time for my turn in the chair. Ending at the shoulders, my wavy locks were of average length for the time. Fidgeting nervously, I took one last glance at my nicely adorned head reflected in mirrors on opposite sides of the walls. The barber didn't say a word to me—his tool did all the talking. Roaring like a hungry beast, his clipper devoured all my hair in less than a minute. The opposing mirrors reflected my now naked *heads* back and forth into infinity. *Jeez, I look weird!* Then I realized, *hell, this place is no fancy salon, so they don't need these mirrors. The only reason they put them there is to humiliate us.*

The barber shooed me out of the chair like a bothersome fly, and the next assembly line victim took my place. Standing in the exit line, I looked forward at the long row of freshly cropped, mostly pale domes. Except for the color, they reminded me of the rows of bowling balls lined up along the racks at the lanes back home.

There can be no doubt the army barbershop represents a significant and symbolic transition from civilian to army life. Enter—Bob Richert of Long Beach, California. Exit—an army assigned eight digit number.

"After a hard day of basic training, you could eat a rattlesnake." Elvis Presley, American rock and roll icon; US Army, 1958-60

I'll never forget the day when about forty of us newbie's, freshly shaved heads shining in the sun, boarded a beat-up old olive drab cattle truck and headed off to our new home at the basic training barracks. Anxiousness gnawed at everyone's guts as we were about to enter into the center of a raging storm. Outwardly I tried to maintain my cool, but inwardly I shook like a scared kitten.

As we pulled up in front of the barracks and even before the truck came to a full stop, three drill sergeants gathered like a pack of hungry hyenas and immediately began barking fire and brimstone. "Get off that damn truck! Now, you maggots, get your sorry asses off my truck!"

Holy shit! This is for real. In a fury of screaming voices and bold gestures, the drill sergeants rushed us off the vehicle and made us line up in four neat rows. We were ordered to place our newly issued duffle bags and gear on the ground in front of us.

One drill instructor shrieked, "Face forward, stand up straight, don't move, and keep your mouths shut!"

The head drill sergeant, a huge, solidly built Samoan, spoke with a slight accent. He stood erect in front of our group with perfect posture and a menacing expression on his bronzed face. *He's like a Greek god—an angry Greek god. I sure as hell don't want to get on his bad side.* As his piercing eyes surveyed the group, I sensed, *he can see right through me.*

With a contemptuous sneering frown, the big Samoan scowled, "You are the sorriest looking bunch of sad-sacks I've ever seen, but we are gonna whip those sagging bodies into shape." He ranted on about how we had better learn to obey orders and submit to our superiors or there would be hell to pay. Pounding a tightly clenched fist on his massive chest, he bellowed, "For the next eight weeks, you are mine!" Everyone stood frozen with fear.

Two drill sergeants cruised up and down the rows checking us from head to toe. Anyone not in compliance or merely appearing out of order became harassed without mercy. One gruff looking DI, face crimson with rage, confronted a young man in the act of fumbling with his accidently scattered gear. Hovering over him like an angry wasp, the sergeant growled, "You need your mommy to help you straighten out your shit? She ain't here, so from now on I'm gonna be your mommy. You gotta problem with that, mama's boy?"

The inductee responded feebly, "No Sir."

"Sir—you call me sir!" Pointing to his collar, the DI raged, "You see any officer's bars here? Your drill sergeants are enlisted men. Only officers are addressed as sir! You got that dumb-ass?" Not waiting for a response, the DI turned to the rest of us, "From now on you trainees will address us properly. Now, let me hear you yell it loud and clear—yes, drill sergeant!"

In unison everyone shouted, "Yes, drill sergeant."

Next, the fiery sergeant made his way down my row and turned to scrutinize me. I stood paralyzed with fear.

"Don't look at me—keep your eyes facing forward!"

Thankfully, he didn't ask me any questions. Any response would likely be wrong and invoke wrath. I learned quickly that for the next two months intimidation would be standard drill instructor MO. *Welcome to basic training private Richert.*

Letter to my Family from Basic Training - January 12, 1969
The First Week

Yech, the army is not my cup of tea. We spent all day today getting cleaned up for inspections. The drill sergeants yell all the time. Just before I started writing this letter, a drill sergeant came into our barracks. We did 25 pushups because no one yelled, "At ease!" as soon as he walked in. Then he walked in again, but this time someone alertly yelled, "At ease!" They keep you on your toes here.

As you know, I'm in for two years. This means I'm not given a guarantee as to school and job, but they let you write your preference. I put in for clerical—I scored well on the test——and chose Germany as an overseas station. Keep your fingers crossed that I get it.

All of this first week has been processing. We start our actual training tomorrow. I've been issued my M14 rifle and tons of equipment.

It has been some week! We get up at 5:30 AM and go to bed at 9:30 PM. Boy, I could go for a pepperoni pizza right now. We only get three meals a day, but I'm used to the usual 10 o'clock snack.

Although the drill sergeants seemed bigger than life and appeared blusterous and menacing, their physical attributes, fitness and mental sharpness impressed me. After all, their occupation is essentially doing basic training. They awakened early and participated during many of our physical activities. Drill instructors always appeared clean shaven with hair cut short, especially around the ears—white wall style. Their olive green fatigues, always neat and tidy, showed not a wrinkle, and their boots shone like the chrome on a fifties show car.

Army bases are not designed to grace the cover of *Architectural Digest Magazine*. They are conceived and constructed strictly for utilitarian purposes. True to military protocol, the dozen or so rectangular, unadorned, and identical barracks buildings lined up like dominoes in neat, precise rows—orderly and antiseptic. The lower floor of my new abode consisted of offices and drill sergeants billets, and we trainees quartered upstairs. Upon arrival inside I noticed, *wow, the floor is as shiny as a billiard ball. I'm impressed.* Then it dawned

21

on me that my soon-to-be-tired arms would be responsible for maintaining its luster.

A row of double bunks ran along the length of each side of the room, which housed about forty men. The bunks had to be aligned precisely from one end of the room to the other. Drill sergeants instructed us how to make them up to army specs. If a trainee failed to comply to the letter with the directions, the DI tore the offender's bedding apart, scattered the components on the floor, and made him put everything back together—sometimes again and again until he got it right. Oh yeah, often twenty push-ups were thrown in for good measure. An old expression says, *you can take the man out of the military, but you can't take the military out of the man.* It must be true because I still make my bed the army way today.

Have you seen movies in which trainees are shown cleaning floors and toilets with toothbrushes? It's not far from the truth. We were required to keep the bathroom and everything in it spotless, as well as the concourse floor and our bunks and lockers. Our socks and clothing had to be folded exactly to specs, and every item in our upright and foot lockers had to be arranged in a specific way. *Boy, the army sure is fussy about details.* For some reason I had difficulty bringing my black boots to the high sheen expected. I spent tedious evening minutes buffing those damn things. Of course, the next day I invariably treaded through dirt and mud, and that evening it was back to shining boots again—and the next evening, and the next.

Each night around 9:30, a drill sergeant barked, "Lights out!" Sound early? Not after a full day of arduous physical activities. Although exhausted, the drill sergeants often rousted us in the wee hours—sometimes for an inspection and sometimes for the hell of it. At 5:30 AM sharp, we rushed like mad to make our bunks, dress, grab our M14 rifle and other gear, and fall in for formation in front of the barracks.

If a drill sergeant noticed any item about your person or clothing not in order—improper posture, collar amiss, boots or brass belt buckle improperly shined, buttons unbuttoned—anything—the offender would be down doing pushups or the dreaded *dying cockroach* routine. One day I improperly handled my rifle, and the DI ordered me to lie on my back while splaying both arms and legs out and off the ground while moving them back and forth. Meanwhile, I yelled repeatedly, "I'm a dying cockroach!" Maintaining this embarrassing posture caused my arms and legs to ache like they had been pounded by a sledge hammer. I dared not beg for mercy because it would only encourage the DI to inflict more suffering.

Letter to my Family from Basic Training - January 25, 1969
Food and Physical Training

We marched around in the rain this week. Boy, it's uncomfortable! I've been learning quite a bit in basic. I can take apart an M14 rifle, clean it, and put it together. I know a little first aid, rules of military justice, how to march, be alert, take orders—all of which I am glad to know. Not that much of the army training is practical knowledge, but they teach you to be alert, physically fit, and mentally quick—and to take a lot of crap. There are times I wish I was dead, but this renders to oblivion around chow time. Food and Sundays are the only things to look forward to and I enjoy them both. This week I've had seconds at dinner every night and stuffed myself—um, um, the food is good! However, I wouldn't complain if you sent me cookies and Cracker Jacks. They go good in the evenings when I get hungry. We can't go to the PX, so this is the only way of getting extra food.

We have been learning hand-to-hand combat (just the basics) this week so I'll really be a tiger when I get home. Next week we go to the rifle range to learn how to fire the M14 rifle we carry around everywhere. I'll have a lot to write on that.

Today we had a test for five events to see how fit we are. One was the *low crawl*, where you get down on your belly and crawl like a lizard for forty yards. Then comes the *man carry*— you carry a person of equivalent weight for 150 yards as fast as possible. That was hard for me, taking 61 seconds although average is about 50. Next we had the horizontal bars—like a horizontal ladder—which is about ten feet off the ground. The object is to go up and then back using your hands from bar to bar until two minutes elapses or you drop. I fell on my thirtieth

23

bar which is just below average. Then we had the *dodge, run, and jump.* You run around these saw horse shaped obstacles and over a ditch, and you are timed. I did average here. Last, but not least, was the mile run. I did that one just below par at eight minutes, fifty seconds. I was really tired after that. I don't know how I have the strength to write because this was an exhausting experience. The test today did not count for anything—it is just used for comparison to our final (same test) to see how we improve. Out of a possible 500, a score of 300 is necessary to pass. I'll make it, although I still don't know my total for today.

I'm going to bed now and dream about the good life at home. Actually, I've got a candy bar hidden away which I'm dying to eat, so goodbye for now from your physically unfit son.

I laughed upon re-reading that the mess hall food was good. When you are physically active all day and drooling with hunger at meal time, a can of Spam tastes like filet mignon with béarnaise sauce.

The *low crawl* while under live fire is one of basic training's most memorable activities. Drill sergeants fire a series of machine gun rounds ten feet above the trainees while they crawl along the ground and through mud for 20 yards. Understandably, the army makes a big fuss about following procedure—like don't stand up and wave at your buddies while bullets are zinging by—duh! Not among the first group to participate, I observed the procedure. At one point one drill sergeant yelled, "Cease fire!" Nothing serious happened, but it was reassuring to see that our leaders practiced extreme caution. When my time came, I felt confident. *As long as I stay down low, there's no chance of getting shot.* Crawling while under fire stimulated an adrenaline rush and I realized that hearing the sound of the bullets whizzing by would help prepare me for potential combat.

**Letter to my Family from Basic Training - Early February, 1969
Rifle Range**

On Friday I qualified on the rifle range. The minimum number of targets to qualify is 30, and I hit 32. On the first range I had a hell of a time. The sun was right in my eyes. What made it even worse is the targets are dull green just like the surrounding bushes. They are shaped like a human silhouette and fall down when hit. The targets are scattered in a lane from 50 to 350 meters in distance. Sometimes one target would appear and sometimes two or three. The idea is to find the target and hit it. The closer targets stay up for 5 seconds, the farther ones for 10. They don't make it easy. If I qualify as a Marksman that is all that counts, so I'm not complaining.

This week is gas week. We get gassed with some nauseating chemical and everyone gets sick. Some guys who have experienced it tell me that this is the worst part of basic training.

A bit of trivia: Our basic training company, winter of 1969, was the last at Fort Ord to train with the old World War II M14 rifle. The army phased out the obsolete weapon and replaced it with the M16. Although less accurate at long distances than its predecessor, its short length, light weight, ease of handling, and rapid fire power better suited the kinds of guerrilla-type combat situations facing US soldiers in Vietnam. I felt much more comfortable handling the new M16 than with the clunky old WW II relic.

Something to get choked up about

Long before entering the service, every Vietnam era young man heard about the dreaded gas chamber. Well, my time was at hand— more accurately, eyes, throat, and lungs. The drill instructors assured us trainees we would come through fine as long as followed their directions to the letter. *Somehow that doesn't make me feel better.* Following directions is one thing, following them under pressure is quite another. Therein lays the objective of the exercise. It's a test of combat readiness. Like everyone else, I feared screwing up, becoming terribly sick, and looking like a whimpering idiot in front of the others. Fortunately, the DI's provided explicit directions. We

25

practiced removing the mask from its case and then placing it over our heads properly, but quickly.

At the last minute, the instructor threw us a curve ball; "Once you are inside, you cannot put on the mask until ordered to do so, and the order will only come *after* the gas is released." *Yikes!* This meant we had better have listened carefully and practiced correctly so as not give way to panic under pressure.

Ten of us at a time, masks packed inside a closed case attached at our sides, marched into a dark, living-room-sized chamber made of cinder block.

One of the men said, "This place looks like a jail cell."

"Or a death chamber," someone muttered with nervous laughter.

A voice emanating from a speaker scolded us; "Do not reach for your masks until given the order." I heard a hissing sound, and suddenly the room began to fill with a menacing looking gray fog. A few seconds later the anonymous voice shouted, "Mask!"

A couple of guys struggled with the equipment and started choking. One of them had to be escorted out because he couldn't manage to put his mask on. Meanwhile, I swiftly removed the device from its container, opened it properly, placed the straps over my head, brought the mask down tightly over my face, and then gulped air. I performed everything quickly and correctly. *Yes!* After a minute or so, a sergeant escorted the group outside. Although the mask worked as expected, I couldn't help but inhale some of the gas and it lived up to expectations. My eyes, throat, and lungs burned, and I felt slightly nauseous. However, the adverse effects dissipated within a few minutes. *Phew, the biggest basic training test conquered. I did it!*

Letter to my Family from Basic Training - February 16, 1969
Bivouac

Next week we have bivouac. We camp out for 3 days out in the sticks. We march about 6 miles with packs on our backs weighing about 75 pounds. It isn't bad though, it might be fun camping out.

Letter to my Family from Basic Training - February 22, 1969
Winding Down

I have been through hell—bivouac! It was cold and wet. During bivouac we had hand grenade. I threw two live grenades and they went boom—ha, ha. Contrary to TV, the pin is easy to pull and nobody does it with his teeth. Also, there is no puff of smoke. Dirt flies up and there is a hell of a shock wave.

I had guard duty last night. This consists of three two-hour shifts. I worked from eight to ten last night, two to 4 AM, then this morning again from eight to ten. It isn't very fun. I was on roving patrol. I rode in a truck with another guy and we went back and forth to four buildings. I got out and checked the doors and windows—got back in and went to the next one—kept doing this cycle all two hours of the shift. No one is around and the buildings are hardly worth guarding, but they want to teach us all this crap I guess.

My time is diminishing rapidly—only two weeks to go. Next week is testing. Wednesday we get tested on the five events of physical training. Friday we are tested on drill and ceremony (left face, right shoulder arms, etc.), hand to hand combat, plus the classes we had like first aid and the rest of the B.S. I'm not sweating it. After this week all we do is drink beer and practice for graduation. This week I get my orders. I'm sweating that one. You will know by my next letter whether or not I go into the infantry.

"Hates California, it's so cold and so damp."
Lyrics by Lorenz Hart, from the song, *the Lady is a Tramp*

Our basic training company boarded trucks for three days of military exercises in the field. The terrain consisted of mostly grassy hills along with scattered brush, including poison oak, as well as oak trees. We set up and slept in flimsy two-man tents. February in the Monterey area is often *cold and damp*, yet we were not issued rain gear.

27

I wore a T-shirt under my long-sleeved fatigue shirt and the only other item issued for warmth was a lightweight cloth jacket.

I didn't sleep well inside the canvas tent. Although snuggled inside my sleeping bag, I felt cold and clammy on the damp ground. Our unit awakened just after sunup, and my body shivered from head to toe. I never liked coffee, but on this chilly morning I needed something to warm my insides. Each day the mess hall staff trucked meals to our location. Coffee was served in one of those typical ten gallon cylindrical metal canisters with a pour spout at the bottom. I filled my tin canteen cup halfway. After warming my hands around it for a few minutes, I took one big gulp, swirled it around the inside of my mouth, and swallowed. "Yech!" Although still shivering and cold, I couldn't force myself to take another sip of that nasty stuff. That cold morning in February provided the ultimate test. I learned for certain I really don't like coffee and haven't sipped a taste since.

The unpleasant weather during bivouac caused even young men from frigid climates like the Midwest and Northeast to complain. Knowing I was a Californian, a fellow from Minnesota approached me. Obviously irritated, he asked, "What happened to sunny California? I thought it was supposed to be warm here. I've never been so friggin' cold in my life!"

I guess that says it all.

D & C

When we trainees weren't hiking, running our asses off, at the weapons ranges, getting gassed, or attending an occasional class, we drilled and drilled. Drill and Ceremony, D & C, is about learning how to stand, hold and move the rifle, and march according to strict military protocol. The classic regimen is designed to instill discipline, but most of us tired trainees thought it a royal pain in the ass.

Not only did our drill instructors require us to learn many different individual moves and positions, but we also had to stay in synch with the rest of the platoon. Therein lay the Catch 22. Like something out of a Laurel and Hardy movie, one or two guys always screwed up. Rather than merely singling out the individuals responsible, the drill sergeants routinely punished everyone in the platoon for the transgressions of a few.

I said to the fellow next to me, "I suppose this form of discipline encourages teamwork—you know, all for one and one for all."

He replied, "Fuck that!"

I, too, felt frustration at having to get down and do push-ups or repeat the same drill over and over just because one or two misfits couldn't get their act together. The good news is D & C was the only physical activity at which I excelled. I could drill with the best of them.

I must backtrack a bit. During the first few days of processing, the army gave all inductees an intelligence test. Of the nearly 100 men in my company, I placed third. In a moment filled with optimism, I thought, *wow, maybe Mom and Dad were right. Surely the army won't send this bright boy into the infantry.* Soon after the test results came in, an army placement officer interviewed each trainee about his skill-sets and job preferences. Of course, this procedure was a bit of a ruse because regardless of qualifications or experience, the army assigned almost everyone into the infantry or artillery and then off to Vietnam.

Upon noticing my high score on the IQ test, the interviewer said, "Richert, I think you may be a good prospect for officer candidate school."

He went on to elaborate about the benefits and various opportunities available. Knowing this meant at least ten more months in the army, plus not feeling cut out for the incessant spit and polish that officer candidates are forced to endure, I responded tersely, "No thanks. I don't want to spend ten more months in the army."

As soon as those words came out of my big mouth I wanted to suck them back in. In a hasty attempt to cut my losses, I asked to become a clerk. Not only did I lack experience, but my typing skills were practically nonexistent. The placement officer sensed my lack of sincerity, and my implicit disrespect for the military surely didn't score me any points. I left the room full of regret. *Dumb, dumb, dumb! This man has the power to alter my future in the army. I should have*

29

offered a polite refusal and boasted about skills and talents that could obtain me a non-combat job in the rear. I blew it big time.

One week before the end of basic training, the dreaded list announcing each trainee's Military Occupational Specialty (MOS) came out. Despite my bad interview, I walked toward the posted announcement feeling slightly optimistic. *I did score high on the intelligence test. Maybe they won't put me into the infantry.* I stood back from the bulletin board for several minutes to reflect on my family and future. Finally mustering the courage, I took a deep breath, walked up and sought my name on the lengthy list. *There it is.* My hopes were instantly crushed—*MOS, Infantry—Theater, Vietnam. No! This can't be happening.* My head and shoulders drooped like the wax on a melting candle. I wasn't alone. All but five men in the company were going to Vietnam.

I called my parents to break the dreadful news. In a downtrodden, cracking voice, I could barely sputter the terrible words, "Well, I'm going into the infantry, and to Vietnam."

After what seemed like a minute of silence, Mom said, "We were sort of expecting it, but your dad and I have confidence in you. We think you'll be okay."

I could almost see Mom's eyes welling up. Dad tried to be upbeat. "Yeah, Bobber, it might not be so bad. Just be smart and don't take any unnecessary chances out there. Don't try to be a hero, okay?"

"Sure Dad, I'll keep my head down. Besides, I'll always have Mom's delicious pies to look forward to and flying gliders with you once I come home. That'll keep me going when times get tough."

We said goodbye for the time being.

The army didn't afford me the opportunity to wallow in self-pity for long. Advanced Individual Training lurked just around the corner.

Before entering the army I never fired a weapon in my life. My dad didn't own firearms, and I never expressed interest in them. During training, I felt out of place at the rifle ranges, and lacked motivation to excel. I couldn't hit a barn door with a bass fiddle, much less a rifle. As a result, my overall score ranked near the bottom. I think the army awarded me a passing grade in their lowest category, Marksman, because they needed more bodies for the war

30

effort. The irony hit me like a pie in the face. *Only in the army can I score at the bottom on the weapons test, in the top three percent in the intelligence test, and yet find myself sent off to the infantry.* This was the bitterest of pills to swallow.

Not everything about basic training was a downer. I end this section with a story filled with a tasty touch of humor.

Letter to my Family from Basic Training - February 1, 1969
Off to Church

Well, today is Sunday and I am going to church as usual. Actually, I'm going to the PX truck to stock up on goodies—if I can.

Although the army fed us trainees three square meals a day, the vigorous exercise we endured greatly increased our appetites. Three meals just didn't cut it. Happily, they allowed goodie boxes sent from home. However, a controlled diet is an essential element of basic training, so each package was subjected to inspection by the drill instructors. They allowed the recipient to keep most items as long as he shared with the other men. Although we appreciated packages sent from home, the nibbles we ended up receiving didn't come close to satisfying our grouchy stomachs. Forget about obtaining food from places like the base PX. Except for supervised outdoor training activities, emergencies, and voluntary church attendance on Sunday mornings, we troops were confined to the barracks area during the entire eight weeks of basic training— including during our few off hours.

By the third week of training, boredom and frustration at being subjected to confinement drove me stir-crazy. On Sunday morning, I decided, *what the heck, I'll go to church just to get away from here. At least it's something different.* The army required us to wear our Class-A dress uniforms. I guess they figured you gotta look good for God. It surprised me that only a half-dozen, including me, of the forty men in the barracks showed up. A sergeant escorted us a few blocks to a modest, snow-white building with a classic steeple. I told the fellow near me, "This church looks like something out of a Currier and Ives painting—definitely out of place here."

He replied, "Who are they?"

Looking at him with the raised eyebrow of a snob, I muttered, "A couple who does art," and moved on.

Normally, drill sergeants remained with us everywhere we went. Unexpectedly, the sergeant who escorted the group left us at the entrance and went off about his business.

Standing with the others in front of the church, I noticed a food truck parked nearby—probably to take advantage of the attendees arriving from throughout the base. While the others went inside, I quietly stayed back. No one seemed to notice or care. Meanwhile, my empty, groaning stomach beckoned me toward the vehicle. *The coast is clear—time to make my move toward heaven on wheels.*

The side of the silvery truck opened wide to my even wider opened eyes. In stark contrast to the olive drab environment at the barracks, layers of shelves exposed a dazzling array of colorfully wrapped sweets, including packaged pastries. Although I had been at Fort Ord only three weeks, it seemed like forever since I indulged in such enticing bounty. Salivating all the while, I purchased a candy bar and one of those half-moon shaped encrusted pies. Candy bars sold for 10 cents and the pies for 15 cents apiece. While scarfing up my fill right there on the spot, an idea struck me—*why not stock up for the upcoming week?* Luckily for me, the Class-A uniform coat abounds with pockets, inside and out. I loaded up with as many goodies as I could, but without showing obvious bulges. The pies fit snugly within the inside pockets, almost as if they were tailored for such a purpose.

Were I to be caught in the barracks with my larder there would be hell to pay, like enduring countless push-ups or spending all future Sundays on KP. However, an insatiable craving for sweets compelled me to take the risk. Fearing being ratted out by a jealous rival or becoming subjected to blackmail, I decided not to tell any of my fellow inductees about my covert activity. I left the items hidden in my coat pockets because during the eight weeks of training we inductees never wore our Class-A uniforms. They just hung idly in our upright lockers.

32

Although the drill sergeants often inspected our lockers, they seldom looked into the pockets of our clothing. However, the last thing I needed was to arouse their suspicion and suffer their wrath. When a drill sergeant discovered any locker even slightly out of order they reacted like a tornado sweeping through a barn. The contents were scattered everywhere. Thus, I made an extra effort to keep my upright and foot lockers squared away. It worked. They were never tossed.

Just after lights out on the night following my trip to *church*, I sneaked my first snack, a chocolate bar. I had to be careful, not just because a drill sergeant might make a surprise inspection, but also because my fellow soldiers might spot me or sniff a whiff of the sweet aroma. I feared they would attack me like starving zombies. However, I felt heartless. After one week and feeling more secure about my surreptitious activity, I decided to share candy with a few of my trustworthy inmates, but not my three precious pies. While nibbling away on one of these coveted crusted treats with its sweet fruit filling, I made an extra effort to keep it hidden from view.

Despite my covert tactics, one night after lights-out the fellow in the upper bunk next to mine caught me in the act. *Uh oh, busted!* In a discreet way so as not to alert the others, Parker began pleading with me to share.

In a voice filled with desperation, he whispered, "I'm starving! You got more pies, don't you? I'll give you 50 cents. Any flavor will do, any. Give me the one you don't like. Come on, be a pal. Okay, here's a dollar, a whole dollar. P-l-e-a-s-e, give me a pie."

Giving in to his persistent pleadings, I plucked the buck from Parker's paw and handed him a pie. I whispered, "Make sure no one spots you with it."

It wasn't a bad deal. I gave up my least favorite flavor, the one with a slightly medicinal tasting lemon filling, plus made an 85 cent profit—extra money for future booty. I don't remember if my bunk neighbor wolfed it down or nibbled daintily, savoring every bite. I do remember savoring the pleasure of observing him in a state of ecstasy.

From my initial visit to the food truck until the last week of basic training, I continued my skullduggery undetected. Each Sunday I put on my Class-A uniform and went to church—well, next to it. I never attended a service, not once. Instead, I sought inspiration at my *sweet-tooth savior* which just happened to be parked next to a house of worship.

My mom and sister Joanne drove up from Long Beach to attend my basic training graduation, which took place on a bright Sunday afternoon in early March. It's a seven hour drive from Long Beach to Fort Ord, and regrettably Dad couldn't attend because of work on Monday. The event was impressive—neat and orderly with lots of pomp and ceremony, as one expects from the military. Afterward, Mom, Joanne, and I hugged the stuffing out of each other. Beaming with pride I said, "Whew, basic is over. I made it!" Mom and Joanne took pictures while admiring me looking fit and sharp in uniform.

Mom, all aglow, bragged, "Son, what a dramatic change I see in you. You never looked healthier in your life."

H-m-m-m—must have been those candy bars and pies.

Advanced Individual Training - AIT

On to eight weeks of Advanced Individual Training for the infantry. *Thank goodness I won't have to endure constant harassment by drill instructors.* However, I would soon discover that one aspect of AIT would be even more physically demanding than basic. In addition to weapons training, the majority of day to day activity consisted of running and *humping*. The term *humping* means hiking, but hiking connotes pleasant activities like camping out and enjoying nature. AIT training was anything but that.

It seemed like we trainees tromped over every square inch of Fort Ord, often while carrying heavy packs on our backs. The terrain varied from flat to hilly and the trails varied from paved to dirt road to rocky or sandy pathways. One thing in our favor was the weather. During March and April, the California coast is cool and pleasant. Although I disliked all the humping and running, knowing Vietnam would be much hotter and the physical conditions much harsher kept me going. Each day I gained strength and endurance.

Lending a Hand

One day, our barracks of young men went on an extended run. About half-way through I came upon a fellow trainee struggling to keep pace with the group. He sweated profusely and breathed heavily. Stout and somewhat pudgy, the young man did not appear cut out for this activity. Our AIT instructors encouraged us to assist a fellow trainee if he fell behind in hikes and runs. Unit cohesion is crucial to effectiveness in combat situations, and helping hands serve to instill camaraderie. Although I didn't know him, I felt duty bound to do my part for the team. I reached out, grabbed the shirt on the back of my laboring comrade's shoulder, and attempted to nudge him forward. Big mistake. Spurred by frustration, he immediately swung his rifle at me.

"Don't touch me, damn it! Leave me alone."

So much for camaraderie. The sight at the end of his rifle barrel struck the web of skin between the pinkie and adjacent finger on my left hand, tearing the skin through to the other side. The wound started bleeding immediately. I considered taking a poke at my angry assailant, but then I felt empathy and restrained myself. Besides, a more immediate problem needed attention—dripping blood.

Leaving him to struggle onward, I sought a medic. Meanwhile, I clenched my left hand into a tight fist and pressed it against my shirt to apply pressure. The company medic put on a temporary dressing and sent me by jeep to the base hospital. The doctor put in several stitches, bandaged my wound, and ordered two days of light duty. *This is fine by me.* Soon after the incident, my assailant sought me out and humbly apologized. To this day I bare a half-inch long *battle scar* from the encounter.

Foot Feat

Each AIT company is required to participate in a twelve mile march. Five weeks into training, our company would begin the long trek early on a Saturday morning, and finish at lunchtime. I felt good in the morning, but nervous. *Hope I can get through this.* For the first seven miles I kept pace fairly well, but then I began feeling pain on the bottoms of both feet. After mile nine, it felt like I kept stepping on burning coals. *Damn, I'm getting blisters. Only three miles to go—gotta keep going.* Somehow, probably out of stubborn pride, I managed to finish.

I immediately removed my boots and socks to see the damage. The bottoms of my feet looked like moon craters. Blisters had popped up everywhere, even on most of my toes. Those on the balls of each foot were the size of silver dollars. I gingerly put on my socks and boots and hiked the half mile back to the barracks with the rest of the unit—*solely* on will power. Fortunately, our company had the remainder of Saturday and all of Sunday off.

I spent most of Saturday afternoon lying on my bunk barefoot so the open air would stimulate the healing process.

Noticing my raw feet, Edwards, one of my barracks buddies, said, "Holy shit, those are awful. Have you seen the doctor?"

"I'll be fine, don't worry about it."

"Okay, but maybe you can get out of some duty."

Not wanting to acquire the nickname tenderfoot and endure endless teasing, I decided against seeking medical attention. Over the weekend I stayed off my feet and kept them exposed to the air as much as possible. It worked. By Monday morning my feet had toughened up. However, not wanting to take any chances and before falling out for duty, I put two pairs of socks on tightly to ensure against excessive rubbing. *Darn, why didn't I think of this before the stupid 12 mile march?* By the end of the week, my blisters had nearly healed and I went back to one pair of socks—always making sure to put them on snugly. Although my solution came late, it proved effective. I never again acquired blisters.

During the two months of AIT, I trained on some new weapons and received extensive practice with those I learned in basic—the 45 pistol, M16 rifle, M60 and M50 machine guns, M79 grenade launcher, M72 LAW (Light Anti-tank Weapon), Claymore mine, and hand grenade. Handling all of these deadly munitions caused me to imagine the incredible harm they could do to the human body or even groups of people. *Scary!* While you might think having access to such sophisticated and deadly weaponry would bolster my sense of security about future combat in Vietnam, it actually made me feel uneasy. Not only did it bring the reality of war closer to home, it made me question, *what kinds of weapons will the enemy be using against me?*

CHAPTER 3

Welcome to Vietnam

My journey to Vietnam began on June 1, 1969, at Oakland Army Base for three days of processing. My Dad's cousin Luella lived in nearby San Leandro, so we planned to meet when I arrived at the airport. I share my aunt's letter here because I think it will resonate with anyone who has seen a relative go off to war:

Letter from my Aunt Luella to my parents - June 2, 1969
Meeting at Oakland Airport

I took a cab to Oakland airport—it is only a bit over 4 miles from us. When Bob's plane was due in, they announced a 45 minute delay. This is normal, right? I sat and relaxed and when his plane was coming in for a landing I stood at the windows and watched them all disembark, but I missed recognizing Bob. Soon I heard him call "Luella!" He looked so good in uniform. He was genuinely pleased to see me.

We walked the long corridor to pick up his army luggage and planned to relax in the coffee shop and chat a while. I wanted to treat him to a very elegant Monte Cristo sandwich, as this sandwich is that good! However—as it is in the service—first he had to find out just what to do and where to go. All of a sudden a group of servicemen gathered and they were told that the bus was right there waiting. We didn't even get a chance to sit and chat or even have a cup of coffee together. We were both so disappointed. Bob was so quiet—in a few moments one feels the whole impact of the war and what it means. It took me right back to WW II instantly—seeing Johnny and Eddy off to overseas. It's been more than 25 years, but it seems like yesterday, for sure.

Bob got right on the bus in front of the airport and I stood there and waved goodbye. God bless our dear boy and watch over him. I'm very fond of Bob and pleased that he thinks as much of me and Gordon. You can't possibly know how much that framed butterfly he gave to me means to me. He is a thoughtful, sensitive fellow—like Gordon at that age.

So that was it, our little meeting at the airport. I know it truly pleased him that I was there. It meant as much to me too. What is needed at such time is for the boys to know that there are relatives who really care about him.

None of us would have ever thought after WW II that we would see it all happen again. It's not fair that any family should have only two sons—and both have to go overseas without even a declared war. Words are inadequate.

My Aunt Luella's comment about "two sons" refers to me and my brother Jim, who served in the Air Force at the time. Although meeting my aunt at the airport in June was all too brief, her compassionate gesture touched me deeply.

Oakland Army Base, also known as Oakland Army Terminal, seemed almost a city unto itself, and it bustled with activity during the Vietnam War. The sprawling complex served as the major transit facility for US soldiers en route to and returning from deployment throughout Southeast Asia. Located on the east side of San Francisco Bay, row after row of huge box-shaped warehouses housing military supplies dominated the landscape. The mega-complex served as a graphic reminder that conducting war requires enormous amounts of logistical support. In 1969, the base teemed with thousands of young men like me, all facing an uncertain future. Although the atmosphere sparkled with activity, the somber gray clouds of war looming across the Pacific muted the mood. Friendly smiles were conspicuous by their absence.

Just after arriving at the base, the army assigned me to a temporary company consisting of about 80 men. We slept in barracks and fell out for assignment on the mornings of the three days there. A Lieutenant divided the troops into groups and sergeants escorted them to perform various work duties around the base. Frustrated, I thought, *how does picking up trash, trimming lawns, and washing the sides of buildings prepare me for combat in Vietnam? It all seems so trivial and pointless by comparison.* I guess the army decided it prudent to keep our bodies busy in an effort to keep our minds distracted. It didn't work. During whatever duties I performed, I couldn't help but think about my future. *What is Vietnam going to be like? Will I be able to handle the hot weather and brutal physical hardships? How much combat will I see? Will I die over there?*

When I first put on the uniform during basic training, I resolved to conduct myself as if the army is one big game. In order to make it through, I must play it the army way. At Oakland it finally hit home this is no game. *In a few hours I am going off to war.* As if this wasn't disturbing enough, another sobering reality revealed itself. Early on at Fort Ord I learned individualism is anathema to military life, but the vast expanse of Oakland Army Base with its thousands of soldiers en route to Vietnam vividly magnified this hard truth. *I am just one amid a vast colony of anonymous and expendable olive drab soldier ants.* The three days I spent at Oakland Army Base awaiting departure to Vietnam were the longest and dreariest of my young life.

Just before leaving Oakland, I made my last stateside telephone call home. I tried to convey an upbeat tone. "I'm going to make it okay, so don't worry about me." No doubt my parents perceived the fear and uncertainty underlying my thinly veiled attempt at optimism. However, my final words were heartfelt. "I love you both very much."

Mom and Dad reciprocated in kind. In a choking voice, Mom said what any concerned mother would say; "I love you my dear son. Take care of yourself."

Dad added, "Don't try to be a hero. Be safe."

I hung up the phone and paused momentarily to hold back tears and regain my composure. Slowly walking away with my head down, I wondered, *will I ever hear their voices again?*

Into the Storm

During the year 1969, 475,200 American troops served in Vietnam. Thus, it wasn't surprising that on the day of my departure from Oakland in early June, every seat on the large troop transport was occupied. As the Tiger Jet roared off the runway and ascended into the azure sky, I kept my face pressed to the window until I could no longer see the beautiful coastline of California. Looking out at the vast expanse of the Pacific, I pondered, *this is really happening. I'm going to Vietnam.* The jet made a brief stopover at a military base near Anchorage, Alaska. We touched down at 9:30 pm. At this northern latitude the sun was just starting to set. As I stepped off the plane, my nostrils immediately filled with sweet, almost perfume-like Alaskan air. I inhaled several deep breaths. Knowing the climate in Vietnam is sweltering, I wanted to savor as much of this wonderful, cool crisp air as I could—*a last olfactory memento of the good ol' USA.* After an hour or two we were off on a long, all night flight to Nam. *There is no turning back now.*

The jet crossed the International Date Line and approached the coast of Vietnam before sunrise on June 3rd. Through my window seat I observed monstrous thunderstorms brewing in the distance, and our comparatively tiny bird headed straight toward them. Interrupting the blackness of the night sky, mighty bolts of lightning illuminated towering thunderhead clouds. Like giant jagged daggers, brilliant white flashes arced from cloud to cloud while others seemed to set off explosions inside immense billowy domes. I had never seen such a violent storm. It seemed as if Thor and other angry gods waged war in the sky. As we neared the foreboding chaos, the jet shook violently in the unstable air. *Jeez, will I even make it to Vietnam?*

Is this turbulent reception an omen of things to come? What the hell have I gotten myself into? Yeah, it certainly seemed like I was entering hell. Somehow, the pilots managed to navigate around the heart of the storm.

As we approached Ben Hoa Airbase, I turned to the soldier sitting next to me and in a sarcastic attempt to quell my nerves said, "Talk about a dramatic entrance, Cecil B. DeMille couldn't have staged it any better!"

The soldier replied, "Yeah, but this ain't no movie."

Letter to my Family - June 3, 1969
My first letter from Vietnam

Well, here I am in the big 'V'. We landed this morning at 5:30am at Ben Hoa Airbase, and it is big! I'll be here for the next four to five days pulling guard duty until I'm assigned to my new unit. Ben Hoa is 20 miles north of Saigon and relatively safe. There are a few pleasures here on base, though not comparable to those stateside. There is a brand new air-conditioned snack bar that has hamburgers, pizza, and cold drinks. It is pretty nice, but the food is all frozen stuff shipped over from the states. I played pool in the service club, and they also have a swimming pool.

It is very hot and humid. It was 85 degrees when we landed this morning at 5 AM. I felt like I stepped off the plane into a sauna. I started sweating immediately. They have a separate building with water faucets and shower heads. The help around the base are all Vietnamese. A woman walked right in while I was showering. They think nothing of it.

We were bused from the airbase. We were lucky enough to go through the town of Ben Hoa on the way. The people are literally stacked up upon one another. They use whatever they can find to build shacks. People were everywhere, like flies—this makes the ghettos of our country look like paradise.

The food in the mess hall is so-so, but at least we have fresh milk. The bugs here aren't bad—there are no mosquitoes in this area.

I know a few of the guys here—some of them were in my AIT (Advanced Individual Training) Company at Fort Ord. Once I arrive at my new unit, I will probably have to make all new friends, but, this is easy here because of the adverse conditions.

It is now June 4th, I pull twelve hours of guard duty per day, but it is easy. All I do is sit in a bunker and make sure that nobody is snooping around out there. There are three guys per bunker. We have a grenade launcher, machine gun, and two M14 rifles at our disposal. I don't believe that any of these weapons have ever been fired, that's how dangerous it is. It rained slightly yesterday, but not at all today. They tell me that it really comes down sometimes, but you dry out so fast that it isn't all that uncomfortable.

I'm going to get some sleep. I'll write as soon as I get to my new unit.

I'll never forget the shockwave of steamy, sticky air that engulfed me when I stepped off the plane. Entering Vietnam's sauna-like atmosphere contrasted greatly with the cool sea breezes I took for granted back home. Living along the Southern California coast most of my life, I had little experience with severe weather. Acclimating to Vietnam's extreme heat and humidity would be a greater ordeal than I imagined. Although I didn't include it in my letter, I anticipated being shot at as soon the big jet set down on the runway. However, I soon learned that Ben Hoa airbase saw very little enemy activity. It felt comforting to be located in a relatively safe place my first few days in country.

"There is no foreign land—it is the traveler only that is foreign."
Robert Louis Stevenson, Scottish writer

My first impression upon seeing the local people and their surroundings left me feeling unsettled. Before my arrival, I understood Vietnam was a poor third world country. Nevertheless, nothing could prepare me for what I saw. Most people wore coolie hats and black or cream colored clothing—soldiers referred to their simple attire, a button down silk shirt and silk pants, as *pajamas*. They looked and dressed alike, but so much differently than Americans, and spoke an odd, almost musically chaotic sounding language. Along the route to base I saw row after row of crude, jerry-rigged structures lining the road. Discarded items like corrugated tin, cardboard boxes, chunks of wood and blanket-like material, haphazardly slapped together, served as walls and roofing for human dwellings.

While shaking his head in disbelief, the fellow on the bus next to me said, "This place looks like a junk heap!"

I replied, "Where do these people go to the bathroom?"

This ramshackle existence represented poverty on a scale I had never imagined. The culture and environment of the Vietnamese people I saw contrasted dramatically with that of my comfortable suburban neighborhood.

Letter to my Family - June 9, 1969
Preparing the Folks Back Home

There is something I want you to remember—the mail system here is not the best. Maybe a few of my letters won't get home. Also, I may be out in the boonies for a couple of weeks and can't write, so if you don't hear from me for a long time—no more than a month—don't worry about me. If something does happen to me, the Red Cross or the army will let you know within 24 hours. I signed a paper that states that if I am lightly injured, they will inform you anyway. This is an option available to us.

When I write home, I'm going to tell you what I am doing. I won't try to sound as if nothing is happening, but I'll never exaggerate or give gory details. I think you should know. I'll say this, I do have a lot of confidence, and you know what I'm most worried about? How hard I will have to work and how much humping I'll have to do. So, what are you worried about?

Although the last paragraph above was sincerely written, later I decided not to write home about any of my combat experiences. I saw no reason to compound the anxiety felt by my parents.

During my stay at Ben Hoa I received orders for assignment at the 23rd Infantry Division, which is called Americal. The Americal encompassed a large section of South Vietnam's northern region and Chu Lai airbase, located on the coast, served as Division headquarters.

Letter to my Family - June 8, 1969
Arrival at Chu Lai

I'm now at the Americal Division Replacement Center in Chu Lai. I'm here until Monday, the 15th for a week of training. I left Ben Hoa on the 7th on a pot-bellied cargo prop with no seats and few windows. Each of us had to sit on our duffle bags for the two hour flight. It is safe here in Chu Lai, so don't worry—yet! I've heard about the units up here and they sound good. They do see action, but not a hell of a lot like the 101st and 1st Cavalry. Americal is the largest division in the army and the most spread out. The only bad thing is that there are mountains about 5 miles out and I may be humping out there.

I took some pictures of the coast. The water is crystal clear, but there aren't any waves. Every night they show flicks outside on the side of a building. They have a place to get ice cream and canned drinks so we live it up around here. It is definitely hot! It usually gets up to 100 degrees at around noon, but cools off and rains later in the day. The really hot days are in August and September. Today I went on a detail. Another guy and I were sent to the motor pool and I had to saw some 4 by 4's and help put in a floor. Boy, did I sweat—that was horrible! I acquired sunburn after just about one hour's exposure.

All the buildings here are just plywood with a tin roof, nothing spectacular. They do the job and that's all that is necessary. There is no nice air conditioned place to go like at Ben Hoa. The Vietnamese who work around here seem to be a

45

happy people. They are very friendly—why not, they love our money—but I still can't get turned on to the local girls. Maybe so in 4 or 5 months!

"It is safe here in Chu Lai, so don't worry—yet!" Yet? Oh, what one small, hastily written word can do to change the meaning of a sentence. I'm sure it sent a shock wave through my parent's nerves. I blew it here.

Letter to my Family - June 12, 1969
Movies and Training

I saw *Rosemary's Baby* at the local outdoor marquis. It was a pretty good flick, but they never showed the damn kid (Rosemary gives birth to the devil—remember?) I saw *Dr. Zhivago* again and *To Sir, with Love*, so at least there is something to do here at night. It's too damn hot in the barracks.

They have a little trailer that sells Wink and Ginger Ale by the ton. I must drink five a day. I'm going to hit the bright blue waters of the sea later this afternoon—they only let us swim between 11 AM and 1 PM and 4 PM and 6 PM each day.

Besides having fun, I have had some training. Tuesday morning, I go down south about 60 miles to LZ (Landing Zone) Jeff. There isn't much humping during this hot season, so most infantry units set up a base and send out patrols to make sure Charlie isn't around (Charlie, a shortened version of Victor Charlie, is phonetic language used in radio communication as a designation for the enemy Viet Cong, which is further shortened to VC).

I enjoyed exploring the warm, crystal clear underwater world of the South China Sea, but for safety, I stayed close to shore. *Look at all these beautiful fish. It's like swimming in an aquarium.* At one point a curious barracuda about three feet long swam around me a few times, and I observed with awe its long, lean shape and subtle, shimmering colors. The artist in me decided it good for my morale to seek beauty wherever and whenever possible in Vietnam.

Letter to my Family - June 15, 1969
Off to the Infantry

Right now, I'm at Duc Pho, 60 miles south of Chu Lai. Duc Pho is the headquarters for the 11th Infantry Brigade. Tomorrow or so, I'll be on my way to my company about five or six miles away in the field. Here at Duc Pho we have an enlisted man's club, actually a shack that sells beer—but, it has a pool table. I won't be at Duc Pho often, but at least I will be able to play when I am here.

My company gets a stand-down in ten days. That is a 3 day break each infantry company gets about every 56 days. We go into Chu Lai and see movies, drink soda and beer, go swimming, and have a groovy time. So, I won't be out in the boonies for too long a time, anyway.

The area I will be operating in is flat rice paddy. But, there are hills which gradually become the Central Highlands about ten miles west. I have been issued my M16 rifle and rucksack out of which I shall live while out in the boonies. The normal load is about 70 pounds—ammo, C-Rations, etc. Yech! But the money is sure good. I'll be rich when I finally go home next June—oh boy. Well, I must go perform a function at the local outdoor lavatory. Then I have an hour's guard of the colonel's bunker—it's no big deal!

Located two miles inland from the coast and named after the local village, Duc Pho served as base headquarters for the 11th Light Infantry Brigade. A high vantage point is a strategic military advantage, so where available, army engineers built most base camps on hilltops. However, Duc Pho incorporated an airstrip, so the engineers constructed it on flat sandy soil near the base of Duc Pho Mountain, actually a steeply sloping hill, which our military had secured. Low lying and heavily sandbagged bunkers spaced about 150 feet apart, and several rows of coiled, barbed concertina wire surrounded the base. Claymore mines dotted the perimeter in key locations.

At night, floodlights lit up the area beyond the perimeter almost like daylight. Most of the buildings were simple wooden structures with corrugated tin roofing. In order to protect soldiers from enemy rockets and mortars, stacked layers of sandbags surrounded most structures. Except for a worn out pool table and cool canned drinks, soldiers had access to few stateside amenities. However, I would soon learn that compared to life in the bush, where I would spend most of my time, any creature comfort, crude or not, is a valued luxury.

I asked a soldier, "How often does the base get attacked?"

He replied, "It's been about a month since the last one. You just never know about those dinks."

"I just hope it doesn't happen while I'm here."

"I wouldn't sweat it. It's been a few months since anyone was killed here. If we get mortared, just go to one of the bunkers."

I did not find his cavalier attitude reassuring.

A Rather Rude Reception

So as to ease my family's anxiety, I wrote the letter below over a month *after* the described incident occurred.

Letter to my Family - August 4, 1969
My First Day in the Field

My company got mortared the night before I was to first come into the field. One man was killed. There were lots of casualties in that area of operations from booby traps before I got there. We were supposedly in the middle of two regiments of North Vietnamese Army. You think I wasn't scared when I first got here to the company?

On a morning in mid-June, 1969, and I, along with another soldier, boarded a chopper for the long, yet all too short, flight to join our infantry unit in the field. The term *field* refers to the fact that for most of its time, the infantry operates and lives outdoors. As the chopper began its descent toward a remote area west of the coast, my gut churned like the inside of a blender. Uncertainty dominated my thoughts. *What am I doing here? I don't belong in the infantry. Will I be shot at as the chopper lands? Will the soldiers in my platoon like me? Will I be able to cut it in the bush?*

The chopper landed at the platoon bivouac area without incident, and we two newbies grabbed our gear and disembarked. I inhaled a couple of deep breaths and tried to slough off negative thoughts. Thankfully, all seemed peaceful and in a few minutes my nerves settled down. The bivouac area bore no resemblance to the comfortable campgrounds and scenery I remembered from my childhood visits to Yosemite. Instead, the setting reminded me of one of those empty lots between old houses in a bad neighborhood—decaying cars, torn sofas, and rusted appliances strewn about among overgrown weeds and other random clutter— only here the clutter was the platoon's gear. I felt dirty almost immediately.

The hilly and highly vegetated terrain surrounding the bivouac area included dense thickets of bamboo, palm, and various other types of trees. Although new to the field, I understood this kind of lush environment is ideally suited to an enemy sneak attack. To make matters worse, North Vietnamese Army (NVA) troops allegedly infested the area. Knowing the bivouac had been mortared the previous night, which led to the death of one young man, I had good reason to be terrified.

The platoon sergeant immediately assigned me to a squad, and introduced me to its eight men. No one seemed friendly. It soon became obvious I was the object of visual scrutiny. Each infantry unit is reliant upon the cohesion of its members, especially in battle situations. The men could see by my lean body and soft hands I had not worked at physical labor stateside. In other words, first impressions indicted I lacked toughness.

One soldier looked me over and asked, "You've had a pretty cushy life, right?"

I muttered something incoherent, but basically acknowledged his observation.

The squad leader, a no-nonsense appearing black man, said, "Stick with your squad, follow directions, and learn from the experienced members and you'll be okay."

"Yes, Specialist 4."

I appreciated his reassuring words, and eagerly sought to comply.

I wasn't on the ground long when I learned our company would remain at this location throughout the night.

One of my squad members blurted, "You gotta be kidding, they can't be serious!"

Confused, I asked, "What's the problem?"

He replied, "Staying at the same place two nights in a row is bad news because no doubt the dinks are still in the area and they know exactly where to find us at night. They'll probably lob mortar rounds at us again and conduct a ground attack."

This is bad. The bitter reality of the previous night's fatality gnawed at my gut like a tapeworm. I couldn't help but anticipate the worst—*will it be me tonight, killed my first night in the field?*

Time to take precautions. During the hottest part of the afternoon, several men in the platoon started digging foxholes. I teamed up with a fellow squad member. The army had previously issued me a portable *entrenching tool,* which is military-speak for *shovel.* My teammate and I started to dig, but we could barely penetrate the hard, rocky ground. After 2 hours of arduous labor, we managed to dig a trench only about 4 feet long by 16 inches wide and 1 foot deep.

My fellow frustrated digger commented; "This puny ditch is hardly enough protection from a mosquito attack, much less mortar rounds or a ground assault!"

I said, "Yeah, this is a bitch! Let's just hope we don't get hit tonight."

Perhaps beginner's luck acted in my favor. By late afternoon we heard the best possible news—our company received orders to move off the location. *Yes, oh yes!* Overwhelmingly grateful and relieved, I gave my fellow digger a high five. By moving out of the area before dark our company would surely dodge a bullet—not to mention several mortar rounds.

At dusk the unit packed up and moved about two clicks—we called kilometers *clicks*—and our leaders found a place to bivouac for the night. We set up in three man groups spaced about 20 feet apart along the circumference of a makeshift circular perimeter. In each three man group, one man is up on guard while the other two sleep, and we rotate shifts. Each man sleeps for two hours and then is up on guard for one hour, twice per night. Sleeping straight through the night is a luxury unavailable to soldiers living in the field.

Although exhausted from the stress of the day, I dared not even think about falling asleep while up on guard duty—especially on my first night. If caught, my fellow soldiers would skin me alive. Sitting up with my legs crossed and M16 in my lap, I stared into the darkness that first long hour. As soon as I felt drowsy, my mind visualized Charlie skulking around nearby, and I became wide-eyed and alert.

During a clear, moonless night, the bright stars and Milky Way seemed within arm's reach. Staring up into the beautiful expanse provided a temporarily escape from the harsh reality on terra firma. My mind wandered in many directions, but not for long. Once again self-doubt and fear haunted my thoughts—*how will I react in a firefight? Will I do something stupid and endanger my fellow soldiers? Am I in over my head? Will I be a coward?* I felt isolated among a group of men I didn't know and some of whom seemed skeptical about my abilities as a soldier. Although in the field only one day, I longed for family and the creature comforts of home.

Fortunately, the night passed without incident. *One day down, 350 to go.* The highly anticipated day I would leave Vietnam seemed as far away as the stars.

Adjustment

During my first ten days in the field leading up to a company pre-scheduled three day stand-down, our unit didn't engage in any battles. The lull in activity created a relatively relaxed atmosphere, allowing me to become better acquainted with the men in my platoon. Growing up in a white neighborhood, I had little social contact with people of other races and ethnicities. At first I felt uneasy among the

51

African American and Hispanic men in my platoon, but it wasn't out of prejudice, but inexperience. I didn't know how to relate, and with racial relations a touchy national issue, I feared saying or doing the wrong thing. However, as I began to know them I realized most of our outward differences were superficial. I learned Seth, a Jewish boy from Brooklyn, earned a reputation as the platoon entertainer. Delgado, a first generation American from New Mexico, was our best marksman, and Tyler, an African American from Washington D.C., served as squad leader. Platoon leader Sergeant Sawyer hailed from Alabama. We were young men from all corners of America compelled to work together under difficult conditions within a hostile environment.

My friendly attitude and sense of humor helped to break the ice.

One day Seth asked, "How are you doin' Richert—gettin' used to things out here?"

In my best imitation of the voice of Disney cartoon character Goofy, I replied. "Garsh, ma boots is sure tight. Oops, I musta put 'em on backwards—ah-hoolk, ah-hoolk, ah-hoolk."

Seth laughed out loud. Sometimes I would switch from one character to another in mid-sentence. The men enjoyed my repertoire of impressions. In no time I formed genial relationships with most of the men in the platoon—black, white, and Hispanic. Instead of feeling like an outsider, I began to feel like part of the team—although my mettle had yet to be tested.

The lull in enemy activity during those first ten days also provided me the opportunity to begin adjusting to the physical hardships of day to day life in the bush. I carried a 70 pound rucksack while trekking long distances, and endured intense heat, frequent and sometimes pounding rain, armies of insects, a perpetual state of dirtiness, and sleeping outdoors in the open. Although Vietnam is located in the earth's northern hemisphere, it is close to the equator and the climate is tropical. The northern section of South Vietnam experiences torrential rains and sometimes typhoons strike between November and January. Between June and October, thunderstorms build up and dump rain mostly during the afternoon hours when heat and humidity are at their max. Under these tropical conditions, we infantry soldiers became exposed to ailments like heat stroke, staph infections, and malaria—and the harsh elements subjected our clothing and equipment to rapid deterioration.

Sweet 16

The M16 rifle served as the principal weapon of the infantry, and I treated mine like a teddy bear. I cleaned it regularly and always kept it close by, including during the night whether up on guard or asleep. The M16 is capable of unleashing devastating fire power. For example, when the expelled round strikes tissue or bone it is designed to fragment into small bits of shrapnel, thus inflicting further damage inside the body. The results are not pretty, but this type of ammunition provides an advantage in combat. A bullet passing through or doing minimal damage may not sufficiently disable the ability of an enemy soldier to continue on the attack.

On the fully automatic setting, M16 rounds fire in rapid succession as long as the trigger remains depressed. However, under this setting the rifle expends rounds so rapidly a soldier can run through his supply of ammo within a few minutes. In addition, the recoil on fully automatic makes the weapon difficult to control. Thus, this setting is inefficient in combat. On the semiautomatic setting, one round is discharged with each pull of the trigger. Repeatedly pulling the trigger expels rounds in succession—like a slowed down version of a machine gun. We soldiers were instructed to fire on semiautomatic in successive short bursts—rapidly expel three to five rounds, pause briefly, and keep repeating the cadence. With the other men firing their weapons in a similar manner, the overall firepower is continuous. This method maximized the effectiveness and longevity of the unit's ammunition.

Each rifleman carried two cloth belts which together held 16 magazines, each of which holds up to 20 rounds. One of the first things I learned in the field was *not* to load each magazine to its full capacity because this greatly increased the potential for a jam. This design flaw became well-known, so our leaders instructed us to load 18 rounds.

Teamwork

53

Shortly after arriving in the field, the platoon sergeant assigned me as squad assistant machine gunner. In addition to my M16 rifle and its ammo, I carried a 15 foot long belt of M60 machine gun rounds by slinging it around both shoulders, Poncho Villa style, and wrapping the remainder around my waist two or three times. Wrapping the heavy belt in this way helped to distribute the weight.

Two men in our platoon carried the M60 machine gun—the platoon's most potent weapon, and therefore the most vital. However, at forty-three inches long and a weight of thirty-eight pounds without ammo, it is a beast to handle, especially while humping long distances in Vietnam's oppressive heat and humidity. Common sense dictated that the M60 be assigned to a soldier with sufficient strength to handle it efficiently. Considering my slim, 142 pound frame, lyrics from a Bob Dylan song seem most appropriate; "It ain't me babe, it ain't me you're lookin' for." Standing about six-foot-two and built like a truck, Ben carried the hulky weapon for our squad.

Ben and I arrived in Vietnam from diverse backgrounds. Before joining the army, Ben had barely roamed away from his small community in America's heartland. He was a big strong farm boy from Nebraska and I was a scrawny Southern California kid. Ben's life was filled with hard work, mine was filled with play. He was reserved, I was outgoing. He was no nonsense and straight laced, I was a jokester. Despite our superficial differences, I liked Ben. He was the real deal, heartland all the way. I teased him about his *Green Acres* life style, but he shrugged it off. During quiet moments I confided my respect for the pride and contentment he felt for life on the farm, and he enjoyed hearing my stories about Southern California with all of its famous attractions.

Ben and I understood the importance of working together as a cohesive unit. In a firefight, a soldier's first reaction is to hit the ground and take cover. Next is to regain his wits, orient himself, and begin firing back while keeping a low profile. Maintaining steady fire with the M60 is critical to the effectiveness of the unit as a whole. A five-foot long belt of rounds remained loaded into the machine gun at all times, so in the event of an attack, the gunner is able to begin shooting immediately. However, with a maximum firing rate of 650 rounds per minute, it doesn't take long for five feet of ammo to run its course. In the event of an attack, I had to quickly attach the end of my belt to the end of Ben's, plus ensure all 15 feet of it didn't become entangled. Not long after being assigned assistant gunner, thoughts began buzzing around inside my head about how our two-man team might work together in the most efficient manner.

One morning I approached Ben to share my concerns. "Don't you think we should develop and practice a routine so we can act quickly while under fire?"

Ben asked, "What do you have in mind?"

"As I see it, we need to devise the best method for me to access the end of my belt and then attach it to yours."

"Sounds good."

First, I had to wrap the ammo belt around my body in such a way that I could easily access and free its right end. I chose to locate it near my stomach area. My second challenge, after removing my rucksack, was to clip the right end of my belt to the left end of his, which hung loosely from the left side of the gun. My third challenge was to find a way to free the remaining length wrapped around my upper body while lying on the ground. Rolling over allowed me to unravel the belt without having to sit up or stand—not a good idea when taking fire.

Ben and I practiced moving from a standing position to hitting the ground and orienting ourselves for maximum effectiveness. Eventually we honed in on a simple, quick routine. We decided that during patrols he and I would always stay as close together as safety permitted. In addition, I would always keep to Ben's left—the side on which the M60 loads. Although these efforts may seem trivial, our leaders taught us that paying attention to small details can make the difference between life and death in a combat situation.

Put to the Test

During mid-morning on a hot August day, our company patrolled in the vicinity of a small village named An Loc. The flat landscape supported rice paddies, scattered palm trees, thickets of bamboo, and various shrubs. Clusters of vegetation provided Charlie with plenty of cover. Our captain assigned my platoon to act as a reserve force for the other platoons in the company while they conducted a sweep through the hamlet. Upon approach, they came under attack. Our platoon, about 100 yards away, quick-stepped toward the village to provide support. My squad spread out laterally in a frontal assault line so we wouldn't be caught in each other's line of fire. Everyone's nerves were on edge.

Ben reminded me, "Make sure to stay close by and on my left."

"Got it—I'll be right here with you Ben."

We arrived within minutes. Almost immediately, our squad came under fire from a machine gun emplacement located near the center of the village. As bullets began flying, it felt like electricity replaced the blood flowing through my veins. "Oh...shit!"

The situation became chaotic. Weapons fired, our squad leader barked orders, and soldiers yelled. Heart pounding out of my chest, somehow I reacted quickly. Ben and I hit the ground—me at his left and both of us laying prone behind an earthen berm about two and a half feet in height. Enemy rounds zipped by above our heads and struck the area in front of us, but the berm provided sufficient protection. Ben propped his M60 on top and began firing from behind it. Although hunkered down and scared, I managed to quickly remove my rucksack and attach the open end of my belt to his. Meanwhile, I rolled my body to free the remainder of the belt. *Our technique is working!* Ben kept firing steady bursts uninterrupted.

The rat-tat-tat sound of Ben's machine gun along with our squad's M16 rifles caused ringing in my ears. Blue-gray smoke from rifle and machine gun fire drifted sideways in the breeze, and the smell of gunpowder filled my nostrils. I fired successive short bursts toward the direction of enemy fire, but probably didn't hit anything but bushes and trees. However, in a firefight it is important to lay down a field of fire if for no other reason than to intimidate the enemy and keep them on the defensive.

Despite being under attack, Ben maintained command of the M60 throughout. With devastating fire power, he sprayed successive rounds toward the direction of enemy fire. I recall thinking—or perhaps wishing—the VC had to be outmatched. Busy making sure

56

the belt of rounds loaded properly into the M60 while alternately firing my weapon, I couldn't pay attention to what other men in the squad were doing. I just listened for orders. Nor did I see the enemy soldiers or their machine gun. It may seem odd, but my viewpoint of the battle constituted mostly the few cubic feet of space surrounding Ben and me.

The battle ended in less than ten minutes, but seemed to last longer. During a firefight, the inevitable rush of adrenaline seems to slow time. The men began taking inventory of themselves, their comrades, their gear, and the situation. I wiped gunpowder residue from around my eyes, and tried to clear my throat.

Squad leader Tyler asked repeatedly, "Is anyone hurt?"

No one responded in the affirmative.

Seth, one of our squad's most experienced members, expressed our squad's collective anxiety succinctly—"Whew, that was hairy!"

Our leaders gloated about pushing the enemy back and killing two VC attackers without acquiring any serious casualties. I don't recall how the enemy soldiers met their deaths. If they were shot, it's likely that in the confusion no one knew by whom.

Interestingly, during those first few moments while under fire I felt frightened, but once on the ground fear became mitigated by the busy activity of helping Ben and shooting at the enemy—along with the aid of a healthy dose of adrenaline pulsing through my veins. In one sense the experience felt exhilarating.

Ben said, "You should be proud that our practice routine worked so beautifully. That was good thinking."

I high-fived Ben and said, "Thanks. You're a rock my friend!"

After twenty minutes, the nerves of most of us had settled down, but Gary remained visibly agitated. I observed him shaking vigorously, and panting heavily.

In a quavering voice, he related, "I was dodging bullets—they were flying by all around me just like in a John Wayne war movie. My God I can't believe I wasn't hit. It's a miracle I'm still alive—I should be dead. It's a miracle I tell you!"

For the rest of the day Gary's closest buddies stuck by him and attempted to quell his anxiety. Understandably, hours passed before he regained his composure.

It is likely a dozen or so enemy soldiers attacked our company. Typical of VC tactics, they hit us hard and then quickly dissolved into the bush. However, in addition to the two kills, our company captured the machine gun directed toward our squad, other weapons, and valuable intelligence documents.

Due in large part to our practice routine, I believe the quick response and efficiency demonstrated by Ben and I helped our squad succeed in repelling the enemy. However, neither of us ever boasted about our teamwork. Along with the other soldiers in our squad, we considered our contribution just part of the job. Apparently someone in authority disagreed. Unbeknownst to the members of our platoon, one of our leaders somewhere up the chain of command submitted paperwork to Division headquarters requesting each member of our squad be awarded an Army Commendation Medal with a 'V' Device—V for valor.

True to my earlier pledge about not telling my parents about combat experiences, I never wrote home about this firefight. Ironically, I first heard about earning the medal, not from the army, but from my parents! Two months after the incident and while on stand-down at Chu Lai, I made a call home. Mom and Dad related that they had recently received an official letter from the army describing the battle and announcing I earned a medal.

Mom said, "We are stunned to learn our son is a war hero."

"Me, a war hero—what is this all about, Mom?"

Surprised, Dad said, "You mean you don't know you earned a medal?"

Embarrassed, I said, "No, this is the first I've heard about it." Mom proceeded to read excerpts from the letter, and it finally dawned on me the medal had been issued for the battle at An Loc.

Not wanting to add to my parent's anxiety and because of my surprise at learning the news, I responded, "Oh no, no, it wasn't such a big deal, really. We just reacted quickly during the firefight. Don't worry about me, I'm fine."

As we said our goodbyes, Dad said, "Your mom and I are very proud of you. Stay safe my son."

Even after learning about the honor, I never thought of myself as a hero. Instead, I prefer to emphasize the importance of preparedness before going into battle. This is the important message of my story.

CHAPTER 4

Day to Day Life in the Infantry
Part 1

War is, "months of boredom punctuated by moments of extreme terror."
Source uncertain, but possibly Guy's Hospital Gazette, 1914

When I arrived at my infantry unit, I feared combat would be the rule, not the exception. Thankfully, the above quotation is closer to the truth, except I seldom suffered from boredom. In the next two chapters I offer a series of mostly short essays about day to day life in the infantry. Each is written around a central theme. Most of the topics are often neglected in books about war. They range from the gritty to the funny, and all are intended to inform, entertain, or enlighten.

The average infantry soldier in Vietnam spent the majority of his active daytime hours trekking long distances while carrying a 70 pound rucksack along with weapons and ammo in over 90 degree heat with extreme humidity. Sometimes my unit patrolled in company sized operations of around 90 men, but more often the four platoons averaging 23 men each separated to work independently.

Sometimes trucks or helicopters picked us up at one location and dropped us off at another, sometimes we worked with track vehicle units, but most of the time we hoofed it from place to place.

Our unit wasn't always on the move. During some assignments we remained at one location for days, usually to provide security. Whether idle or on the move, enduring the harsh conditions of life in the field proved to be a day to day grind. We soldiers were constantly pestered by bugs, day and night, and always dirty, sweaty, and tired. The heat, humidity, pests, and unsanitary conditions took a toll on our stamina, health, and morale.

Letter to my Family - September 20, 1969
Wet

Today we go on bunker guard at Charlie Brown just down the road apiece. At least I'll be dry for four days (we slept inside fortified bunkers). It has been raining every day for the last week. Today it's windy and partially cloudy, but no rain. When we moved to our night location we went through a lake of water about two feet deep. These lowlands are getting wetter every day. At night we build hooches (a simple lean-to made with a rubberized poncho and tent stakes) to keep dry, but sometimes the wind screws it up.

Upon re-reading the above letter, my thoughts drifted to the brave men (and recently women) who served before me in WW II and Korea, and after me in the Mideast. They all endured nasty weather conditions—be it the bitter cold of Europe and Korea in winter, the sweltering humidity, and intense storms of the Pacific Theater, or the blistering dry heat and sandstorms of the Mideast. Climatic conditions have always been a priority consideration in the design of military equipment and clothing, construction of base camps, planning of battle strategy, and maintaining morale. Historically, weather has changed the course of battles, even major wars. Consider Hitler's disastrous offensive into Russia during the winter of 1941.

Soldiers cope with adverse weather in various ways, often by griping, but occasionally by making light of it—like the day when several of us sought relief from a downpour by huddling together under the overhang of a dense tree.

Frustrated, Larry asked, "Hey Richert! Why aren't wars fought in places with nice climates like Southern California where you live?"

"Hey man, forget Southern California. We like to make love, not war. We go to the beach all day and party all night."

The chatter helped to lighten the mood, but Larry had a point. Southern California, especially along the coast where I grew up, is known for one of the most pleasant climates anywhere. Thunderstorms occur, but mostly inland. During my youth I heard thunder, saw lightning, and felt the rain from these infrequent events, but they didn't prepare me for the storms on steroids I endured while living outdoors in Vietnam.

July, August, and September rains usually resulted from the build-up of localized thunderheads during the hottest part of the afternoon. Observing small, innocuous cotton puffs rapidly swell into ominous billowing towers stretching higher and higher into the upper atmosphere and then unleashing their fury, was both spellbinding and frightening. *What bitter irony if I were killed or injured in Vietnam, not from enemy fire, but from lightning or a flash flood.*

Sometimes Vietnam's thunderstorms unleashed massive quantities of water. The precipitation seemed to explode upon us soldiers like the cascade of bullets pummeling down on the enemy from the mini-guns of a Cobra helicopter. Exposed in the open, sometimes we hunkered down under bushes or trees, but mostly we had no choice but to soak it up. Eventually the hot sun fought its way through the breaking tempest and at least partially dried our equipment and clothing—until the next round of cloudbursts arrived. It wasn't all bad. Summer showers often provided a welcome period of refreshment. The water felt cool. Sometimes we stripped down naked and washed days of dirt and grime off our bodies. Once the hot sun reemerged, our wet clothing dried out quickly. Of course, *dried out* is a relative term in Vietnam's extremely humid climate.

July and August rains occurred sporadically and with varying intensity throughout the day and night with one exception.

62

Curiously, almost daily near 4 pm, clouds opened up and dumped heavy rain for up to an hour—nature's version of an alarm clock. This prompted a daily warning from the men in my platoon. For example, Reynolds, who hailed from Florida, warned, "It's almost 1600 hours—batten down the hatches—Niagara falls will soon be on us."

Whereas periods of hard, pelting rain interrupted the mostly sunny days of summer, November and December rains persisted day and night in an almost uninterrupted drizzle or light mist. In the northern section of South Vietnam, winter rains arrive around late October and last through January. Records from November, 1969, reveal an unusually damp and cold month for Vietnam. I can attest to that! Every day an overcast sky stretched from horizon to horizon. I don't recall seeing the sun once during the entire month. Daytime temperatures seldom rose above the mid-seventies, and some nights went down into the fifties. When you are accustomed to unrelenting heat in the nineties and hundreds, temperatures in the fifties feel like those of a Minnesota winter.

In Chapter 2 I related comments offered up by my fellow AIT trainees from the east coast and Midwest. They complained about the cold, wet weather at Ford Ord, California, during January and February. November in Vietnam seemed like déjà vu all over again.

Conway from South Dakota griped; "I thought Vietnam is supposed to be hot all year around. What's with this continuous cold drizzle?"

"Yeah", added Jennings. "I'm from Northern Michigan. I've been through minus 40 degree freezing spells, but this cold, damp shit is almost as bad."

Knowing our fatigues provided inadequate protection from this unusual weather, in early November our platoon lieutenant requested a chopper bring waterproof rain suits. The rubberized *Farmer John* style pants and jackets helped, but somehow the unrelenting dampness managed to penetrate all the way to my skin. Whereas summer's heat and humidity made me feel sweaty and grimy, November's dampness made me feel clammy. Heads you lose, tails you lose.

One day while undressed, I inspected my crotch. "Geez Andy, with this weather who knows what kind of crud can be growing there. Any day now I expect to see moss growing on my balls."

Andy laughed; "So, is this why you are always scratching those damn things?"

Although keeping our bodies reasonably dry proved an annoyance, maintaining our weapons was critical to the safety of our unit. The M16 will function when the exterior is wet, but moisture inside the barrel, bolt mechanism, or other vital internal parts could cause a malfunction. Coming under attack only to discover a significant percentage of rifles wouldn't fire is a platoon nightmare. Our leaders rightfully ordered us to keep our weapons well maintained, and as dry as possible. During patrols I kept my M16 pointed downward so the water would roll off and not enter the barrel, and during idle time I usually kept it under a palm leaf or my poncho. Our rucksacks were made water resistant, but not waterproof. Thus, we soldiers sealed our cameras, writing materials, and other valuables inside double plastic bags.

In addition to physical discomfort, November's weather induced mental miseries—especially depression. Living outdoors day after day under sunless, damp, gloomy gray gets you down—especially when your morale is already low. We soldiers compensated by keeping busy during our idle time. We played cards, clowned around, and shared stories about our families and life at home. When alone, I sheltered under my poncho and wrote letters or read a paperback. November's cool, misty environment did provide a few benefits—far fewer bugs, zero potential for heat stroke, less need for drinking water, and because of rising rivers and flooding, less enemy activity.

"If you don't like the weather now, just wait a few minutes."
Mark Twain, American writer

Audiotape - February 9, 1970
Rain

One day on a mission into the mountains, we went out on a light patrol during the day. That means without our heavy

64

rucksacks. The plan was that some soldiers stay back at camp during the day while my group went on patrol to check out a valley. We were to come back in the afternoon and then move a few hundred meters from our day camp to another location for the night.

We always moved off a daytime location after dark (to bivouac for the night) because if Charlie is out there, he wouldn't know where we were going. Anyway, during the morning we went out on a light patrol and on our way we had to cross a stream. It was no problem because the water was only ankle deep. This was monsoon season. Everyone was wearing rain suits—the bottoms are similar to a Farmer John and it keeps you dry. However, when we waded through water, it came up through the bottom near the ankles. That wasn't too bad. We went out in the morning about 10 AM or so, and it had been raining lightly the whole time. We moved out and checked out the valley, but didn't see anything unusual. It continued to rain the entire time, but not hard, just a drizzle.

When we came back in the early afternoon to the same spot along the river we crossed earlier, the water was up to our necks! We sought out the best place we could find to cross. I don't know how the first guy got across, but somehow he did. The rest of us formed a chain. Everybody grabbed the arm or weapon of the man next to him and somehow hung on. We made our way across, but slowly. A couple of guys went under, weapon and all. The water was rushing really fast and if they hadn't been hanging on, they would have been pulled way down stream. The brush was so thick around the stream that they wouldn't have been able to get out. They would have to fight their way back up along its bank to rejoin us. I went under water all the way up to my neck. My weapon and I got totally soaked, and the water was cold.

We finally made our way back to camp about 2 PM. The rest of the day I sat around in a make shift hooch made of ponchos, like a pup tent. We burned heat tablets and anything else we could find to help keep us warm. We took off our rain suits, but kept our clothes on. The goal was to allow the fire to

65

slowly dry us, but it never did. The fire was just too small. The only part of my body that got dry was my knees because they were closest to the fire. That night we had to sleep all wet, cold, and soggy—yech! If you get dirty or wet, you can't change clothes out there. We had to stay that way for the five days in the mountains.

After our mission, we came back in to Charlie Brown to change clothes. We couldn't even take a shower because it was too cold. The temperature was about 50 degrees and the showers are all outdoors. The wind was blowing and also cold. People think it is always hot in Vietnam, but not during this time. Sometimes after returning from one mission, we were unable to shower because of the cold, and we immediately went out on another mission. The longest period I went so far without showering was about two weeks, which isn't too bad for Vietnam. That was better than I did at home—ha, ha!

Creature Discomforts

In addition to coping with the weather, a cornucopia of creeping, crawling, and sky cruising critters tormented us weary soldiers. During my first couple of weeks in the infantry, I frequently heard the warning, *watch out for the two-stepper!* The two-stepper, also called three-stepper in some units, allegedly topped the list of Vietnam's most dangerous snakes. Once bitten, after taking two or three steps you fall dead, thus the name. I never saw one of these legendary serpents or heard about a verified death, so I wondered, *is the two-stepper a mythical creature?*

In writing this section, I decided to search the internet for information. It turns out Vietnam hosts some of the world's deadliest snakes, including numerous vipers and pit vipers, coral snakes, cobras, and kraits—ouch! However, no known species of snake on the planet can kill a human within a few seconds. The world's most venomous land dwelling snake is the black mamba, a species native to Africa. Its neurotoxin can kill in two and a half minutes, but only if the fangs penetrate a blood vessel leading straight to the heart. This rarely occurs. Most toxic snake bites require hours to kill their victims. That being said, more than 30 of Vietnam's 140 species of snakes are venomous. The most likely candidate for the two-stepper legend is the banded krait. Its venom is extremely potent, but normally requires hours to cause death. The record fatality rate for a bite is 30 minutes.

It appears the two-stepper story was just so much wartime snake oil...venom. No doubt the deeply entrenched human phobia of these slithering serpents added *scale* to the legend.

I once asked Seth, who had been in country for six months, about the two-stepper.

He replied, "I think the military keeps the story alive to keep us scared of all snakes."

I said, "Not a bad idea, considering how many of the damn things must be out there."

Actually, I don't recall seeing large numbers of snakes in Vietnam. I never saw a cobra, but I did see an occasional unidentifiable species, a few boa constrictors, and the small, slender green vine snake. Fortunately, the infamous reptiles never posed a major problem for our company in the field. To my recollection, no one ever received a bite.

One reptile in Vietnam was real, not a rumor, and known by its profane nickname, the *fuck-you lizard*. With a little imagination, its call is clearly audible, and sounds like—you got it! In an effort to attract mates or announce its territory, the call is repeated over and over during the night. The fuck-you lizard's more formal, but less colorful name is the Tokay Gecko. Search Tokay Gecko on YouTube and you will find images along with recordings of its distinctive call. After researching this intriguing reptile, I regret I never observed one in Vietnam. I had no idea the lizard is so large—up to 20 inches in length. The reason why I never saw one during all those months living outdoors in the field is because this species of gecko, uncommon for reptiles in general, is primarily nocturnal. It probably hid under rocks or deep inside thick brush during the day. I frequently heard its audible call mostly while sitting up on guard during the stillness of the night. One day in an act of mischief, I decided to fool my fellow grunts by learning to imitate it. Although I practiced repeatedly, the fuck-you lizard's memorable and unique sound proved too difficult to duplicate.

At one location along the coast near Chu Lai, I encountered an impressive group of *water monitors*. The prehistoric looking reptiles, some over six feet long, lived where I didn't expect any lizard would thrive—along a sandy beach within feet of the surf. In fascination, I watched them scurry about and move in and out of holes mostly hidden within clumps of grasses. Presumably, water monitors dig these holes for shelter and to lay their eggs. They didn't appear to be aggressive. Several scooted by me like I wasn't there. However, I chose not to sneak up on one for closer inspection. After all, water monitors are close relatives to the largest lizards on earth today, the famous Komodo dragons of Indonesia. These relics of the Cretaceous are known to attack and eat humans. Thankfully, water monitors feed on small prey like fish, rodents, and crabs—not children or lean GI's like me.

Enemy Aerial Assaults

While reptiles proved more a curiosity than hazard in the field, bugs posed a persistent problem. Mosquitoes were the worst. Like the Viet Cong, what they lacked in size, they more than made up for in numbers, aggressiveness, and determination. At dusk, clouds of them hovered over rice paddies, marshes, or any area with still water—in other words, almost everywhere.

A few years ago I viewed a video recording featuring a large congregation of starlings performing a sky dance over England (search *clouds of starlings* on YouTube). The undulating motions of these small birds brought back memories of the shifting masses of mosquitoes I saw in Vietnam—except starlings don't try to eat you alive. Our leaders strongly advised us soldiers to take our malaria pills regularly and budget our use of repellent. The latter proved easier said than done. Sometimes resupply arrived late, or we soldiers ran out of the precious juice prematurely. The following letter is one of my more colorfully written. My choice to compose it in the third person reflects sarcasm born out of frustration.

Letter to my Family - September 11, 1969
Mosquitoes

Boy, last night was miserable—mosquitoes all over the place, and no repellent. You could hear a mess of them circling over your head, and then, biz-z-z-z, one at a time they come dive-bombing at your ears, arms, back, and ankles. Then you cover up with your poncho liner head to foot and listen to their spine shivering shrills as they hover over you mercilessly—as if they know that you are boiling under that poncho liner and can't breathe. They make a few swoops over you, sometimes landing for just a few seconds just to annoy you—hovering and swooping impatiently until you give in—you just can't stand suffocating and sweating under that poncho liner, so you pull it off. Then, biz-z-z, it seems like there are millions of them dive bombing you, and you start scratching and swatting at places where it doesn't even itch. Finally, after endless hours, morning comes and the mosquitoes are gone, their bellies full of your blood. You heat some water and laboriously with great care, make your cocoa. Peace at last. Then just as you are about to take a sip, biz-z-z, oh no, here come the flies!

Every time I started to nod off, an irritating, high-pitched chorus of vibrating wings rousted me. After a nerve wracking night without sleep, next morning it was back to hauling my heavy rucksack on extended patrol through the bush. From that day on, I decided to manage my repellent more efficiently. In order to work effectively, the juice must be applied liberally and over all exposed areas of the body, including the face—sometimes twice per night. The platoon received re-supply about once a week, so I calculated a dozen of the four ounce plastic squirt bottles would suffice to get me through nights between deliveries. My calculations worked. I never again ran out of the liquid armor. Although I could not avoid encounters, none of my subsequent bouts with the pesky blood suckers measured up to the miserable night I describe in the above letter.

The dry climate of Southern California is not ideal habitat for mosquitoes, so their numbers are far lower than in the tropics.

During my youth they bred mostly in stagnant drainage ditches. I never endured their presence during my frequent visits to the beach. On one particularly hot evening in early August, our platoon set up in a relatively safe area within a hundred feet of the South China Sea. The azure blue water, white sandy beaches, and rows of coconut trees looked like something out of the movie *South Pacific*. My first time at bivouac close to the ocean, I assumed that, like back home, mosquitoes were less prevalent by the sea. Deciding it's better to be safe than sorry, I spread a layer of bug juice on my exposed arms and face. It turned out to be a wise decision because I would soon find out that Vietnamese mosquitoes are not as reluctant about going to the beach as their Southern California cousins.

As darkness settled in, the thermometer didn't seem to drop even a millimeter. The temperature had to be well into the nineties, and the evening air hovered in dead stillness. *Oh, how I miss the cool, refreshing sea breezes back home.* Although the long-sleeved fatigue shirt offered better protection from mosquitoes, wearing it on a hot, steamy night becomes unbearable. Instead, we soldiers wore our T-shirts, but this left our arms exposed.

The Competition

Just after dark, my buddy Greg and I sat next to each other on our poncho liners spread over sand still warm from absorbing a day of sizzling sunrays. Greg was new in country and still learning the ropes. In an effort to distract our minds from the heat, we talked about life back home and other mundane matters. He and I shared much in common. Like me, Greg grew up in a suburban environment, except he hailed from Ohio. Like me, his thin build made adjusting to the hardships of day to day life in the field difficult. I offered advice to help make his days in the boonies more endurable, including the need to carry plenty of insect repellant. Claiming the mosquitoes didn't bother him, Greg refused to smother his exposed skin with the protective liquid.

"Hey, we have lots of these back home in Ohio, so I'm used to 'em."

I quipped, "Maybe, but this ain't Ohio."

Greg's exposed arms soon became an irresistible lure for hungry aerial hunters on the prowl. Sure enough, the mosquitoes dive bombed him without mercy.

Greg said nonchalantly, "I can handle this. I'll just slap the little buggers away."

As for me, heavy layers of repellent kept most of the pests at bay.

While Greg made busy with his game of swatting mosquitoes, I looked up at the magnificent, cloudless night sky with a half-moon. Back home the bright lights of suburbia obscure the view, so under the pristine conditions of rural Vietnam, I marveled at the expanse of star-filled sky and Milky Way.

The Perseid meteor shower occurs each year during August, and for astronomy buffs like me, this night did not disappoint. Every few seconds, I saw one or more shooting stars flash across the purplish backdrop. Actually, the term *shooting star* is a misnomer. Meteors are not stars—most are vagrant baseball to sofa sized chunks of asteroids or comets. They burn up upon entry into the earth's upper atmosphere. It seems hard to believe that objects so small and far away can burn so brightly, but traveling at over 30,000 miles per hour when striking the earth's dense atmosphere, the resulting friction releases tremendous amounts of energy.

I kept nudging Greg while exclaiming, "Wow, did you see that flash? It was really bright. Oh, look at the green one—it's breaking up!" Greg didn't share my enthusiasm. He remained preoccupied with swatting mosquitoes. Apparently his earlier boast was no exaggeration. The invaders didn't seem to bother him. In fact, he enjoyed making a game out of killing as many of the pests as possible before they could sink their proboscises into his irresistible arms.

After ten minutes of this activity, the proverbial bulb lit over my head. "Hey Greg, I have an idea. Let's make a bet. When I say, 'Go!' you start counting the number of mosquitoes you kill and I'll count each meteor I see. Let's time it for two minutes. Only mosquitoes you kill, not just swat at, will count, so look to see you got 'em and keep track. The winner gets his choice of any item in the other guy's C-rations. What do you say? I'm gonna beat you buddy!"

Greg couldn't resist my challenge. I checked my watch and asked, "Are you ready?"

Nodding approvingly he said, "Ready when you are."

I snapped, "Go!"

Instantly, Greg started swatting, I started observing, and we both busied ourselves counting. For the first ten seconds or so, the race seemed close.

I shouted enthusiastically, "Number 11—it's a small one, but I'll take it. Oh, there's 12 and 13—both at once. You're in trouble...!"

Greg interrupted, "Cool it! You're making me lose track of my count."

I shut up and kept tabulating my sightings. On occasion, I glanced over at my opponent. By three-quarters through the time limit it became obvious I had fallen behind. Greg swatted mosquitoes with a flurry of flailing arms, sometimes killing more than one with a single slap.

I called time, and in a timid voice said, "I counted 34 meteors. How did you do?"

Greg nonchalantly quipped, "I lost track after 56."

My last precious can of *Beef Spiced with Sauce* became his well-deserved trophy. Despite the excitement of his victory, a few minutes later Greg began to show signs of exasperation. He still swatted at the persistent pests, but at a much less frenetic pace. In a *vain* attempt to take respite from his attackers, Greg slumped head down and folded his arms into his chest and between his knees. I tried to lift his spirits; "56 dead mosquitoes in less than two minutes—not bad my man. That's one helluva story for the folks back home." Finally, reason overrided his ego and he decided to grab some repellent.

While Greg scrambled for bug juice, I looked up toward the sky and my mood became philosophical. "Jeez, Greg, there must be billions of stars up there."

Greg paused from rubbing repellent over his splotchy, tired arms, looked up toward the sky with me, and sighed, "Yeah, and just as many mosquitoes down here!"

We both agreed they were true winners of the competition.

Violators of the Right to Privacy

When it came to insect pests in Vietnam, bigger didn't necessarily mean badder. One day our platoon set up bivouac on a gently sloping hill—more like a mound really. Atypical for Vietnam, only a few scattered bushes and trees dotted the mostly rocky landscape. Except for the humidity, this area reminded me of the semi-desert terrain one sees in San Bernardino County, California. Too hot to go on extended patrols, our 23 man platoon sat idle during the day. All remained peaceful until late morning. At about 11 am, the enemy struck. Zillions of tiny black gnats, each about one-quarter inch long, suddenly emerged from out of nowhere.

I told Andy, "They're everywhere! Where did they come from?"

Andy replied, "You studied biology, you tell me."

The unrelenting pests began swarming around my head and body. Wherever I moved, the mass moved with me. As if the bugs would heed my desperate plea and back off, I yelled, "Get away from me—you're driving me crazy!"

Probably in search of moisture, the gnats tried to enter my mouth, eyes, ears, and nose. I busily tried removing those with the fingers on one hand while shooing the rest away with the other. The black blizzard became so annoying I couldn't keep still. I waved, moved, and cussed, but with little effect. The implacable invaders persisted and persisted—the insect version of a Tet offensive.

I've got to find someplace, any place, to find relief. Visibility was impeded because I narrowed my eyes to slits in an effort to keep the bugs from entering. Ambling about in search of an oasis, but finding none, I wanted to scream, *I can't take this anymore. I give up!* However, opening my mouth would only serve as an invitation for my adversaries to enter. The intense heat added misery upon misery. After over an hour of this onslaught, I became sweaty, exhausted, and thoroughly frustrated—battle fatigue.

The invasion let up slightly in the early afternoon, just in time for lunch. The bugs stayed away while I unwrapped and munched cheese and crackers, but I sensed the juicy fruit cocktail would be an irresistible lure. Sure enough, as soon as I began to dip my spoon into the can, the plunderers got wind of my sweet meal and came back in spades. My attempts to finish quickly became *fruitless* because each time I scooped up a spoonful I had to swish flies away and pick out those landing on my utensil and inside the can.

Somehow I managed to finish the fruit, along with a few accidental bits of insect protein, but a half-inch of the precious juice remained at the bottom. To my chagrin, several of the black buggers had engulfed themselves in the sticky nectar. *Damn, that's the best part.* My patience at an end, I yelled, "Fuck it!", and flung the can and its prisoners away like a Frisbee.

What were the other guys doing during the siege? I'm sure they suffered equally, but because of my preoccupation with the peppery cloud of pests, I didn't take notice. For much of the late morning and early afternoon I felt like a shipwrecked man isolated on an island—alone, helpless, and surrounded by a tiny air force of dive bombers. The ordeal waxed and waned at various levels of intensity for the next two hours. I can't imagine what would have happened had Charlie chosen to attack us during the height of the onslaught. *Please, one enemy at a time is enough!*

By late afternoon and as quickly as they appeared, the swarms of gnats seemed to dissolve into the bush like Charlie after an ambush.

As he raised his canteen for a toast, my buddy Larry said, "Whew—here's to peace at last!" Everyone raised their drinks in agreement and then shared their own harrowing story.

Reynolds, while rolling his tongue around the inside of his mouth remarked, "Shit, I must have spit out two dozen of the damn things. I swallowed some, too."

Tyler, while blinking, rolling, and rubbing his eyes, said, "I'm still trying to get pieces of the bastards out!"

Greg's defensive strategy showed creativity; "I lit a cigarette hoping the smoke would scare them off. It kept most of them away from my face."

In terms of pests, I never endured anything in Vietnam as intense as the two previously described insect assaults. It is amazing creatures so tiny can wreak so much havoc upon one's body and morale. If I had to go through nights and days like these on a regular basis in Vietnam, I would have gone insane.

Letter to my Family - August 1, 1969

There are bugs, and then there are bugs!

What's green and black, looks like a butterfly, a grasshopper, and a bee all in one, and flies silently? I don't know, but something like it just flew by. Every day I see an insect I've never seen before, and some weird varieties. One day I saw this *thing* that looked like a bunch of long feelers with just a small pair of wings holding it in the air

I didn't stray far from exaggeration in writing home about seeing a different type of bug every day. I saw eight-inch long centipedes, large and small spiders, butterflies, moths, beetles, bees, wasps, flies, ants, mosquitoes, gnats, plus things like I describe above that seemed to have blown in from another planet. Having to live with these pests on a daily basis provoked sarcastic comments from us grunts like, *the worst enemy in Vietnam is the damn bugs!* Then again, we soldiers were also forced to endure the heat...and the rain...and...

"There's a sucker born every minute."
P. T. Barnum, founder, Barnum and Bailey Circus

I cannot end this section without mention of the infamous and detested Vietnamese leeches—the *bug* kind, not the black market kind. Before joining the army, I heard unnerving stories about these slimy, slug-like critters, notorious for feasting on soldier blood. Leeches are not insects, they are segmented worms, and in Vietnam some species reach over six inches in length. That's a large tank to fill. They attach to their prey at the mouth and tail ends—double trouble! Sharp teeth sink firmly into flesh, and at the rear is a powerful sucker. The parasites thrive in moist tropical climates, and Vietnam provided plenty of ideal habitats.

In our region, leeches dwelled in slow moving streams and ponds. Most averaged about three inches in length. Like living magnets, they attached to our ankles, legs, and even our groin areas. A soldier's first reaction upon discovering the pests, besides disgust, is to swish them off as soon as possible. However, leech removal is not a simple task. It is impossible to obtain a firm grip on their soft, slimy, bodies, and once they latch on you almost need a crowbar to pull them off. The most common removal techniques included burning them with the lit end of a cigarette or saturating them with bug juice. These two methods usually caused them to release their grip, but the more stubborn among them had to be scraped off with the edge of a knife blade.

Once a soldier discovered one or more clinging to his body, he immediately notified the platoon because the other men likely carried the creepy critters. You would think when a leech sinks its teeth into your skin and attaches its sucker, the ensuing discomfort would raise a pain alarm. Not so. Leeches produce an anesthetic which numbs the affected area. This allows them to go about their bloody business undetected. Often, we wouldn't discover the hitchhikers until bothering to raise or lower our trousers and look. Of course, a soldier cannot visually inspect his rear end. For this unpleasant task he needs another pair of eyes.

One late morning, our platoon had just finished trudging waist deep through muddy water, and the men busied themselves at removing leeches.

Larry, said, "Damn, I think I may have one in the crack of my ass. I feel something squishy there." He asked me, "Can you check it out?"

"Okay", I said reluctantly. Larry dropped his drawers, bent over, and spread his cheeks.

"Is one there?"

I took a quick peek. "I think you're okay. It looks like some mucky green stuff."

Larry sighed, "Thank God!" He proceeded to wash the clump of muddied algae away with water from his canteen.

Meanwhile, I had planned to open a can of C-rations, but having lost my appetite, decided to write a letter home.

Although my body became a gourmet meal several times, thankfully, the suckers never acquired a taste for my genitals. Nonetheless, it was unsettling to look down and see three or four of the bloated buggers clinging to my legs and ankles.

I conclude this section of the chapter with a bit of advice. Next time you hear a veteran say, "Vietnam sucked," you have my permission to take him literally.

Letter to my Family - September 20, 1969
Hippies

Hippies seem to be searching for some fantasy-like world where everything grows on trees because they sure don't want to work. Almost all of the guys here are down on the hippie way of life. One reason is because in a way we out here in the field live like they try to—with very few material possessions, and man you can have that! All we can think about is cars, pepperoni pizza, our own bed, stereo, TV and all those other great things that hippies say they can do without.

None of the soldiers in my infantry unit claimed to be former hippies. However, with so many young men receiving draft notices during the late sixties, many hippie-types must have ended up serving as grunts in Vietnam. How many, after coming home, returned to their former lifestyle? I think this chapter and others in my book offer many clues toward answering that question.

CHAPTER 5

Day to Day Life in the Infantry
Part 2

Creature Comforts

The army furnished us grunts with clothing and amenities to make our lives more comfortable in the field. For example, I previously mentioned rain suits, ponchos, and occasional hot food sent out from base camp. The following section expands on the topic. Some of the creature comforts the army provided, although well intended, were unpopular with us grunts. Sometimes other sources provided items we enjoyed or made us more comfortable.

Jesus Christ Saves my Sole

Unlike the all leather black boots issued to us in basic training, portions of our jungle boots were made from a porous, pale green colored textile which allowed our feet to breathe. Although more comfortable than the all leather variety, I didn't like wearing them. I noticed the Vietnamese managed well with simple sandals or flip flops. *Why can't I wear those?* Back home I routinely wore Jesus Christ sandals, or JC's for short. The irreverent nickname came to be associated with then popular Clark sandals because of their resemblance to those worn in Biblical times. JC's could hardly be called official military attire, but regulations were considerably looser out in the bush than in rear areas.

I asked our platoon sergeant if I could have my sandals sent to me so I could wear them in the field. I argued, "Most of the gooks, including the VC, wear sandals and their feet don't rot off." To my surprise, Sergeant Sawyer acquiesced, but with the proviso I wear them only in pacified areas and those in which we went on light patrol. I wrote home and asked my parents to send the pair otherwise gathering dust in my closet. Three weeks later, my JC's arrived and I started wearing them immediately. Meanwhile, I kept my boots tied to the back of my rucksack. At first, several of my comrades poked fun at me.

Reynolds said, "Look at Richert the sissy gook!"

"Worthless hippie," chortled Seth.

After a few days of this good natured harassment, the men couldn't help but notice that my feet felt more comfortable and cooler than theirs stuffed inside bulky boots. Next thing you know, some of them began asking permission to write home requesting sandals or other comfortable footwear.

Andy commented, "Looks like you're starting a fashion trend."

Smiling, Larry added, "Yeah, maybe bell-bottomed fatigue pants will be his next request."

I came back; "Nix on that idea. It would just give the damn leeches an open invitation to crawl up my legs."

My fellow soldier's requests for haute couture didn't have a chance to get off the ground. Knowing the situation could get out of hand, or should I say foot, our platoon sergeant put the boot to it. He allowed me to continue wearing my JC's, but whatever envy men in the platoon may have felt became short lived. Despite their high quality construction, the elements quickly took a toll. In less than a month, my JC's fell apart. I gave them an appropriate burial, and no, they did not *rise* after three days.

Although I trudged my nearly bare feet through mud, bacteria infested rice paddy water and other nasty stuff, I never suffered from

79

an infection or other foot related problems—and certainly not silver dollar sized blisters like those I acquired during the 12 mile long march during stateside training. Could it be my JC's possessed divine healing powers?

"You want boom-boom?"
Solicitation for sex by local Vietnamese prostitutes

The above became a standard phrase because sexual encounters between horny US soldiers and local Vietnamese prostitutes usually lasted briefly—*boom, boom*, and it's over. The price for a quickie was two dollars for about two minutes of pleasure. In July, our platoon bivouacked for one week at a location where two local prostitutes, who we called, "Boom-boom girls," paid us nearly daily visits. Still relatively fresh from the states, I didn't find the village girls appealing. They wore cheesy, flimsy dresses, coolie hats, flip flops, and excessive makeup ineptly applied. *Not exactly Red Carpet attire.* Their attempts to walk and pose in a sexually alluring manner appeared clownish. At times I covered my mouth to hide laughter.

One of the girls attempted to solicit me; "Hey GI, you beaucoup horny? I make you feel like real man. You have good cum."

Ah, such romantic, poetic verse—ha! Elizabeth Barrett Browning must be turning over in her grave. Lacking the slightest motivation to partake in the services, I politely declined. My answer wasn't entirely due to disgust. During that first grueling month, the unsanitary conditions, suffering exhaustion from daily patrols, and the added stress, caused my sex drive to go into hibernation. *Who needs saltpeter?* Later, and after coming to accept a permanent patina of grime all over my body, the girls began to appear more attractive. If everyone is dirty and smells of body odor, the effects tend to neutralize each other. You just don't notice it. In addition, I became accustomed to the Vietnamese language, their unsophisticated clothing, and demeanor.

Highway 1

My platoon spent many days providing security alongside National Highway 1, the main north to south route in South Vietnam. Within our sector near Chu Lai, the thirty-foot wide paved road meandered along the coast—not unlike Pacific Coast Highway, also called Highway 1, in California. Typical motorized transportation included the moped, motor scooter, motorcycle, and small electric busses. Add a mish-mash of bicycles, two-wheeled human powered carts, pedestrians, and an occasional water buffalo accompanied by a man or child ambling along the shoulder. Despite the frenetic activity, no center line separated the two lanes of traffic moving in opposite directions.

Our military vehicles and convoys used the road, but I don't recall ever seeing a civilian automobile, truck, or school bus. Instead, small three-wheeled electric powered taxi buses—more like overgrown golf carts—served as public transportation. I stood watching with amazement at the amount of cargo, including large burlap bags stuffed with rice, hanging on the outside and strapped to the top of these fragile putt-putts. The accumulated mass, often larger than the bus itself, looked like a cancerous tumor. Judging by their awkward appearance, the vehicles had to be unstable. Yet, I never heard about one overturning or becoming involved in an accident. Traffic on Highway 1 would be best described as organized chaos.

Life along the highway appeared colorful as well as busy. Quaint fishing villages dotted the coastline, and a mosaic of rice paddies extended to the west. In a sea of coolie hats, numerous locals milled about and conducted commerce alongside the road near their villages. The Navy had built a small, but nicely afforded base at the end of a peninsula across a narrow, shallow bay opposite of Sa Huynh, the largest fishing village in the area. Sometimes our leaders obtained permission for us to visit and have lunch. We always looked forward to devouring some excellent Navy chow.

Road security along Highway 1 was, by far, the best of our rotating duties. The majority of Vietnamese civilians in this area had long been loyal to our forces and the South Vietnamese government. Thus, we seldom saw action there. In addition, securing the road all day meant we didn't have to go on extended patrols. We just sat around playing cards, writing letters home, sharing stories about our civilian lives, enjoying the numerous kids hanging around, or just goofing off. On those days when the platoon pulled security close to the beach, we went swimming.

Audiotape - February 9, 1970
"You want soda?"

During the day along the road, two soda girls visited regularly. One girl called herself Love—really—and the other was named May Lee or Maylene, I never could understand which. The two friends were about 17 years old. They weren't boom-boom type girls—no! These girls were nice (conservative). They made all their money selling sodas and lived in Bong Son, which is one of the larger towns in this part of Vietnam. Bong Son is located about 30 miles south of our location. I heard that it is pretty nice—it had streets and two story buildings, which we never saw in our area. I guess the soda girls had to take off pretty early, about seven in the morning (in order to visit all the GI bases and bivouacs along Highway 1). On the back of the motorbike was a cardboard C-ration box filled with sodas and beer attached on top of a large block of ice.

We saw them riding everywhere on Highway 1. A typical sight was a black Honda. A young man drove the motorcycle with the soda girl hanging on right behind. Right behind her, the C-ration box was tied down with rubber from old tires or something similar. When they saw us GI's, they would say, "You want soda?" The price was 50 cents for soda and 50 cents for beer. Much as I hated to pay it I did because, boy, the weather was hot! I would rather pay it than have nothing at all to keep me cool out there.

Our resupply brings out sodas and beer. We have to pay 15 cents for each, but they are usually warm. Rarely was there any ice and if ice was included, it had melted down to, at best, fist sized chunks by the time they arrived. Beverages and ice was brought in large, red colored vinyl bags (which lacked insulation—the bottoms were usually wet from melted ice). Sometimes we traded our warm sodas for one of the soda girl's

82

cold ones. They didn't mind because they usually sold two cases a day. They made ten cents off each soda and the Mamasan, who I assume is the middle man they buy from, makes ten cents, and some crummy GI character back in the rear sells the sodas and beer to the Mamasan. Of course, the GI makes the biggest profit.

Down highway 1 there are more salesmen than you can imagine—little kids selling dirty pictures—if the young girls aren't selling sodas they're selling a whole barrage of junk from mirrors to photo albums, bush hats to knives, jewelry— anything you want. It's like a portable store, and they come by every day. One of the guys took a picture of me wearing some of this junk.

The canned drinks sold by the young entrepreneurs were not Asian products, but American made beverages like Coca Cola, 7-Up, and Budweiser. At the time, a soda at your local supermarket cost about 10 to 15 cents, and a can of beer about 35 cents. Our price for a soda or beer, 50 cents, provided the Vietnamese with a considerable profit. I never learned the details about how the beverages came into the hands of the local soda girls. American soldiers working in supply on large bases must have pilfered and sold the beverages, making this a black market operation.

In contrast to the cold beverages provided by the soda girls, those brought to us by chopper always arrived warm. I never understood why the guys in rear supply couldn't provide sufficient ice to keep our beverages cold for the duration of the flight to our location. Our platoon made several requests for more, but our efforts always fell upon deaf ears.

Collins quipped, "Is the problem the heat? Maybe the chunk of ice has to be the size of a boulder to last the trip, but this may make it too heavy to haul on a chopper."

Collins' sarcasm provoked a few chuckles.

I added, "Or maybe they think the puny amount they toss in the bag won't melt during the long journey here—duh!"

Johnson nodded disapprovingly; "That ain't it. Those lazy assholes in the rear just don't give a shit about us grunts."

Andy offered a provocative response; "Maybe they want us to rely upon the soda girls because they're the ones supplying them and making a nice profit."

Whether due to inattention, indifference, or intent on the part of army supply staff, the warm beverages they sent didn't satisfy our cravings for something cool and refreshing. Thus, we frequently turned to the Vietnamese soda girls. This enabled them to make money from a flourishing black market business along Highway 1. No real harm done.

"What foods these morsels be."
A *Mad Magazine* parody of a line from Shakespeare, circa 1960's

The army supplied soldiers in the field with three main types of food—canned goods called C-rations, freeze-dried, dehydrated rations packaged in foil bags called LRP (Long Range Patrol, pronounced *lurp*), and occasionally hot food prepared at base camp and flown out by chopper. In order to supply adequate nutrition, each individually boxed C-ration contained a balanced meal—one single serving can each of a main protein, diced or sliced fruit in juice, crackers, cheese, bread, and pound cake—yes, bread and cake in a can! Main protein dishes included scrambled eggs, sliced pork, turkey, and beef spiced with sauce. We grunts agreed that the best protein item among the *C's,* as we called them, was *Beef Spiced with Sauce*. Although stringy and sometimes tough, the well-seasoned sauce provided for a juicy, tasty entre.

On the other side of the coin, or can, if you will, was the worst C-ration item. Just about every grunt agreed the winner of that competition went to the scrambled eggs. If you viewed the contents without reading the label, it is unlikely you would be able to discern egg was the major ingredient. The scrambled mess looked like congealed snot in a can, and tasted like it looked—terrible. Few soldiers ate the awful glop. Even the rural Vietnamese—we occasionally gave them food we didn't want—usually passed on this item.

Stateside workers portioned and packed C-ration units by bulk in cardboard boxes, so this eliminated the possibility of custom ordering individual cans. In addition, because of the variety of main protein items, only two or three out of ten individual units in the box contained a can of highly valued *Beef Spiced with Sauce*. Limited availability resulted in shortages of the most popular C-ration items, and surpluses of those deemed undesirable—Adam Smith's economic philosophy in a can.

Members of the platoon bartered cigarettes or paid cash for the delicacies most in demand, and discarded the unpopular items or gave them to the Vietnamese. Due to the limited availability of the tastiest main dishes, sometimes I went for days living mostly on my morning cocoa, cheese and crackers, canned fruit, and pound cake. It's a wonder I kept up my strength on such skimpy rations. No one gains weight living in the field, that's for sure.

Tropical chocolate scored second as most detested item. The bars arrived in our sundries packet along with cigarettes, matches, toilet paper, toothpaste, soap, and other personal items. Tropical chocolate was shaped and wrapped like any other chocolate bar, but that is where the similarity ended. Instead of a medium or dark brown, the color appeared an unappealing, anemic tan. What did it taste like? Just grab your everyday blackboard chalk and take a big bite out of it. Yeah, nearly as bad.

Why the dry, grainy texture and bland taste? Ordinary milk chocolate melts rapidly in tropical heat, so some brilliant stateside chefs—more like chemists, I think—conjured the brainstorm of adding a chalk-like ingredient to impede the melting process. It worked—the bars didn't melt in the heat. I'll give them that. The problem is each bar contained far more chalk than chocolate. *Did these guys ever sample their creation?* Perhaps the culinary chemists have improved the taste and texture since those days, but as far as I am concerned, tropical chocolate should be renamed *Tropical Chalk-olate*.

We soldiers ignited heat tablets to warm our food. The two-inch wide discs burned evenly for about two minutes. In order to retain heat, sometimes we placed them inside a shallow depression dug in the ground, but empty C-rations cans served our needs more efficiently. Using a can opener, we cut holes in the sides of the little makeshift stove to allow for air circulation.

Most of us restricted use to between three and five discs per hot meal so our inventory would last until resupply arrived. This amount provided sufficient heat to warm some items, but not enough to fully cook others, or boil water. I always looked forward to my morning ritual of preparing hot—well, warm—cocoa in my metal canteen cup. I added the powdered mixture into water and stirred it over three heat tablets. Unlike tropical chocolate, the cocoa looked and tasted much like today's modern supermarket counterparts. I found it satisfying. Little things like morning cocoa helped to get me through the day.

In 1964, the army developed freeze dried foods called LRP. Items included chicken and rice, beef hash, chili con carne, and spaghetti with meat sauce. All a soldier need do is heat a pint of water inside his canteen cup, add the contents, stir, and allow a few minutes for the ingredients to hydrate and warm. The *Catch 22* is four or five tablets didn't produce sufficient heat to reconstitute some of the items, especially fibrous vegetables. For example, despite the fact they had been pre-cut to one inch lengths, the green beans never became malleable. Chewing through their woody texture felt unpleasant, so I opted to separate out and discard them. Despite the difficulty at heating some items, LRP's tasted much better than C's and provided additional variety to our palette and diet.

Letter to my Family - August 27, 1969
Gourmet food

I still have the can of smoked lobster—I'm saving it for a special occasion.

Letter to my Family - September 15, 1969
Garbage from home

I received your latest *garbage box*, as Dad puts it. That pudding is good—I still have the lemon flavored one. Mom, that goulash was surprisingly good—things like this are what

86

really hit the spot out here. I warmed up some onion soup over heat tabs the other day—for breakfast would you believe? I gave some to a couple of my buddies, and they loved it. And you said I couldn't cook!

After living day to day on C-rations and semi-cooked LRP's, I really looked forward to receiving what Dad sarcastically, but affectionately, called, "Garbage boxes." The long flight across the Pacific placed limitations on the types of food products shipped—for example, perishable items that are not hermetically sealed. Nonetheless, my creative Mom managed to include a nice variety of tasty delicacies. Her boxes contained a variety of canned goods, but these were no C's. I relished each can of crab, salmon, smoked oysters, ham, and even lobster.

I can't believe it. I'm having lobster, way out here in the field. It's amazing! Sitting on the ground, open can and rusty fork in hand, I envisioned sharing my meal with a beautiful female companion on fine China set upon a white table cloth under soft candle light. Considering the circumstances, this effort required a vivid imagination.

Those of us receiving these tasty treasures usually shared with our buddies—but for me not the best items, like lobster.

A Fish Story

We soldiers greatly appreciated packages sent from home and the warm food occasionally brought out by chopper, but after months living mostly off of field rations, most of us craved freshly prepared meals. *Oh, I would give anything for Mom's fabulous roast pork dinner with her wonderful, fluffy dumplings and a piece of her made-from-scratch cherry pie.* Fantasies aside, some types of fresh food could be accessed in the field. In September our platoon bivouacked near a narrow lagoon next to a fishing village. The enticing, emerald waters appeared so clear I could see to the bottom twenty feet below. I waved at my fellow soldiers and yelled, "Hey guys, there's lots of fish swimming around down there!" Spinning off a famous line by English poet Samuel Taylor Coleridge, I added, "Damn—fish, fish everywhere, but not a pole in sight!"

As if bitten by a bug, Seth stood up quickly and exclaimed, "So, who needs a pole when you have...hand grenades!" He pointed to one hanging from his rucksack strap.

Squad leader Tyler interjected excitedly, "Yeah, I've heard about other guys doing this. We can drop a grenade down there and the explosion will kill or stun some of the fish—maybe enough for everyone. I'll ask Sergeant Sawyer—"

Sawyer interrupted, "Sure, let's do it, but make sure to follow safety procedures."

We noticed three Vietnamese fishermen working on their Sampans nearby. Sawyer instructed me and Andy; "Go over and see if one of them will help us. Offer some of our catch—that should do it."

One of the fishermen understood English and agreed to our request. He grabbed a basket and joined our group at lagoon's edge. When everyone was ready and a safe distance away, Tyler yanked the pin, yelled *fire in the hole*, and heaved the grenade smack into the middle of a forty-foot wide section of the waterway.

Collins yelled, "Good shot! You should be pitching for the Yankees."

We all heard a mild thud, and the waters churned upward before settling down. Soon thereafter, over two dozen fish, most over a foot long, floated to the surface.

Our local *hired temp* stripped to his shorts, plunged into the water, basket in hand, and retrieved the bounty. Next, he spread them out on the sand.

Gary said, "Look at all these fish! Most are in one piece. You were right Tyler. The concussion, not shrapnel, did 'em in."

I added, "And look at the variety. I wonder what these reddish ones are."

Reynolds, who was an experienced angler from Florida, said, "Sometimes the most colorful ones are not edible. We better ask the fisherman."

Our local expert picked the two reddish ones, and said, "Number 10," meaning bad. Curiously, he added these to his batch—hmmm. We didn't care. Plenty remained for everyone to share. Reynolds and Collins grabbed knives and began the task of cleaning our bounty.

Greg asked, "How are we going to cook them?"

Reynolds replied, "We'll leave the heads on so we can run a branch through the mouth down to the tail end—like on a skewer. I need a couple of guys to gather some three foot long branches at least a half-inch thick. Find ones that are straight and sturdy, and strip off the twigs. We'll soak them in seawater, run the ends through each fish, and hold them over the fire until cooked through."

Greg said, "Sounds like you've done this before!"

"Well, sort of, but not with branches. I just hope they don't catch fire and the fish don't fall off."

Seth and I made a nice hot fire with dry palm fronds and local wood. Others gathered and prepared the branches, and we proceeded to roast the fish over open flames. One slipped off into the coals, but was recovered. Reynolds' plan worked well.

Growing up near the Pacific Ocean, I learned to enjoy all types of seafood, so this meal made me drool. Raising a chunk on my fork, I proclaimed, "Hey guys, look how white and tender this meat is, and it's cooked just right. Man, this is s-o-o-o good!" I gave Reynolds a high five and exclaimed; "Great job!"

Prideful, Reynolds replied, "Glad to be of service men. Maybe the army should have made me a cook."

"Too late now," jibed Collins. "Besides, the army would never make someone with your gourmet skills into a cook."

The spirits of the men rose as high as a dolphin's leap.

After stuffing ourselves, we enjoyed telling stories around the campfire. I reminisced, "This reminds me of beach parties back home. On some evenings we used to build fires and roast weenies and marshmallows right on the beach. The only thing missing here is Beach Boys music and some cuties in skimpy bikinis."

Reynolds replied, "Yeah, it was like that in Florida, except instead of surfing we went sailing or fishing. My girlfriend would kill me for telling you this, but she liked to sunbathe naked on my sailboat. She has a great body. Damn, I miss her!"

Gary interjected, "Cool it guys. You're making me homesick...and horny."

As the sun began to set and the fire dimmed, warm thoughts about home and loved ones enveloped the men in the platoon.

"The two basic items necessary to sustain life are sunshine and coconut milk."
Dustin Hoffman, Oscar winning actor

The fresh fish tasted great, but how about fresh fruit? Coconut palms grew abundantly in some places along the coast. The flesh and juice provides nutritional benefits well-suited to soldiers living mostly in the field. They boost the immune system, provide quick energy, and enhance physical stamina. The problem is gaining access to it. We feared eating those lying on the ground because they might cause illness. Unfortunately, the ripe fruit grows in tight clumps under the fronds at the top of the tree—as high as fifty feet above the ground. Only an expert can safely climb the long, branchless trunk, so once again a weapon became converted into a culinary utensil—this time a rifle instead of grenade.

Shooting coconuts out of trees is not as easy as it may seem. The M16 round is designed to disintegrate into shrapnel when penetrating an object. We all knew this would shatter the fruit into pieces. Thus, the challenge is to free the coconut intact. For this you need to hit the connecting stems or branch, and for that you need the talents of a sharpshooter. Enter Spec 4 Delgado—we called him Gado—our platoon's crackerjack marksman. He was the only man in the outfit who carried the old M14 rifle. Its long barrel enables greater accuracy than the M16.

Just as Sergeant Sawyer was about to make a request, Gado waved him off with a growl. "I hate coconut—it makes me wanna puke!"

Our wise leader knew just which buttons to push. "Yeah, I doubt even you could hit the right spot from 20 meters away."

Delgado's uncooperative, sloping body language abruptly transformed into the erect posture of a soldier steeped in pride. He couldn't resist this challenge to his ego, so he agreed to give it a shot. Gado stabilized himself against a nearby palm tree, aimed carefully, and fired several rounds. Some missed and some struck the fruit directly, but eventually a clump of five coconuts fell to the ground intact. Larry and I rushed to gather them up.

Time to show off. Having learned how to juggle with three pool balls and a few times with two light bowling balls, I had to try my hand with three of the smaller coconuts. "Hey guys, check this out!" I managed to juggle three coconuts through four complete cycles before losing control and dropping them to the ground. "Hey, where's my applause?"

Unimpressed, platoon leader Sawyer barked, "Quit clownin' around Richert! Let's get these things open. We've got to go back out on patrol soon."

Opening coconuts is not a simple matter—the outer husk is thick and fibrous, and the brown shell surrounding the white flesh lining the juice-filled interior is almost as hard as bone. We required the services of our platoon strong man. Johnson, who had hacked through many miles of jungle with his trusty machete, skillfully opened the fruit without losing all the milk.

Displaying a large chunk, Tyler yelled, "Gado, are you sure you don't want to try some? Look how nice and white this meat is!"

Gado shook his head; "No gracias. Back home I work construction. I put up tons of drywall, and that shit is too much like the plaster they make it out of. I can't stand to even look at it."

Not to me, but then again, I've never put up drywall. I relished the refreshing nectar and snow white flesh, and saved some leftovers for later meals. The meat provided a healthy supplement to my otherwise skimpy diet.

Taste Temptation

One day our platoon inspected a rice farming village. Noticing a local family preparing food in a makeshift kitchen just outside their hut, I approached. A stew-like concoction in a beat up old pot cooked slowly over an open fire. The mixture included vegetables and what looked like large chunks of pork. It smelled rather bland— neither bad nor appetizing. Most of us grunts wouldn't eat the local peasant food. Some of it looked disgusting and we were understandably wary of becoming sick.

Feeling adventuresome—not to mention extremely hungry—I began to pull out a couple of MPC bills (the locals eagerly accepted American Military Payment Certificates) and gestured to purchase a bite. Then I remembered Vietnamese peasants are proud people and considered payment for a meal an insult. I put the money away. The cook, a skinny, elderly man with a friendly, but betel nut blackened smile, offered me a two-inch thick portion. I thanked him and placed the morsel in my canteen cup to cool. What looked like pepper covered the dull gray, fatty meat. *I hope this is pepper, not fly specks.*

I grabbed the warm meat with my fingers and took a bite. *Yuck, it tastes awful, like old stale beef.* I didn't want to insult the elderly man or his family by displaying a grimace. Somehow I managed to force an approving smile and said, "Number one!" The cook offered more, but I politely declined. Once out of view, I tossed the leftovers into a bush and gulped down water. *No more local peasant food for me.* Probably because the small portion was thoroughly cooked, I didn't later become sick.

"Water, water, everywhere, nor any drop to drink."
From *the Rime of the Ancient Mariner,* by English poet Samuel Taylor Coleridge

Most soldiers carried two or more one-quart plastic canteens of water. Choppers brought the precious liquid to the field by chopper in fifty-gallon reinforced rubber blivets or five-gallon metal cans. Both containers left a noticeable aftertaste, but considering the thirst we soldiers acquired under the scorching Southeast Asian sun, our canteen water seemed as refreshing as Perrier.

During mid-day our platoon entered a village for a routine inspection. This village was known to be friendly, so we felt relatively secure in our surroundings. During the hottest part of the day, we sat around in the shade. I noticed a boy about ten years of age sponge bathing alongside a well. My canteens were low on water, so I approached him and asked for a drink. He readily complied. I felt wary about tasting the water, but it smelled fine so I took a drink. I detected a slight mineral taste, but otherwise found it surprisingly cool and refreshing.

With resupply overdue, I told the thirsty men, "Hey guys, there's a well over there. The water is cool and tastes fine."

Squad leader Tyler said, "Man, you shouldn't be drinkin' that shit. Who knows what kinds of bugs live down there? Besides, Romeo Sierra (resupply) will be arriving soon."

"Great, now you tell me."

None of us soldiers could have known about the potential danger at the time, but after many years of US bombing missions, toxic chemicals like Dioxin had gradually seeped through the soil into the Vietnamese water supply. Luckily, I suffered no ill effects from the well water.

Under conditions of extreme thirst, people will do almost anything to wet their whistle. On yet another scorching day in the field, Romeo Sierra was overdue and most of us grunts needed water. Although my canteens were down to drops, I refused to beg my buddies for a taste. At the time, our unit had set up next to rice paddy fields. Rice crops require large amounts of rainfall, and the paddies are flooded during part of the year—mainly during the peak of the wet season from November through February. Although in September the paddies are not flooded, some retained pools of water from frequent summer thunderstorms.

Our leaders often warned us grunts about the health dangers of drinking local water. All kinds of nasty critters thrive in nutrient rich rice paddy water, and I occasionally saw Vietnamese defecate in it. However, desperation overwhelmed my caution. I didn't want to be observed taking the risk, so I told the guys I was going off to take a piss. I found a spot behind some bamboo trees and out of view of the others. Eyeing a section of relatively clear surface water, I cupped my hands and scooped some up. First I sniffed it. It smelled like the pond water I gathered for pollywogs as a kid, but milder. With trepidation, I took a drink. To my surprise, the mouthful tasted okay—not good, but bearable. I scooped up another handful and before I could change my mind, gulped it down. Then, having second thoughts, I quickly stepped back. *What the hell have I done? I'm going to get horribly sick!*

Happily, I suffered no ill effects from the dubious drink. Although I bucked the odds, the episode provoked a vow: *From now*

93

on and no matter how desperate my thirst, I will never chance swallowing rice paddy water again. I kept my promise, but not because of a strong will. After that day, resupply became more reliable, and our platoon never again had to endure a prolonged shortage of water.

Letter to my Family - September 3, 1969
Inspection

I finally got a haircut. I look like the Bob Richert of Long Beach again. There was a big inspection by the new Brigade Commander, a colonel, here on Charlie Brown today. Boy, I must have policed up every piece of paper and tin can on the peninsula—reminded me of Basic Training. I shouldn't gripe—it sure beats humping in the bush. Everyone has a haircut and shave, but you should have seen these guys before—long sideburns, beards—like a bunch of hippies!

Spit and polish neatness on a military base with facilities is one thing, but it's impractical under the crude conditions of the field. After weeks of missions in the boonies, our unit arrived at Division headquarters in Chu Lai for a three day R & R. Talk about hippies— I hadn't shaved or bathed for two weeks—phew! Although anxious to clean up, I first stopped by the PX to send out film mailers and grab a cold soda.

The PX at Chu Lai compared to a stateside five-and-dime store— well, at least until I walked through the door. The employees and others stared at me as if I was a Neanderthal who just crawled out of his cave. My crumpled fatigues bore caked-on splotches of dirt—my boots could barely be seen through layers of dried mud—grime covered my body from head to toe—my matted hair looked like someone had combed it with an egg beater—and a half-inch of grubby stubble protruded from my worn out face. I overheard a base soldier whisper to a colleague, "Look at that guy. Aren't you glad we're not grunts?"

After finishing my business at the PX, I immediately sought the nearest shower. I couldn't peel off my cruddy clothing fast enough. The cool, clean water raining down on my tired, dirty body felt wonderful. I stayed under for what seemed like an hour. Afterward I put on clean fatigues and new boots. If the original gawkers at the PX saw me just after freshening up, it's doubtful they would know it was the same person. The Neanderthal had evolved into *Homo sapiens.*

Letter to my Family - September 25, 1969
Point of View

I got a chance to see more of this country today. I went by truck from Charlie Brown to LZ English, 20 miles south. On the way were some fairly large villages, one had two and three story buildings. It would still be a slum by our standards. Kids run around naked and dump their loads any ol' place. So do the old people.

Like most of my comrades, I reacted with disgust upon witnessing people, especially the elderly, doing number two out in the open— mostly in rice paddies next to their villages. However, it's not like rural Vietnam was *flush* with bathrooms or Port-a-Potties. Defecating and urinating in view of others was taken for granted, and not perceived as offensive. On the other hand, we Americans are taught from an early age to do our business in private.
Obviously, we soldiers didn't have access to individual bathroom stalls in the field. We went outside our bivouac area and dumped our loads, "any ol' place." I suppose the moral of this story is, *when in Rome...*

Letter to my Family - August 30, 1969
I Miss a Photo Op

The chopper ride was nice yesterday. We took off just after sun-up, and the countryside was beautiful. Naturally, I forgot my camera. I could have had a fantastic picture through the side of our chopper—the next chopper was about 100 feet away, and another chopper 100 feet behind that. The sky had

95

billowing clouds along with the ocean and gold hills behind. Oh well, I'll get some pictures from choppers later on.

Although onboard choppers frequently, I don't recall taking any pictures while airborne. It's difficult to hold the camera steady and take pictures while the chopper is maneuvering and shaking from engine torque. Fast shutter speeds are required for crisp, clear photographs, and my cheap Instamatic didn't cut it. I missed many potentially interesting shots.

Audiotape - February 9, 1970
More Photo Ops

· I wish I had my Minolta camera during the infantry. Actually, in many ways I don't because it might have been ruined by the elements or stolen. There are some things out there I would really like to have photographed. For example, a couple of months ago it was rice harvesting time. All along Highway 1 I saw all these colorful patches of rice—all different shades of brown for miles. The farmers wrap the rice up into bales and it's really pretty—they are like haystacks scattered among the rice paddies and going off into the distance as far as the eye can see.

In a nearby village there is one scene I just have to shoot. There is a little marketplace and at times all the Mamasans (women, mothers) are gathered into a tight space. Every one of them is wearing their gook hats (18 inches wide, off-white in color, and conical shaped). As you pass by in a truck it looks like just a big gathering of coolie hats all moving around in this crowded marketplace. It's packed with people and they are all jabbering away. I guess they are bartering. These people can be really funny. I have come to respect them in a way because although they don't have any of the luxuries we do, they live pretty well.

Viewed from the elevated perspective of the passing truck, the rhythmic pattern of dozens of tightly squeezed and thus seemingly bodiless white conical hats would have made for a fascinating photo, but an even better video. Although my company passed by the marketplace several times, I never saw it crowded like on that day—another opportunity for a prize winning photo missed. Sometimes I wanted to kick myself for not taking more pictures in Vietnam. Then again, I wasn't sent there as a tourist, much less a Nat Geo photographer.

Both the slide and print film I purchased in the rear came with mailers. The processed film arrived back to our unit via chopper within two weeks. I appreciated this efficient and reliable system. It is unfortunate that due to the heat, humidity, and harsh environment of the field, only about 30 of the numerous slides I took with the Instamatic camera survived. Sadly, most of those became badly faded. I'm frustrated so much interesting imagery from my first few months in the infantry succumbed to the elements. I'm reminded of the old saying—*a picture is worth a thousand words*. I learned my lesson. After purchasing a Yashika 35mm camera in early October, I began having my processed film sent to my parents.

Rumors

One constant in the army, especially within the infantry, is the persistence of rumors. Stories about enemy activity, troop withdrawals, and other happenings circulated from soldier to soldier throughout Vietnam like those staph infections that had spread across my body. Invariably, the scuttlebutt turned out to be exaggerated or false. Probably due to wishful thinking, the most common rumors told of early troop pullouts or a forthcoming end to the war. Sure enough this hopeful theme reverberated throughout my infantry company.

Letter to my Family - August 4, 1969
Home for Christmas?

Not a prediction, but this war may be over by Christmas. Our CO has a close friend in intelligence—a high ranking individual who knows what's going on in Washington.

Yesterday, our CO said he is confident this mess will be over soon. He just got back from a meeting with intelligence people, but didn't say how, why, or what. Perhaps something is cooking—I hope so. There has been a general feeling among the officers and high ranking NCO's that the war is going to end. Most of the grunts are pessimistic—not me, though.

Another thing, there have been persistent rumors that my brigade may be next to catch the freedom bird! It's about time—the ARVN were supposed to be given control over Duc Pho and all its operations a long time ago. The ARVN would replace us grunts, but the Americans would still back them in the rear—chopper pilots, artillery—things like that.

Letter to my Family - August 6, 1969
He knows a guy who knows a guy

I found out about the statement the CO made in regards to the war ending. It seems his uncle is way up there in Washington and he told the CO that the 11th Brigade would be pulled out with the next group to go. I sure hope he knows what he is talking about.

Letter to my Family - September 10, 1969
Majority Opinion

According to all sorts of people, officers, sergeants, etc., the 11th Brigade will be the next to be pulled out. That is if Tricky Dickey (President Nixon) ever announces pullouts. Boy, I hope so.

We infantry soldiers wanted desperately to get out of the field, so it is understandable we clung to any sliver of hope it might happen. Of course, rumors being what they are, paying attention to them inevitably set us up for disappointment. However, once in a while rumors do indeed bear fruit. It turned out a nugget of gold lay buried under the barrage of bull circulating widely. Ah, but I am getting ahead of my story. Stay tuned, more on this later.

CHAPTER 6

The Good

Life in the infantry varies from the calm and mundane to episodes of humor, to moments of inspiration and enlightenment, to periods of discomfort and exhaustion, to situations of extreme emotional intensity and anxiety. Like most young men who served, I experienced all of the above during my one year tour in Vietnam. My emotions rode a roller coaster of highs and lows, mostly lows, and sometimes receded into numbness. On the positive side, my mind and heart opened to many things I could never have experienced back home. This chapter focuses on the *good* things. It is also about some bad things, but I include them because they taught me *good* lessons.

Letter to my Family - August 6, 1969
My Buddies

I never have mentioned much about the people I'm with out here. One of my best friends is Andy from Florida. He was an English teacher and got into the infantry because he got fed up with OCS (Officer Candidate School), and dropped out. We have about four college educated men in our platoon—seems like all the duds are in the rear with the gravy jobs. Seth is an Israeli, and although he lives in Brooklyn, he stills retains an Israelite accent. Squad member Reynolds is a college graduate from Florida.

Like many Americans, before joining the army I believed the stereotype that only society's dregs ended up in the *lowly* infantry. Wealthy, upper middle class and otherwise bright young men avoided the draft by going off to college, with the aid of influential family members, cooperative doctors who faked or exaggerated ailments, or by some other means. To my pleasant surprise, I found that many college students and even graduates ended up in the infantry. In addition to those mentioned in my above letter, Larry studied English literature before the army gobbled him up. We college boys often talked about a wide range of subjects, including religion and politics. Most of us expressed skepticism about US involvement in Vietnam and felt embittered about having to serve in a war we believed to be a fruitless effort with no end in sight. You might think this attitude would undermine our performance as soldiers, but it didn't. More immediate concerns faced us grunts on the ground—mainly to ensure the safety and survival of ourselves and each other. All of us, whether for or against the war, cooperated in this effort.

Not everyone I admired had been to college. The ages of the soldiers in my platoon averaged in the early twenties, except for our platoon sergeant. By the time I arrived, our 32 year old leader had already earned the nickname, *Old Man Sawyer*. His rugged hands and skin, like deeply tanned leather, revealed a life working outdoors at manual labor. Although from Alabama, not well educated, and missing a front tooth, Sergeant Sawyer did not otherwise fit the redneck stereotype. A man of few words, his quiet demeanor displayed humble confidence. Years of hard work and self-reliance provided the kind of mental and physical toughness necessary for a platoon leader in Vietnam. Before I joined the unit in mid-June, Sergeant Sawyer had seen considerable combat and gained valuable soldiering experience.

During the many times our company split up into independently working units, our captain rotated his time between the four

100

platoons. Sergeant Sawyer took charge during his absence. Our company captain projected an aggressive, gung ho attitude and held contempt for Vietnamese civilians (Chapter 8). Sawyer's demeanor and leadership style contrasted sharply. He knew how to lead men and maintain discipline effectively, but he wasn't gung ho or a hard-ass. Instead, he displayed caution when entering potential danger, and treated Vietnamese civilians with respect.

Sawyer's leadership style demonstrated the right combination of toughness and compassion. Directly or indirectly through the squad leaders he mentored, Sawyer's hard-earned wisdom filtered down to most men in the unit. He instilled in us the necessity of preparedness, and taught us many things that helped to ensure our survival. Sergeant Sawyer earned great respect from the grunts under his command.

Chieu Hoi! (Pronounced, chew-hoy)

Early on during the Vietnam War, the South Vietnamese government initiated a program called, Chieu Hoi, which means *open arms*. They aired radio messages and dropped tons of leaflets encouraging the Viet Cong to defect to the South, and guaranteed their safe conduct. Of the thousands of defections recorded, only about twenty-five percent proved genuine. I assume the remaining seventy-five percent became prisoners of war. Despite these and other problems, our military regarded the program as successful. Once thoroughly vetted, some of these former Viet Cong became *Kit Carson Scouts* for US and ARVN forces. By assisting our troops in searching villages for hidden tunnels and weapons, and serving as interpreters, their intimate knowledge of the enemy provided the American military with a valuable resource.

One day our platoon patrolled among the flatlands of rice paddies and scattered villages located between the coast to the east and the Central Highlands to the west. 23 of us snaked out in a line along a trail with our squad in the lead. The front portion of the patrol is often targeted first during an enemy attack or is most likely to trigger a mine or booby trap. Thus, the lead squad must be on high alert, and the point man doubly so. Any startling noise or action resembling enemy activity usually prompts the man on point to immediately open fire. Better to shoot first than hesitate and end up dead or wounded. Squad leader Tyler led the platoon on this day, and I marched fourth in line behind him.

Intermittent clumps of bamboo trees and other vegetation separated rice paddies on each side of the trail, providing Charlie with excellent cover. Suddenly and from behind a thicket, a young Vietnamese man wearing typical black pajamas jumped out on the trail less than twenty feet in front of Tyler. Open hands raised high over his head, he screamed "Chieu Hoi, Chieu Hoi!" Although the young man's hands were free, an inexperienced or high-strung soldier might have panicked and immediately began firing. Not Tyler—he showed remarkable restraint. Instantly gathering his wits and assessing the situation, he made the quick decision not to shoot. Meanwhile, being so close to the action, I nearly crapped in my pants.

Using gestures, Tyler instructed the young man to kneel down and place his hands on top of his head. The prisoner's thin body twitched in fear. I can't imagine what thoughts ran through his mind, but, judging by his deep breaths and slumping posture, feelings of relief seemed to surface through the anxiety.

Our platoon sergeant issued orders; "Johnson and Collins—keep your rifles aimed at him. Gado and Reynolds—check him for a hidden weapon and documents. Let's get his hands tied up. Clarkson, call in a chopper." No weapons or documents were found. A chopper arrived twenty minutes later and hauled the Chieu Hoi away. Perhaps in time, he became a Kit Carson Scout.

Some of us soldiers speculated about our reactions had we been in Tyler's boots. Most of us expressed uncertainty because the young man's gestures, cries of Chieu Hoi, and open hands clearly indicated submission. However, considering the abruptness of his appearance and our readiness to defend ourselves, it would have been a close call.

Billy Caleb, one of the platoon's most brash, crude, and gung ho members, boasted, "I would'a dusted that stupid dink."

In an attempt to lighten the mood, I offered sarcasm. "If I fired at the poor son of a bitch, I would'a been so startled I probably would'a missed."

Speculation aside, I believe Tyler's ability to remain calm and in control during an instant of high tension and quick decision making demonstrated excellent leadership.

"Oh, what a beautiful mornin', oh what a beautiful day. I've got a beautiful feelin' everything's goin' my way."
Lyric from, *Oh, What a Beautiful Morning,* **by Rodgers and Hammerstein; from their musical** *Oklahoma*

The soldiers in my platoon preferred pulling security along Highway 1 because the location saw little enemy activity, the beach was nearby, we didn't go on lengthy patrols, and kids and soda girls visited us daily. Thus, the mood of the platoon generally remained high-spirited. Seth hailed from Brooklyn, a city known for producing entertainers, and he fit the bill. He stood at average height with a lean, well-proportioned body. Recessed, dark brown eyes somehow managed to appear bright under the roof of bushy brows and full head of dark brown, curly hair. Seth always shared a broad, white-toothed smile and sparkling sense of humor.

I once told him, "With your good looks and charisma, the girls back home must be waiting in line for your return. Unless you're married—"

He interjected, "No—too many hot Jewish chicks to choose from in Brooklyn!"

I boasted, "Good for you, but Southern California girls are the best."

In many ways Seth reminded me of the great entertainer, Sammy Davis Junior. Like Sammy, Seth displayed multi-talents and seemed to be possessed by boundless energy. A variety of jokes, stories, and songs supplemented by deft dance moves brought broad smiles to our tired and grungy group. Nearly every morning, his rendition of, *Oh, What a Beautiful Morning,* aroused sleepy eyes and induced good cheer among the men. To this day, whenever I hear that song, I think of Seth. Those optimistic, joyful lyrics performed by an optimistic, joyful soldier boosted platoon morale. Only a few special people are endowed with the ability to maintain an upbeat attitude and lift the spirits of others under the adverse conditions and stress of war. Keep 'em smilin' Seth, wherever you are!

There's a Moon out Tonight
Popular 1961 doo-wop song performed by the *Capris;* written by Al Gentile, Joe Luccisano, and Al Striano

The above lyric brings me to memorable incident involving my buddy Andy. Before I relate it, I must explain in detail how our 23 man platoon set up for the night. We set up our bivouac after sunset away and out of view of a village and Highway 1 on sandy soil amidst scattered bushes and palm trees. Our platoon divided into three-man units spaced about twenty feet apart and forming the perimeter of a circle—seen from above, like the numbers around the circumference of a clock face. Two men slept while one sat up on guard, and we rotated shifts. Our platoon leader, medic, and radio man set up in the center. In addition to our individual weapons, for added protection we set three Claymore mines outside and around our perimeter.

The M18 Claymore mine contains 700 steel buckshot-like pellets backed by a layer of C-4 explosive. It is set off via a thirty-foot long cord which extends to the soldier's location. Its face is gently curved so upon detonation, the pellets fan out like a shotgun blast. It is *effective* (military-speak for deadly) up to 150 feet. If the enemy approaches, the soldier simply squeezes the trigger and it's as if 20 shotguns go off at once. As you might imagine, the Claymore mine is one nasty weapon.

Sitting up on guard during the darkness of night without the ability to spot the enemy is disconcerting. Enter a signaling device called the trip flare. Each is about the size and shape of a toilet paper tube. The flare is attached a few inches off the ground to a tree or bush adjacent to a pathway or trail and outside the perimeter. A thin wire with a pull-pin attaches to the flare and is extended a few inches above ground across the trail and tied to a stake, tree or bush. When Charlie unknowingly trips the wire, the flare lights up the area like a fireworks fountain. Soldiers are prompted to immediately start shooting their weapons and setting off Claymores.

104

One night I sat up on guard at 2 AM staring into the blackness and listening for any suspicious sounds. Half-way through my shift, Andy, one member of my three man group, came over and whispered in a distressed voice, "I have to take a shit really bad. I just can't hold it anymore."

Soldiers in the field seldom carried out number two in the darkness of night, but when you gotta go, you gotta go. I told Andy, "Okay, but as you know, this requires some planning." I reminded him about the location of the Claymore and trip flare, and we agreed upon the spot he would do his business. Just before going out, he informed the soldiers on guard to our left and right of his intensions and location. He moved out about 20 feet in front of me, but even at this distance I could barely make out his silhouette.

The other two men up on guard to our immediate left and right went on high alert because with one of our own out there this is not the time for Charlie to show up. Andy could be caught in the middle of a firefight. For the time being, all was calm. I heard only the rustling of vegetation and disturbed ground caused by Andy shuffling about.

Two minutes later—ZAP! The trip flare went off and instantly lit up the area like a bonfire on the beach. Knowing all hell could break loose, I immediately started shouting as loud as I could, "CEASE FIRE, CEASE FIRE, CEASE FIRE!" With Andy out there and exposed in a most vulnerable position, I wanted to give clear warning to the others.

Meanwhile in a heart-pounding, frantic panic, Andy started screaming, "Don't shoot me, oh my God, don't shoot me"! He feared some of the men would react on autopilot and squeeze the Claymore detonator or fire their rifles in his direction. Squatting with his pants down to his ankles and pale bare butt illuminated by the flare, poor Andy struggled to simultaneously maintain a low profile and pull up his trousers. Still screaming "Don't shoot me!" he hopped about like a crippled rabbit. Fortunately, cool heads prevailed. Everyone in the platoon heeded our highly amplified pleas to cease fire. Meanwhile, Andy attempted to regain what was left of his composure.

105

During the immediate aftermath everyone began asking questions and expressing concern about our now compromised position. Thanks to the fireworks show, any enemy in the vicinity would know exactly where to find us. Sergeant Sawyer decided it impractical to move at the late hour, so our nervous platoon stayed in place. Adrenaline still gushing through our veins and thoughts drifting to what might have been, neither Andy nor I managed to catch a wink the rest of the morning. The remaining three hours of darkness ticked by at a snail's pace, but thankfully without further incident.

Oh, did I forget to mention the culprit responsible for the calamity in the first place? No, it wasn't Charlie. Believe it or not, the flare tripping trespasser was *Felis catus*—a common house cat. Just as the flare lit up, I saw the frightened feline fleeing the scene of the crime. Knowing kitty, not Charlie, caused the chaos prompted my immediate and vociferous call to cease fire.

Always concerned about the welfare of his men, our platoon sergeant approached and asked me, "Are you sure it was just a cat?"

I reassured Sergeant Sawyer and the others, "I'm positive. I saw it running off just as the flare lit up."

Although it would have added *color* to my story to incorporate a *white* lie, I must report forthrightly—the cat was not *black*.

The incident wasn't the least bit funny at the time, but later in the day we grunts shared many laughs at the expense of our well-mannered platoon aristocrat. Dare I say—he became the *butt* of our jokes? I told everyone, "A full *moon* came out last night. Andy's pale cheeks lit up the area brighter than the flare."

Seth asked, "Andy, drop your drawers. The medic needs to treat your tush for flare-burn."

Andy didn't cooperate.

Larry added some dry sarcasm; "Looks like Andy was the real scaredy-cat. With all of the stress you put up with last night, you must be pooped!"

On and on it went. Everyone got in their kitty-licks and some of us laughed until we ached.

True to his nature, poor Andy handled the incessant kidding gracefully, but in truth, the episode literally scared the shit out of him.

Letter to my Family - June 28, 1969
Stand-down

This is the second day of Stand-down. It's a ball—live entertainment, movies, good food, soda, beer, and a comfortable bunk to sleep in. I'm going to hit the beach after lunch today.

About every two months our infantry company received a well deserved break from the drudgery of the field—three days of stand-down at the 23rd Infantry Division home base at Chu Lai. The sprawling facility provided nice amenities such as clean bunks, indoor showers, and an enlisted men's club. One of the first items of business for the motley group was to shower weeks of ground-in dirt off our bodies, shave a half-inch of bristle off our faces, and put on fresh, clean fatigues. Although I had been in the field only a few days, it felt good to be clean again. I can only imagine how good it must have felt to the men who had been in the boonies for the previous two months. The mess hall fed us steak for dinner, ice cream for dessert, and provided us with all the cold soda and beer we could guzzle.

Inevitably among rambunctious young men winding down from the stress of life in the field, some consumed too much alcohol and became rowdy. A couple of fights broke out, but were quickly squelched. One soldier who had been in country for several months became increasingly drunk and raucous. On his way to a nervous breakdown, he lashed out in a flurry of uncontrolled rage and had to be restrained by several of his buddies. I'll never forget his crying screams. "Don't make me go back out there. I can't take this shit anymore, I won't go out there, no, no, I won't go out there!"

Although I didn't know the soldier, observing his highly agitated behavior shook me to the core. I had never before seen anyone lose their composure to such an extreme degree. Even more disturbing is that I couldn't help but wonder—*will this be me in a few months? Am I going to lose my mind and end up in the loony bin?* Stand-down releases the steam inside the pressure cooker that has built up from weeks in the field. Eventually, the lid just has to blow. Interestingly, except for a nasty hangover, the soldier seemed fine the following day. Observing his apparent recuperation gave me a glimmer of hope that built-up emotional stress is survivable as long as it is allowed to be released.

During stand-down, the USO provided entertainment, mostly musical groups from the Philippines. Much to my surprise, they performed with skill and flare. The usual act consisted of a mix of four to seven young men and women. Not only were they talented singers and musicians, I was amazed by their impressions. Proficient at disguising their accents, the performers mimicked popular singers and rock groups of the time, and also the sounds of musical instruments. Listening to my favorite songs brought back many pleasant memories from home. My belated thanks to the USO and the many groups from the Philippine Islands who entertained US soldiers in Vietnam.

Letter to my Family - July 26, 1969
Starved then Stuffed

We had a mission two days ago that required us to stay overnight at LZ Low-Boy, an LZ (Landing Zone) for the engineers. I had eaten hardly anything since bunker guard two days before because I didn't take any C's and we didn't get re-supplied. So, I was starving by the time by the time we got back to Low-Boy about 5 PM. The mess hall had more food than I've seen since I've been here. As I went down the line, my tongue hanging out, I came first to the roast beef. The server gave me two slices and I asked for more knowing that they give you seconds in the army. But, this guy piled it on and asked if I wanted more still—I couldn't believe it! I had mashed and au gratin potatoes, salad, beans, tuna fish, kosher pickles, olives, a big slice of cherry pie, and I washed it all down with a quart of chocolate milk. I also had all of the ice tea I could drink and I don't know what else. I was so stuffed that I could barely move.

We had to get up at three in the morning the next day and the cooks were nice enough to get up and make us breakfast. I had eggs, good French toast, and cold cereal. We got back at noon and had an equally fabulous lunch. It was a mini R & R.

I had never consumed so much food at one sitting my entire year in Vietnam—or, for that matter, my entire life. I'm reminded of a film I once saw that featured a python swallowing whole an adult pig three times the snake's width. Stuffing my belly like a python almost made up for all those days in the field in which I lived off nothing more than canned fruit, cheese and crackers, and my morning cocoa.

Kids, Kids, Everywhere

My dad spent many hours in his garage tinkering with various household projects, working on his car, and building model airplanes. His friendly, good natured personality and interesting hobby attracted many curious neighborhood kids. Dad exuded affinity toward them, and they responded in kind. I thought about those happy days in his garage while stationed along Highway 1. Numerous youngsters from the local fishing village often gathered around our bivouac and we enjoyed their company.

Letter to my Family - September 15, 1969
Kid with Calf

Right at this moment, some little kid about two feet high is chasing his equally small calf down the road. There—he got him, and promptly swatted the calf on the rear.

I grew up in a suburban environment, but we neighborhood kids had access to plenty of nearby open space. I occasionally saw wild jackrabbits and coyotes, and I collected pollywogs and lizards. However, I had zero experience living on a farm among domestic animals. In my neighborhood, kids didn't guide calves down the road. The confidence and control Vietnamese children exhibited over their domesticated animals would impress any rancher. On numerous occasions I saw kids half my size taking charge and guiding 1,000 pound water buffalo, their main plow animal, through rice

109

paddies and along roadsides. By contrast, some of my adult neighbors have great difficulty controlling their yappy Chihuahuas.

Audiotape - February 9, 1970
Kid Helpers

At one point we were receiving hot chow about 3 PM every day along with our resupply. We made the little kids clean up the area where we stayed because we would eventually come back. They picked up all the C-ration and coke cans. They even dug a hole so that we could put all our trash in it and then burn it. They even dug us foxholes—anything we needed, they would do it.

Some of the guys gave kids money to go into the village and buy a bottle of Jim Beam Whiskey and bring it back to them. The kids would have done all these favors for nothing, but since we didn't finish our hot chow all the time—there was always some mashed potatoes or bits of meat left—we let the kids get in line and help themselves. Sometimes we even served them. They sure loved the hot food. We would also give them the C-rations that we didn't like. They would beam and their eyes would light up. These kids were poor—most had only one set of clothes. I guess we really helped them.

With so many kids hanging around us throughout the day, I often wondered, *where are their parents? Are some of the kids orphans? Why aren't they in school?* It's possible the parents approved of their children hanging around us soldiers because we gave them food and treated them well. Perhaps they received an education, but where and when this took place I haven't a clue. I don't recall seeing any schools. It's a shame because the kids visiting us almost daily appeared bright and eager to learn. Despite living in poverty amidst the turbulence of war, the kids along Highway 1, like their counterparts everywhere, exuded tons of energy and loved to laugh and play.

Letter to my Family - September 27, 1969
Games

The other day, one of the guys was playing with the kids—making up games and so on. It's funny, this colored guy is mean looking, but the kids love him. It was heartwarming—the kids were having so much fun you'd think it was Christmas. They were running relay matches and the colored guy just couldn't get them to do it right. About nine of them took him on in a tug of war—darn near beat him! Then, they all chased him around and wrestled with him. It was hilarious. I don't know what we'd do without these kids.

Although of average height, Tyler was strong and stocky with sausages for fingers. Outwardly, he appeared tough and intimidating, and when it came to soldiering, he was a no nonsense squad leader. Observing Tyler play games with the kids allowed me to gain a glimpse of his warmer, softer, and lighthearted side.

Letter to my Family - September 27, 1969
Surf's up!

Another *rough* day in the field—the beach was perfect today, I just got back. Big, body wompin' waves—honest, today I had more fun than I have had in Vietnam until now. Some of us guys had air mattresses and were riding the waves on them. I did, and got dumped over. This place would be a surfer's delight. The weather is real nice, no complaints.

My parents worried constantly about my welfare in the infantry, so in my letters I made an effort to over-emphasize the *good* things and minimize the bad. The above is one of my best examples, but this time I didn't have to exaggerate. While writing the letter, I thought, *if only there were more days like this.*

During my youth I spent many summer days enjoying Southern California beaches near home, including Huntington Beach, known as Surf City, USA. I didn't think it could get any better than this, but the coast of Vietnam is equally beautiful and alluring, if not more so. In most places the sand is fine grained and almost sugar-white, plus the water is warm—over 80 degrees. However, the "big, body wompin' waves" we soldiers enjoyed on that September day turned out to be the exception, not the rule. The surf near Chu Lai is small most of the year. The clear, tranquil waters are more suitable to snorkeling and scuba diving.

A memorable, but violent scene in the movie *Apocalypse Now* depicts a gung ho Lieutenant Colonel, portrayed by Robert Duvall, calling in helicopter gunships to blow away a VC village located along a section of coastline. In a spectacularly violent scene, napalm explodes, people scatter, and many die. Incredibly, the captain's actions are not motivated solely by military objectives, but also to cordon off a section of beach so he and his men can go surfing.

When our platoon gained access to the sea and wanted to swim, we didn't bring in dozens of helicopter gunships to blast the hell out of the surrounding area. Sorry, I don't have any dramatic, "Secure the beach" stories to share. Quite simply, half of our platoon stood guard while the other half went swimming, and then we traded places. We stripped to our olive drab army shorts and eagerly dove into the welcoming surf. Compared to the stifling air, the dip in eighty degree water felt refreshingly cool.

Swimming in the South China Sea felt invigorating, but once we soldiers got out and dried off, sea salt and fine sand stuck to ours bodies like the residue left after old tape is removed. Our skin itched and felt tacky. The only effective way to eliminate the patina is to rinse off with plenty of fresh water. Regrettably, we lacked access to a fresh water source and couldn't waste our limited supplies of canteen water. We brushed off our bodies as best we could, but with minimal effect. Having spent many days body surfing at local beaches and not showering until I arrived home, I developed a tolerance to the discomfort of sandy and salty skin. Not so for the platoon landlubbers. They suffered miserably.

Nebraska corn husker Ben commented, "My skin feels sticky and, boy, does my back ever itch."

Observing him squirming around and brushing his back against a palm tree for relief, I said to Ben and the others, "It won't last long. After an hour or so of sweating and moving around, the stuff will wear off. You'll be good as gold."

Ben and others continued to scratch and squirm, so I don't think my pep talk helped much. That being said, I had to believe that even for the landlubbers, the experience of swimming in the South China Sea must have been worth an hour or so of aggravation—if for no other reason than to feel cool and wash off weeks of accumulated terrestrial grime. For me, riding those waves on my air mattress rekindled many happy memories of fun-filled days at my favorite Southern California beaches.

X-rated?

One day at the coast we enjoyed the pleasure of female company. Three local soda girls in their late teens joined us for a romp in the water. Like us, they stripped down to their shorts. They wore no tops and thought nothing of it. Although stunned at seeing these young cuties displaying their bare breasts without the slightest embarrassment, I couldn't help but enjoy the view.

Looking is one thing, touching is another. I noticed crosses hanging from the girl's neck chains. Up to 20 percent of pacified village residents were conservative Catholics. The religion was infused into Vietnamese culture from the long French occupation. Out of respect and because we had access to prostitutes for sex, I didn't try any funny business, and neither did my comrades. To my surprise, it didn't take long for us to become accustomed to our topless companions. We joked around and frolicked in the surf like innocent school kids. Except for the initial attraction distraction, our interaction turned out to be like a day at the beach back home.

The company of the bare-breasted girls brought to mind images of Paul Gauguin's paintings of Tahitian culture. For centuries, women in many South Pacific and Southeast Asian cultures have publicly exposed their breasts. It's a cultural norm. The apparent conflict between Western Catholic attitudes toward nudity and native tradition became resolved by accommodation—or the church just looked the other way. The two girls swam bare-breasted because they were not taught to feel shame about it. However, I wonder if things changed when the communists took over Vietnam. In many

113

ways pertaining to sex and nudity, they were known to be conservative. Go figure!

Letter to my Family - September 30, 1969
False Alarm

We moved down here today (south of Duc Pho) by two trucks. We stopped on the road to let some guys off and shots rang out from atop a nearby hill. We thought we were getting hit so everyone jumped off the trucks, took cover and then opened up on the side of the hill. Finally, someone yelled, "Cease fire!" and it was explained to us that there were ARVN's up there. They are always shooting their weapons—they are like kids with toys. Some guys got skinned-up jumping off of the trucks. The ARVN's were on top of the hill out of sight, but our rounds coming over the hill probably scared the hell out of them.

The above letter is my *Reader's Digest* version of the incident, but some details are in need of illumination. After a couple of men were let off the trucks, I and others remaining on board heard what sounded like rifle fire coming from the steep, rocky hillside to our left. For the time being, confusion hung in the air. A few seconds later the rifle fire became distinct, and I started yelling "Incoming!" I was the first soldier to leap off the vehicle and take cover behind it. It was a risky jump. I scrambled over the fence-like railing surrounding the flatbed and hit the hard ground below—while carrying my rucksack and other heavy gear. Fortunately, I landed unscathed. A couple of seconds later the rest of the men began leaping off and behind the trucks for cover.

I knelt at the rear and started shooting toward the hillside. Not seeing any movement, I decided to aim between rocks where I thought the enemy might be hunkered down. Meanwhile, the other soldiers in the convoy began firing toward our invisible enemy. Oddly, no incoming rounds zipped by us or struck the trucks. Our platoon leader called in to headquarters. It turned out ARVN soldiers located on the other side of the hill had been firing weapons,

114

but not toward us. They were probably taking target practice or just messing around. Giving them the benefit of the doubt, they couldn't see our convoy from their location over the crest of the hill, and their ongoing rifle fire suppressed the noise of the trucks.

When I first found out we were never under attack, I felt embarrassed. *Some of these guys are down on my soldiering abilities, and surely my hasty reaction didn't help matters.* I said to members of my squad, "Sorry guys, all this hubbub was for nothing. Hope no one got hurt jumping off the trucks." Before anyone could respond, Carter, one of the platoon squad leaders who previously expressed doubts about my capabilities as a soldier, came up and patted me on the back. "Richert—you were the first to warn us and you reacted quickly. I didn't think you had it in you. Good job!"

Carter's praise came as a shock, and it caused me to pause and reflect. *Yeah, what if things had been different? What if we had come under enemy fire while exposed on this road? Maybe my alertness and quick action would have saved lives. He's right—I did the right thing. I shouldn't feel embarrassed, I should feel proud.* My morale rose to new heights.

Esho Funi

The subject of religion is relevant to war because a soldier's values and beliefs are tested to their fullest capacity in a combat environment. Much of my book is about ethical and philosophical challenges I faced, and the lessons I learned from them.

My parents raised the three of us kids without religious beliefs and practices, but they did not encourage us to be hostile toward Christianity or other faiths. Instead, they decided to allow us to make our own choices once we reached maturity. Before joining the army and at community college, I studied philosophy, including the beliefs and rituals of the world's major religions. When I arrived in Vietnam, I did not believe in God or life after death. Thus, it may sound odd coming from an atheist in a foxhole, but during my tour I underwent what many people would call a religious experience.

On a drizzly, gray November morning, our company began heading down a mountain after a week-long mission into the Central Highlands. The vegetation consisted of tall trees, but also unusually

115

dense, bushy ground cover. The landscape reminded me of the nearly impenetrable chaparral found in some of Southern California's foothills. In search of the North Vietnamese Army, the four platoons in our company had earlier separated from each other laterally by over 500 feet. Trails being nonexistent, our platoon was forced to meander through the thick brush toward the valley below.

Our trip through the tangled terrain quickly became arduous. At one location we took turns hacking our way through with machetes. One hour of hard labor earned us only a few hundred feet. It seemed like we would be stuck in the labyrinth forever, but eventually we managed to slash our way toward a rocky, shallow stream.

Our platoon leader ordered us to trek down it instead of laboring through the bush. That seemed a welcome order. However, the stream provided its own set of obstacles. It angled down at about twenty-five degrees on average, and in some places became steep. Abundant rocks varied in size from pebbles to boulders the size of a small car. Thankfully, in most places the rushing water reached only to mid-calf. Navigating down a rocky, wet streambed is quite difficult, especially when you are tired and weighted down by cumbersome gear.

My buddy Larry said to our squad leader Bryant, "What are we gonna do if one of us slips and breaks an ankle? There's no way a chopper could land around here to pick him up."

"We'd have to carry him between two guys or make some kind of litter," Bryant replied. "Let's make sure that doesn't happen, so spread the word for everyone to be extra careful."

Like the tedious hack through thick brush earlier that day, the afternoon trek downstream continued at a snail's pace. Before heading out that morning, our leaders had planned for the four platoons to hook up in the valley below by dusk. By late afternoon it became obvious that wasn't going to happen. Over two miles of rough terrain still remained ahead, and the men were exhausted.

I asked my machine gunner, Ben, "Where in this maze are we going to find a place to set up for the night? The stream is too rocky and the brush is too thick."

Holding the bulky M60 machine gun over his right shoulder, Ben replied, "I haven't a clue, but I'm so tired I could sleep on a bed of nails."

As if preplanned, toward sunset our platoon finally stumbled upon a rare patch of open ground next to the stream bed. The small clearing provided just enough space for the 23 of us to hunker down in a tight bunch. *Ah, relief at last!* A full day of laborious trekking drained everyone of energy and we all welcomed some well-deserved shuteye. Lieutenant Fredericks decided that only one man at a time need be up on guard for a one-hour shift during the night. He selected me to be one of them.

For the first time since arriving in Vietnam, I didn't worry about the threat of an enemy attack. I told Ben, "This wilderness is so remote and rugged, I doubt humans have ever set foot in it."

The big Nebraska farmer replied, "I can't imagine how anyone could live out here. There's certainly no place to grow food."

A few minutes later, Ben curled up on his poncho liner and fell sound asleep.

Have you ever been so exhausted you can't sleep? That's how I felt after a hard day's journey into night. My body felt limp, but my mind remained active. I hadn't caught a wink when my guard shift arrived at midnight. I sat with legs crossed in front and M16 rifle nestled in my lap. While the men around me slept, I listened to the many sounds of nature surrounding me—insects, frogs, and perhaps monkeys calling in the distance.

After a snack of crackers and cheese, I relaxed and stared upward at the sequin-like stars and Milky Way arching across a cloudless, moonless sky. The magnificent panorama filled me with wonder and awe and inspired many philosophical questions. *Why is the universe so big? Does it ever end? What, if anything, is the meaning of it all? Surely intelligent beings must exist out there. Have they learned to live in peace with one another, or do they also wage war?* One thought dominated all the others; *Here I am stuck in the middle of nowhere in a strange country far from home. Compared to the grand scale of things, my existence and purpose here seems insignificant.*

Just then, five months of pent-up anxiety and hyper-alertness from life in the infantry began to melt away. Like a comforting, protective aura, an overwhelming sense of calm and peacefulness enveloped my mind and body. *What a strange quirk of irony—here I am in the middle of a war and yet at this moment I feel safer than at any other time in my life.*

Soon, my mind and body seemed to transcend ordinary time and space, yet simultaneously I felt deeply connected to everything around me. I wasn't a soldier, I wasn't flesh and blood, and I wasn't in Vietnam. My body and the earth became one, and my mind enveloped the entire sky. My essence melded with the universe. The episode gradually faded and I came back down to earth. Although calm, I felt emotionally spent.

Buddhists call a feeling of oneness with the cosmos Esho Funi, which literally means, *two, but not two.* A Christian might interpret a similar episode as a spiritual closeness to God or Christ. Whatever one calls it, the sensation felt amazing and I have never experienced anything like it since. Although awesome and deeply moving, I didn't feel religious in the sense of a connection to the supernatural or God. My parents didn't indoctrinate me to think that way. Instead, and perhaps because I have always loved the outdoors, I felt an intimate relationship with nature.

It's not a romantic conclusion, but I believe my Esho Funi episode was produced solely by neuro-chemical activity within my brain. These experiences are known to occur during times of sleep deprivation, high stress, and anxiety—a permanent condition in the infantry. For me, this explanation in no way undermines its profound effects. Although the philosophical and psychological issues such experiences raise are interesting, I chose to relate it here because of its uniqueness and the incredibly good feelings it aroused.

My Ritual

Trekking all day while carrying a 70 pound rucksack in blistering heat and stifling humidity, along with knowledge that an enemy attack could occur from anywhere at any time, is physically and mentally exhausting. As the sun goes down, you just want to curl up and sleep the night away, but no such luxury is available to soldiers in the field. Each night every man in the platoon performed two

118

separate one-hour shifts on guard, which disrupted our sleep. It was a bitch to remain awake, especially in the quiet and blackness of a moonless night. However, a soldier dare not nod off. Sleeping on guard could result in death or injury to himself and others from an enemy attack. This very real fear motivated me to stay awake, but occasionally I sought additional aid in the form of snacks.

Often while up on guard at night I fantasized, *oh, what I wouldn't give for a juicy cheeseburger hot off the grill or slice of pizza fresh out of the oven.* Although fantasies couldn't satisfy my hunger, all was not lost. A few tasty snacks remained from a goodie-box my mom had sent me a few days earlier. One of those, the pepperoni stick, helped to quell my craving for spicy food. The mini-sausages, vacuum sealed in cellophane to ensure a long shelf life, easily endured the long journey across the Pacific. Most of the sticks I received measured only about one-quarter inch in thickness and five inches in length—not much more than a mouthful. Although I usually received a half-dozen of the tasty treats, I limited my ration to no more than one per day.

I faced a dilemma. *How do I simultaneously enjoy my pepperoni stick while making it last for one full hour while I'm up on guard? This is gonna require planning and discipline.* I hatched a strategy—a precise ritual of sorts. First, I had to select on which of my two shifts to savor the treat. This depended upon the time of night and the degree of my hunger and weariness. For example, if really tired, I saved the treat for my last shift to help keep me awake during the wee hours of the morning.

To ensure for success, I made careful mental calculations. *At 2:10 am, I bite off a one-quarter inch piece then slowly move the morsel around in my mouth while chewing delicately in order to absorb as much flavor as possible. I must always remind myself—don't rush, make it last. Five minutes later, I repeat the process and keep repeating until—hopefully—near the end of the shift I enjoy my last precious morsel.*

Unfortunately, sticking to my self-imposed time table posed too difficult a challenge. Despite rigorous planning and my best efforts, I couldn't maintain the discipline to make the five-inch long treat last throughout my one-hour shift—on that night and for any of the others in which I indulged in the ritual. Patience and discipline couldn't compete with my cravings. However, one night I managed to finish the snack forty minutes into the hour. I felt pride in this noble accomplishment.

From the comfort and security of home life, some people may see my act of creating a detailed ritual out of eating a snack as bizarre. Granted, but practicing the routine preoccupied my mind, which helped to keep me awake on guard. Most importantly, it taught me a valuable life lesson. Besides reinforcing the importance of planning and discipline, I learned that a key element to coping with adverse situations is to always look forward toward something enjoyable— even if it is only a modest pleasure. In Vietnam, the pepperoni stick and other rituals, like preparing and savoring my morning cocoa, helped to get me through many hard days and nights.

CHAPTER 7

The Bad

Candy Ass!

Not one of the physically stronger members of the platoon, those first two months adjusting to the physical hardships of the infantry stressed my stamina to the max. On long, exhausting treks, sometimes I struggled to take the next step. We stopped for breaks about every thirty minutes, but they never seemed to last long enough. Too tired to perform the simple task of removing my rucksack, I often sat down on the trail and leaned back against it. I nodded off almost instantly—only to be awakened five minutes later by a squad leader barking, "Let's move out!" Somehow, probably out of stubborn pride, I always managed to keep up with the group. After two months, my body finally began adjusting to the rigors of the field. Nonetheless, I remained physically sub-par to most of the soldiers in my platoon. Sometimes in good natured fun, and sometimes not, the men called me a pussy, candy ass, or California faggot.

In September my physical prowess would be tested further. Nebraska cornhusker Ben, our squad's big strong machine gunner, was scheduled to leave for one week of R & R. Squad leader Tyler informed me, "While Ben's gone, you're gonna carry the 60. As Tyler walked away I muttered to myself, *damn! I'm not sure I can I handle the beast. Why did Tyler have to pick me, just to see if I could cut it?* The day after Ben left, our platoon went on patrol through rice paddies and scattered villages west of Highway 1. *Thankfully, this territory is flat—no steep hills to climb.* The standard method for toting the 38 pound machine gun is to sling its strap over the shoulder, grasp the grip behind the barrel with one hand, and hold on under the rear handle with the other. The behemoth is less burdensome when the weight is distributed. The macho method is to carry it Rambo style—hold it in front with both hands, but without the support of the shoulder strap. Some soldiers slung the big gun on top of a shoulder. Holding the weapon Rambo style or, alternatively, over the shoulder for extended periods requires great strength, but my thin build and spaghetti arms weren't up to the task. I carried it in the conventional manner at all times.

After two hours on patrol, the thick strap began digging into my trapezius muscle, and my arms ached. As the day went on I had great difficulty handling the weapon. Fatigued and irritable, under my breath I kept bitching, *I hate this fucking beast! It's killing me. When are we gonna take a break? This job sucks. I can't wait for Ben to get back.* Once again stubbornness and pride helped push me through, but I wondered—*how will I make it through tomorrow without collapsing?* Sure enough, day two at lugging the 60 became even more difficult. By midday I became awkward and wobbly, like a top running out of spin. Discomfort and exhaustion distracted my attention and dulled my senses, causing me to become less alert—all of which could result in a delayed reaction time. During an enemy attack, these inhibiting factors could jeopardize platoon safety.

My tenuous condition did not go unnoticed. Toward the end of the day squad leader Tyler approached me and stated empathetically; "Looks like you're having a little trouble carrying the 60. Are you okay?"

I wanted to blurt out, "Hell no!" but pride held me back. Although my face drooped like that of a wounded bloodhound, I told him, "I'm doing okay. It's taking me some time to get used to carrying the gun. I'm not strong like Ben, but I can handle it."

Tyler could see my words did not match my demeanor. He didn't say anything further, but I sensed he considered taking the beast away from me. Sure enough, the next morning he and Sergeant Sawyer decided to place the M60 in the hands of a more physically able platoon member.

Tyler and Sawyer's main priority was for the safety of the men, and rightfully so. The M60 is the platoon's most vital weapon. It should only be in the hands of someone with the strength to handle it, and handle it with confidence. Most of the soldiers agreed with the decision, and a few viewed me with contempt. I overheard snide comments like, "Squad candy ass," and "Worthless." Those words hurt. They hurt not only because of the embarrassment I felt at my inability to physically handle the M60, but more so because I literally could not carry my share of the weight for our platoon. I let myself and everyone else down. Luckily, during the two days in which I carried the big gun, we didn't make enemy contact.

The plain truth is ever since day one I had serious doubts about my ability to cope with the physical hardships of the infantry, and obviously so did some of the other soldiers in my platoon. Like my sagging shoulders, my morale sank to a new low. *I don't belong out here. I'm not cut out for the infantry.* Then, like a punch in the arm, I decided, *okay, Bob, time to stop feeling sorry for yourself! Ben's coming back in a couple of days and I'll be back to my job as assistant machine gunner.* Once back in my comfort zone, my depression waned, along with the snide comments of my critics.

To the point

"Richert, you're gonna lead the company today." So ordered platoon leader Sawyer one August morning just before we were to move out on an extended patrol. I had walked on point before, but only briefly and on platoon-sized missions in familiar areas known for little enemy activity. On this mission, the entire company would patrol through unfamiliar territory known for a heavy VC presence, and with our squad in the lead.

Squad leader Tyler took me aside and offered some of his hard earned wisdom. I listened attentively for any information that might

123

enable me to better perform this dangerous job. Knowing my wimpy reputation among the platoon, the last burden I wanted weighing on my sagging shoulders would be to screw up and possibly imperil myself and the others. The point man must be a keen observer and remain on high alert at all times. He must not only visually sweep the surrounding terrain for the presence of the enemy, but also look down at the trail ahead for signs of booby traps. This is easier said than done when you are stressed, exhausted, and your eyes are full of dirty sweat from unrelenting heat and humidity.

The trail we followed meandered away from the villages and rice paddies in the flatlands toward a group of hills rising in the distance. Our route did not appear to be well worn—a good omen because those with the heaviest traffic were also the most frequently booby trapped. The VC planted two main types of booby traps on trails. One is a mine with a pressure sensitive detonator. It is buried a few inches under the dirt. A few of the mines we encountered in Vietnam were capable of killing or seriously maiming within a twenty foot radius, but most severely impacted only the individual who stepped on it—provided soldiers had spaced themselves more than eight feet apart.

Sometimes the VC made crude mines from our own discarded C-Ration cans. Only three other ingredients are necessary—C-4 explosive imbedded with buckshot or nails, and a pressure sensitive triggering device. The VC designed these homemade devices not so much to kill, but to maim and demoralize US soldiers. While patrolling roads, trails, or walking on rice paddy dikes, we always remained wary that potential harm could be buried inches below our feet.

Underground planted mines cannot be detected visually. Given a column of twenty or more men, someone is likely to step on the device and detonate it. One of the soldiers near the lead of the column usually triggers a mine, but the soldiers at the rear could never feel safe. A month earlier a young man from another platoon stepped on one. In defiance of the odds, the soldier was located near the middle of column of 90 men. My platoon was at the front of the column when the explosion occurred.

Shortly after, Ben turned to me and said, "That could have been any one of us."

I replied, "That's what's so scary. It's just dumb, blind luck who steps on one."

A medic attended the young man until a chopper arrived twenty minutes later to take him to the base hospital. I heard shrapnel from the mine badly tore up the soldier's legs, but he survived.

The other common type of booby trap we encountered on trails consisted of a trip wire attached to a camouflaged grenade or other type of explosive device. A thin wire is extended across a trail about six inches above the ground. When a soldier unwittingly trips the wire, a pin is released causing the device to explode. These mines were often concealed in highly vegetated places. Even on bright, sunny days, trip wires are difficult to detect among the dappled light or shadowy places between shrubs. Whereas anyone in a column might detonate a buried pressure sensitive mine, the point man is most likely to trip a wire strung across a trail.

With all of this weighing on my mind, plus the probable presence of VC ahead, I began to lead our company forward. Squad leader Tyler followed right behind me.

"I got your back, Richert," he said reassuringly.

"Thanks Tyler." His presence and encouraging words boosted my confidence.

Knowing the potential dangers in this area, our company moved at a cautious pace, and the men spaced themselves at least ten feet apart. Soldiers clumped close together are prime targets because Charlie gets more bang-for-the-buck when he shoots at a cluster. The column stopped briefly upon occasion for rest breaks, or when the captain and platoon leaders needed to assess the situation.

We patrolled through the flatlands toward the distant rolling hills. *So far, so good.* Bamboo thickets and palm trees, which provided good cover for Charlie, punctuated the rice paddies on both sides of the trail. After twenty minutes, a thickly vegetated, steep hill appeared off to our right—ideal conditions for an ambush. Moving forward, I kept my M16 at the ready while adrenaline gushed through my veins. I felt nervous, but also determined. My eyes darted back and forth between the terrain and the trail ahead of me. Tyler kept a close eye on me while others down the line kept an eye on the ominous looking hillside at our right. We passed by it without incident and everyone felt relief, especially me. However, I wasn't about to let my guard down. Like a tiger on the hunt, I remained highly focused as we moved toward the unpopulated hill country—unpopulated by civilian rice farmers, but not necessarily Charlie.

In order to minimize the chances of tripping a booby trap, instead of walking directly on a trail and if the terrain permitted, soldiers walked to one side. After three hours on patrol and with no signs of the enemy, the vegetation became thicker, including along both sides of the narrowing path. For the next few hundred feet, the column had no choice but to walk directly on it. *Gotta watch for trip wires.* Nerves frayed and physically exhausted, I tried not to let it show. I led the company forward toward the base of a hill.

Just as we were about to lead the company up the incline, Tyler placed his left arm on my shoulder and whispered, "Hold up."

"What's up?" As we gazed at the hill gently rising in front of us, Tyler seemed to feel a premonition of foreboding. I'm sure in the imaginations of most of the men, including me, menacing apparitions of Charlie—weapons at the ready—glared at us through the bushes and trees ahead.

Tyler and our company captain consulted while our squad and the rest of the column remained in place. As he broke away from the brief meeting, Tyler abruptly commanded, "I'll take point from here on." The decision hurt my pride, but I simultaneously felt relief. This is not the time for rookie mistakes. I realized they were right so I swallowed my pride and moved to the back of the squad.

After a few minutes of rest and with Tyler in the lead, the company advanced cautiously up the gently sloping hill. We moved about 300 feet and then abruptly stopped.

Ben, standing in front of me, said, "Something's up."

"Yeah, maybe he spotted some dinks," Gary replied.

Tyler held his arms up and gestured everyone to move back. Along with Tyler, the entire company retreated about 100 feet. Word came down the line quickly that Tyler stopped about two feet short of tripping a wire attached to a hidden grenade. He managed to spot the device just in the nick of time. Our experienced squad leader didn't seem outwardly agitated by the fact he came within inches of death or serious injury, but I had to believe his insides were doing summersaults.

Following standard procedure in such situations, our company captain ordered two men to move forward and set a Claymore mine next to the booby trap. Like a series of echoes, men down the long line repeated, "Fire in the hole!" A soldier detonated the Claymore, which destroyed itself and the booby trap. Soon afterward our company proceeded on its way up the hill, and the remainder of the day passed peacefully.

Although happy all turned out well, the episode put a lump the size of an apple in my throat. *What if I had remained on point? Would I have spotted the booby trap? Probably not.* Although my innards quavered for a while, I decided to turn a positive into a negative. I became more determined than ever to remain sharp and at the ready at all times during patrols—point man or last in line.

"Life is far too precious to waste it complaining. If you don't like where you are change it—it's just that simple."
Sanyo Jendayi, American writer, *Girl, get Empty*

Something tells me Ms. Jendayi never served in combat. Many things in life are beyond our capacity to change. You just have to make the best with what you are handed—and sometimes the effort is futile. During my first few months in the infantry, I earned a reputation as one of the platoon's most vociferous complainers. My personality type is outgoing, so expressing my misery out loud helped to shed anxiety and frustration. The problem is members of the platoon were forced to endure my acid tongue.

Squad leader Tyler once told me in uncertain and raw terms, "I got my own shit to deal with. I don't need to hear your constant bitching, so button it!" I tried, but the button didn't hold. In early November, our platoon pulled all night guard at a fire base south of Chu Lai. My squad slept in tight quarters inside a perimeter bunker. The weather became cooler and damper. Instead of the afternoon cloudbursts of summer, November ushered in days of steady, misty rain.

After one year in the bush, Tyler had recently left for a well deserved trip home. Stocky of build with dirty blonde hair, a pudgy face, and ruddy complexion, Spec 4 Bryant became our new squad leader. Although he demonstrated a no-nonsense type of leadership style, Bryant wasn't the gung ho type. He didn't volunteer to serve in Vietnam, but had a job to do and took it seriously.

On day two at the firebase, our squad awoke at 3:00 AM to go on an overnight mission into the Batagan Peninsula. Known for a heavy presence of Viet Cong, the infamous My Lai incident took place just to its southwest a year and a half earlier. Cranky and pissed off upon hearing the news, I started going off; "How come we have to get up so fucking early? Can't the assholes in the rear wait until daylight to send us into this shit? It's pitch black out there. That peninsula is bad news, and—"

Squad leader Bryant had enough. Grabbing my shirt by the lapels, he pushed me back to a wall and yelled, "I'm sick of hearing your Goddamn whining. Shut the fuck up!"

The other men in the squad stood by and watched, but I'm sure most silently cheered Bryant on. Literally taken aback, I nonetheless didn't react with anger because I deserved the shove and lecture. "Sorry Bryant. I will try and cool it from now on." He let go without further comment and I moved away feeling isolated and low.

Our mission left little time for me to dwell in despair. We soldiers gathered our gear and moved out toward the peninsula. With visibility near nil under a black blanket of thick clouds, we inched our way along a winding trail until morning's light expedited our progress. By mid-morning, the temperature reached the mid-seventies, and a light misty rain began to fall. I detected the faint odor of salty air gently blowing in from the coast not far away. *Smells good—reminds me of June Gloom back home.* The light rain penetrated through my fatigues, but after months of oppressive heat, the cool moisture felt refreshing.

Our platoon trekked over six miles the first day, and at dusk we set up bivouac in a remote section of the peninsula. I made a makeshift lean-to with my poncho and slept reasonably comfy during the night. *No signs of the enemy so far.* The morning mist lightened up and we worked our way back toward Highway 1. Late in the afternoon, trucks picked us up and hauled us back to the firebase. After humping a dozen miles over two full days through the notorious Batagan Peninsula, we never saw even a hint of the VC.

The two day mission turned not to be the terrible ordeal I had anticipated, so all my previous bitching only served to cost me mental angst and alienate me from some of my comrades. If the army gave medals for putting one's foot in one's mouth, I would have been a shoe...boot-in! *This is a wakeup call. From then on I'll try harder to curb my tongue.* I mouthed off from time to time, but no more so than the others. After all, bitching is to soldiering what scratching is to a mosquito bite. At least Bryant never grabbed me by the lapels following that embarrassing day.

Seeing Red

One day in July, the extreme heat made patrolling over long distances impractical. Our platoon sat around idly on a sandy mound a quarter mile inland from the beach. Other than some waist high shrubs and scattered palm trees, the area consisted of mostly open terrain. During the height of midday, shade was scarce. One of the members of my squad—we called him Red because he fit the stereotype of a freckle-faced, hot-tempered redhead—had been riding me all week. From out of nowhere and for no apparent reason, he would curse at me or call me nasty names. Sometimes, I told him to knock it off and leave me alone, but I usually just let his harassment go unanswered. However, on this searing day he raised the temperature even further by riding me harder than ever.

"Richert, you're a chicken shit, sorry-ass excuse for a soldier. I bet you don't even know how to fight. Come on, I'm calling you a coward, are you just gonna sit there and take it?"

That does it! My anger thermometer reached its bursting point. I stood up, raised my fists, and rushed toward him. "I'm gonna shut your big mouth once and for all!" Before I could dig into him, a couple of the guys rushed in and separated us. After a few minutes we both calmed down. The same oppressive heat that stoked our tempers also drained our energy.

After the blowout, Red quit harassing me. We weren't friendly, but remained cordial. Puzzled by his sudden change in attitude, a few days later I decided to have a talk with him. "Red, why were you riding me so hard?"

"I was testing you. I wanted to see how long it would take you to get pissed off enough to want to stand up for yourself. I wanted to see if there was a man inside there somewhere."

"So once I challenged you, you were satisfied I was okay?"

Red replied, "Yeah, that's about it. It sure took you one hell of a long time to react. You have more patience than anyone I ever met."

"Yeah, it takes a lot to make me really mad. You know the old expression, *sticks and stones may break my bones, but names will never hurt me?* That's what I was taught, but that only goes so far. But, now I understand why you did what you did, and I'm okay with it."

After Vietnam, Red and I ended up serving our last few months in the army together at Fort Hood, Texas. We became friends. He introduced me to the base craft shop and we went to movies in the local town.

Something to be sore about

We infantry soldiers carried most of our gear on our backs via the army issue Lightweight Tropical Rucksack. A water resistant nylon bag with one large compartment and three external pockets is attached to a tubular metal frame. Like modern backpacks, two adjustable straps attach to its top and bottom. Any hiker knows that carrying a heavy pack for a long time period places stress on the muscles of the upper body and compresses the discs of the lower back. I can attest to the latter because I have suffered from lower back problems since leaving the army. Oops, there I go griping again.

During my first few days in the field, it seemed like our platoon humped a thousand miles, and the weight of my rucksack began taking its toll on my upper shoulders. The constant pressure and shifting of heavily weighted straps caused increasing irritation to my sunburned skin. Several sores broke out. Both shoulders became raw, but because I unconsciously shifted more of the rucksack weight

130

to my right shoulder, it became more adversely affected. After only four days, the rounded, reddened sores became more numerous, larger, and skin began peeling away. The hot, steamy climate and grime of the field resulted in an infection. Puss began oozing out, so during breaks I tried to clean them as best I could.

In an effort to facilitate healing, I shifted the bulk of the rucksack's weight to my less affected left side. Meanwhile, I folded my towel and placed it between the strap and my right shoulder to serve as a cushion. Despite my efforts, the sores became larger and more infected. The largest one increased to over three inches in diameter. The affected area eventually covered my entire right upper shoulder down to the top of my scapula.

During the eighth day of my ordeal, Sergeant Sawyer happened to see me with my shirt off. Upon closer approach, a look of disbelief appeared on his face.

"Holy shit, these are bad! Why didn't you tell someone about these sores? We've got to get you treated." Sawyer called over our medic, Michelson, who the men called Mick.

After one brief look at my raw shoulder, he gasped, "Whoa!"

Mick began treatment by cleaning my sores with cotton balls and a liquid antiseptic. Next, he applied a layer of gelatinous antibacterial salve, added a dressing, and gave me antibiotic pills with instructions to take two per day. Michelson had been a field medic for seven months. Obviously, I wasn't his first patient suffering with this affliction.

After dressing my wounds, he scolded, "You shouldn't have waited so long for treatment because these sores grow fast, and if left unchecked they could become a serious problem."

I confessed, "I've only been in the field eight days, and I didn't want to look like a cry baby in front of the others."

Mick nodded, "I get it, but you have to think about your health first, and you are no good to the platoon in this condition. If the sores come back, make sure to see me right away. Don't mess around with this shit!"

"Okay, thanks doc." Mick's treatment eased the pain, and with only two more days in the field followed by three days of stand-down, my wounds healed quickly.

131

In WWII these staph infections were called jungle rot, but in Vietnam someone coined the disrespectful term, *gook sores,* and the name stuck. Many infantry soldiers contracted them, but with varying degrees of adverse affect.

Letter to my Family - July 26, 1969
More Sores

Remember me telling you about the gook sores? The ones on my arms have pretty well disappeared, but now they are on my face. I've got a scab on my left ear that just won't heal. The damn flies love to land there, it drives me nuts! But, these are the small sores—I still have some big ones on my lower legs. On my left leg below the knee I have ten good sized sores mostly around the shin bone and arch of my foot. They just won't heal. I've got stuff to put on them, but if I don't get results in a week I'm going to see the doc. I've got a mess of small ones starting to appear on my upper legs also. They are just a scab under which is puss—if I push down on the scab, puss oozes out. Blech!

Letter to my Family - August 1, 1969
Treatment

I had our field medic look at my legs and he fixed me up. He cleansed the sores with some stuff and then put on a medication. He wrapped up my bad left leg in a bandage to keep dirt and flies off. The flies are murder! It's hard to sit here and write because the damn flies are continually landing on my exposed open sores.

Letter to my Family - October 3, 1969
They're back!

Well, I've got those bad sores again. They got infected and progressively worse on my ankle and the cheek of my ass on the right side. So I went into Duc Pho yesterday and the doc

132

gave me pills and five days of rear duty. It started raining. I'm glad I'm here instead of out in the field. Anyway, I have a very raw ass. It is too tender to sit or put my weight on. These sores got larger because of my scratching them, but the itch was too much to bear. I couldn't stand it.

Any small scratch or abrasion on my skin became enlarged, infected, and then offshoots spread like monster-sized zits on a teenager's face. I suffered from this problem to a greater degree than anyone else in my platoon. In the eyes of some of my fellow soldiers, this provided yet more proof of my status as platoon candy-ass. I confided to my buddy Andy, "Maybe those guys are right about me. I can't carry the 60, and no one trusts me to walk point. Now this shit."

"Yeah, I guess I'll call you a tenderfoot, like in one of those TV westerns."

Andy noticed by my dejected posture his attempt at humor didn't work.

"Hey, don't let it get you down, and ignore those guys. These sores are something you can't help and have no control over. We're all living in the same dirty conditions, yet you just happen to be the one the germs are most attracted to. Are the girls back home as attracted to you as these germs?"

This time I chuckled. Andy's empathy lifted my morale when I needed it most.

By late September, the sores had grown more numerous and moved up my legs and all over the right side of my butt. Sitting stung like hell and the puss stains on my trousers became easily visible. This time our platoon sergeant sent me to the field hospital at Duc Pho. I clearly remember lying face down on a table while the doctor used a tweezers-like tool to pull off dozens of scabs—one at a time—from my raw legs and butt. I saw no purpose in mentioning these sordid details in my October 3rd letter home. I had already shared more than I should. Happily, this was the last time I needed treatment for the so-called gook sores. Oh, they eventually came back, but never as bad. *Thank goodness—one less enemy to put up with.*

Letter to my Family - July 9, 1969
If you can't take the heat...

I spent two days in the hospital ward at Duc Pho because of heat exhaustion. In the field I was out in the sun too much and then got weak and nauseous. I ran a temperature of 102 degrees. They called in a dust-off. A helicopter came out, picked me up and took me to Duc Pho. That first day I was really weak. It was hard to get up and walk. The next day— July 6th—I felt normal again, so they sent me to my company in the rear at Duc Pho for two days further rest.

When I arrived at the base hospital I feared the worst, so the first question out of my mouth was, "Do I have malaria?" When the nurse informed me I suffered from heat exhaustion, I felt a degree of relief. Fever, nausea, and extreme fatigue are symptoms of both disorders, but malaria is a much more serious illness. The day before my symptoms appeared, I spent too much time under the sun minus my bush hat, plus I didn't drink sufficient water. Our leaders often cautioned us about such risks, so I should have known better.

During the afternoon of my first day in the hospital, platoon sergeant Sawyer arrived to check up on me. Weak and groggy, I had difficulty remaining awake. The only words I recall him saying were, "Hey Richert, how you feeling?" I muttered something incoherently, and then my lights went out. By the time I reawakened, Sergeant Sawyer had been long gone. I felt badly about our brief visit because he had to catch a chopper and be away from his men. Of course, upon my return to the field he kidded me mercilessly.

With a twinkle in his eye, Sawyer barked, "Richert, you're lucky I didn't give you an *Article 15* for the disrespect you showed to your platoon leader that day. Get your ass in gear, young man!"

I nodded, "Yes, platoon sergeant," and smiled. I knew underneath the feigned bluster lie the compassion of a leader who cared about my welfare.

Déjà vu all over again! A couple of months after the above episode, I underwent a turbulent night with tossing in my sleep. I awoke so weak I couldn't even get up on my feet.

134

While our platoon sergeant picked up a radio to order a dust-off, Billy Caleb growled, "He's faking it! He just wants to get out of the field."

Fortunately, Reynolds spoke up in my defense. "I don't think he's faking. I slept next to him and he stirred, groaned, and talked to himself all through the night. He woke me up several times."

The dust-off was called in, and two soldiers had to help me to my feet and assist me to the chopper. I don't recall what caused this latest bout of heat exhaustion, but thankfully, it never laid me out again. During my first four and a half months in the infantry, the platoon medic regularly treated me for staph infections and choppers brought me to the hospital three times—once for the sores and twice for heat exhaustion.

Letter to my Family - July 12, 1969
O.P.

I'm back out in the field. You can tell because as soon as I got out here it started raining and didn't stop all day or night. Then it started raining intermittently until today, and now it is very hot again. The first night out here, I had O.P. (Observation Post). Three of us went out about 200 meters from the perimeter and stayed up all night listening for the enemy. No enemy, but beaucoup (abundant) rain! Then yesterday, we went out on a patrol of about five miles altogether. What was bad is we got up at 3 AM to do it. Ah, but today I got caught up on my sleep, cleaned my weapon, and have done nothing else all day.

The above letter briefly describes my first assignment at Observation Post. OP is usually set up at an elevated position alongside a trail a few hundred feet away from the platoon. The team is assigned to keep watch throughout the night for enemy movements and forewarn the platoon leader via radio of their location. They are not supposed to initiate contact unless spotted or attacked because their isolation puts them in great jeopardy. Sadly, many soldiers who served on OP and came under assault are not around to tell their stories.

Each man on OP must remain highly alert, and no one is supposed to sleep. However, on this rainy night one soldier was allowed to sleep while the other two kept lookout. We left our rucksacks with the rest of the platoon and brought a radio along with our weapons, ammo, and water. I decided to bring my air mattress.

Gary, one of our three man team, saw me with it and said, "Leave the air mattress. We don't take those out on OP."

"But I need it because it's supposed to rain all night and I sleep on my stomach."

Gary came back, "So, don't sleep! Laying on it makes squeaky noises that will alert the dinks, so forget it!"

Just then Seth, one of our most experienced soldiers, intervened. "No, no, it's okay. You can bring the air mattress, but just fill it ti-ti (pronounced tee-tee, Vietnamese slang for a small amount) with air. That way you won't make noise laying on it."

I agreed to comply and after hearing Seth's explanation, Gary and Red, the other soldiers in our group, approved. During the night my half-filled cushion worked as Seth predicted. Not a whisper of noise, and considering the rain, I felt reasonably comfortable. However, I slept less than one hour. As soon as my eyelids became heavy, I envisioned ghostly images of Charlie aiming his AK47 at my face. Luckily, Charlie never showed. The next time I went on OP, I left my air mattress behind.

Things that go bump in the night

Rather than setting up for the night in the standard circular perimeter, one evening the 90 men in our company formed a U-shaped line around the base of a broad, gently sloping hill. In order to make a circle, the circumference of the hill's base would have required spreading the men too far apart for safety, so our captain nixed the idea. Instead, he called this unusual U-shaped formation a company-sized ambush. The problem with the configuration is the enemy could conceivably penetrate through its unguarded open end and attack us from the inside and perhaps outside simultaneously.

To our benefit, the densely vegetated hill greatly inhibited potential movement by the VC, especially under darkness. Also, in the event of an attack from inside the U, the hill's elevation provided a natural barrier thwarting crossfire between our soldiers located on opposite sides.

Seen from above, my three man group was located at the lower left side of the U. Behind us about 200 feet away lay a large, quiet lagoon. A wide open mudflat, interrupted only by a few small bushes and clusters of boulders, lay between us and the placid waters. Due to lack of cover, our squad leader determined it unlikely an attack would occur from the mudflat. Thus, he told us to observe both areas, but direct most of our attention toward the inside of the U. The first 50 feet between my group and the base of the hill consisted of mostly open space, but the terrain beyond transitioned into thick vegetation.

As always, each man must know precisely where the groups to his left and right are located, and 90 feet of open space separated us from each other—four times the standard distance. We had little choice in the matter. Lack of cover compelled each group to set up within available clusters of large rocks for protection.

Next to my group sat an old concrete Vietnamese grave. Its flat main section rose about a foot and a half above the ground, almost like a bed, but slightly larger. To complete the picture, a four foot high, decorative scalloped wall on one side looked like a headboard. As we set up after sunset, my two comrades decided to sleep on top of its flat section.

Norquist said, "This will be much better than sleeping on the wet ground." His buddy Blake agreed.

Although the three of us were the same rank, I had accrued more time in country. I stated firmly, "Bad idea! This elevated exposed position will make both of you easy targets in case of an attack. Set up on the ground next to the grave marker so you'll have cover."

Norquist and Blake ignored my suggestion. For protection, I decided to sleep on the ground adjacent to a granite boulder the size of a small sofa. Daytime winds had diminished to a soft breath of a breeze. As night set in, overcast skies made visibility beyond 25 feet near zero. I told my comrades, "It's dark out there, so we all have to stay extra alert on guard tonight."

Around 11:30 pm, shots rang out from the other side of the hill on the upper right end of our company U—over 100 yards from my group's location. The commotion aroused everyone on our side, but in a few minutes things settled down. Our three man group didn't have a radio, and thus, no way to immediately determine what had happened. Whatever the cause, you would think this incident would have motivated my two comrades to move off of their cozy concrete *bed*. Instead, they stubbornly decided to stay on top. All had remained quiet when I began my guard shift at 3 AM. However, knowing Norquist and Blake were exposed in a vulnerable position, I decided it best to remain hyper-vigilant.

A half-hour passed peacefully, but then I heard bushes rustling about 120 feet away at my eleven o'clock position. *Is it the wind? Can't be, it's too still.* I knew it couldn't be the group to my left because they were at my nine o'clock position. *What is it?* All remained quiet for a minute or two, and then I heard more rustling. I couldn't see a thing and wondered, *is this Charlie or an animal? But, we never see any animals out here. Please, be a deer or something.* Wishful thinking aside and considering my exposed comrades, I was not about to take any chances. I stabilized my arms and rifle on top of the granite boulder's rounded surface, set my weapon on semi-automatic, and aimed toward the direction of the disturbance. I heard what sounded like someone walking slowly toward my direction. *Damn!* My heart pounded so I took long, shallow breaths. I dare not call out to Norquist and Blake or move to awaken them because the noise would surely give away our position—plus, I didn't want to be distracted from the potential threat. With eyes opened wide like an owl and ears perked like a wolf, I stared into the black and kept motionless with finger on the trigger. My aim remained steady, but my insides quivered. Although all of this took place within a few minutes, it seemed like forever.

I faced a serious dilemma. *If I shoot into the darkness and the enemy is out there, it is likely I will miss. They will surely shoot back in my direction. Norquist and Blake could easily be hit. On the other hand, if I don't shoot and it is the enemy, they may spot our silhouettes against the open backdrop of the lake and, thus, have the advantage of shooting first. What do I do?* I decided to remain at the ready. *Please guys, now is NOT the time to start snoring or shuffling in your sleep.* Thankfully, Norquist and Blake continued to remain quiet. Meanwhile, the soft patter of slow steps, only about 70 feet away, now seemed to be moving parallel to my location. Finger tensed on the trigger, I made a decision—*if those steps start to move toward me in the slightest degree, I will start shooting.* I waited...frozen. The sounds gradually began to diminish as they moved away and off to my right. I remained at the ready for another couple of minutes, but heard only silence. After taking several deep breaths, I took my finger off the trigger. *Whew!* Somehow, whatever lurked out there managed to vanish like a ghost in the night. The remainder of the morning passed peacefully.

After sunup, I asked members of the groups to our left and right if they heard any footsteps passing near their location at around 3:30 AM, and they said no. I wasn't surprised because the sounds were faint and probably too far away for them to hear. To this day, I am not sure whether they were caused by an animal or human. Later in the morning I speculated, *if the sounds I heard were due to Charlie sneaking around and I began shooting, what would have happened? Nothing good, I'm certain.* If it was an animal and it suddenly moved toward me in the darkness, it is unlikely I would have realized it before deciding to fire my weapon.

I am proud I kept my cool during those tense early morning minutes. Good soldiering isn't always about shooting first and asking questions later. Interestingly, I felt more frightened during this incident than a previous firefight. While I posed frozen with fear with finger on the trigger, the seconds ticking away like seeping sap only served to amplify my anxiety.

After sunup I cornered Norquist and Blake, told them what happened, and scolded, "By sleeping in a highly vulnerable position, you two placed me in a terrible situation. You can't imagine the fear I felt! Not only did I have to worry about facing Charlie in front of me, I had to worry about you stubborn jackasses exposed on top of that stupid slab. Don't ever put me in this situation again, damn it!"

They half-heartedly apologized and I skulked off. Although I should have explained the incident to my squad leader or platoon sergeant, I decided to let it go. I doubt my inexperienced comrades would make that mistake again—at least not around me.

I never found out what prompted the rifle fire on the other side of our U early that evening. I have often wondered if the soldier responsible heard noises similar to mine and decided to shoot into the blackness. Although next morning a squad inspected the area, no evidence of animal or human presence, such as tracks or footprints, was discovered. *Ghostly weird!*

"Oh, what a beautiful mornin', oh what a beautiful day. I've got a beautiful feelin' everything's goin' my way."
Lyric from, *Oh, What a Beautiful Morning,* by Rodgers and Hammerstein; from their musical *Oklahoma*

It wasn't Seth once again serenading the platoon that aroused me from sleep one morning. At this location an eight-foot high railroad berm meandered alongside Highway 1, and our platoon bivouacked next to its base. The long, wall-like structure barred our view of the road and beyond, so Sergeant Sawyer assigned Greg, Larry, and I to set up a nighttime observation post on top. At dusk, we each ambled our way up the steeply sloping sides to the top.

Larry commented, "It's nice up here—a flat surface to sleep on. We should be comfortable tonight."

I blew up my air mattress and placed it next to the tracks on my right. My two companions set up on opposite sides of the rails about ten feet to my rear.

Greg, still new in country, queried, "What if a train comes by during the night?"

I replied, "I doubt any trains have been by here for years. I've been in country three months and I have never seen one."

"Okay, but aren't we going to be easy targets for Charlie up here?"

Larry came back, "We seldom see any action in this area, so we should be fine tonight. Just don't take anything for granted and fall asleep on guard."

Each of us completed our two shifts of guard duty, slept comfortably in between, and the night passed quietly as Larry had predicted. Well, almost!

At sunrise, the sound of soldiers yelling abruptly awakened me from a deep sleep. The first thing I saw, as if in slow motion, was a six-inch long twig along with some pebbles and dust float up in the air in front of me. The sight seemed surreal, and for the briefest moment, I thought I must be dreaming. Just after observing the twig defy gravity, I heard the distinct whistling sounds of rifle rounds zinging by my exposed body. *Shit, I'm bein' shot at!* Just then something struck my right calf. "Ouch! Am I hit?"

Guys below kept yelling, "Incoming, incoming!" and my two buddies Greg and Larry, who scurried down just before I awoke, shouted, "Richert—get off now!"

Just like that, I found myself sitting in a crouch at the base of the berm. It happened so quickly I have no idea how I moved from point A to point B. Beam me down, Scotty?

Meanwhile, the men in the bivouac area had been firing their weapons toward the source of the attack. The incident lasted only about five minutes, and I never got off a single round. Whoever hit us probably scurried off. Once my nerves began to settle down, I pulled up my trouser and inspected my lower leg. At the same time, Sergeant Sawyer came over to check up on the three of us.

"Are you guys okay?"

Sawyer saw me rubbing my calf, and before he could comment, I replied, "Yeah, just a bruise—no blood or anything. One of the rifle rounds must have hit a rock and sent it flying at my leg. It just stings a little. No big deal, I'm fine."

Larry responded with sarcasm; "Hey Richert, why don't you apply for a Purple Heart?

We all chuckled. I said, "I know you're joking, but I would be embarrassed to receive one for this over-sized mosquito bite. Purple Hearts are for real wounds, not this shit."

Larry said, "Amen to that!"

Turning to Sawyer, Greg said, "We're alright—just a few scrapes and bruises from scrambling down and landing on the hard ground."

Sawyer came back, "Okay, but see the medic if you guys need bandages or something."

Later I said to the men standing nearby, "With bullets flying so close by, I was amazed none of us got hit. Those VC must be really bad shots."

Platoon sharpshooter Gado started shaking his head *no*, and pointed toward the distant hill from which the enemy fire originated. "That hill is what, maybe 300 meters away? The range of the AK 47 rifle is 400 meters, so you're wrong, Richert. That VC wasn't a bad shooter. Only a good marksman can group AK47 rounds so close together from so far away. You guys were very lucky he didn't kill you."

Gado's comment sent a chill up my spine, but, paradoxically, during the episode I never felt frightened—just excited. With things happening so quickly, I didn't have time to think or feel fear—or pain.

Later, Larry, Greg, and I became the objects of good natured ridicule.

Our machine gunner Ben asked, "What's it like to be ducks at a shooting gallery?

I responded in a Donald Duck voice, "Quack, quack!"

With a twinkle in his eye, squad leader Tyler quipped, "Richert—I never saw you move your sorry ass so fast!"

Seth wanted to know if we would welcome a similar wakeup call the next morning. "After all" he smirked, "It seems the only way to roust you lazy bums."

Greg smiled, "No thanks Seth. We much prefer your singing."

Joking around after enemy contact greatly helps to boost platoon morale.

Letter to my Family - July 17, 1969
Bunker Guard

This is the second of seven days on bunker guard. There are various isolated base camps called LZ's (Landing Zone) around Duc Pho and Highway 1. They are usually high hilltops overlooking the flat farmland below. They are strategic areas that we have secured. Around this base is an irregular perimeter with bunkers spaced about 100 feet apart. Since

142

these base camps are favorite targets for dinks, the bunkers must be manned by five or more of us—two men stay up at night while the others sleep. Since us *legs* can't be out in the boonies all of the time, someone must man these bunkers, and we get the job from time to time.

We have plenty of firepower. Starting about 9 pm, each bunker starts shooting off everything from M-16 rifles to tossing grenades down the hillside below. This is to deter Charlie from trying to sneak up and inside our perimeter. We also have parachute flares (launched into the sky by mortar tubes) that make it almost as bright as daylight. This goes on all night.

Surely, with the knowledge that he hasn't a chance in the world of really doing damage, Charlie tries nonetheless. Last night, trip flares went off down at the bottom of the hill on my left. I didn't see any movement. As soon as that flare lit up, all kinds of weapons opened up, raining firepower all around. I never found out whether we got the intruders—how they could possibly escape such a bombardment is beyond me. But, often they do, only to come back and try again another night. When the dinks come up here, they know they will likely die—I suppose for them, that one in a hundred chance of getting at us and inflicting damage is worth it. Many of them are doped-up—add this to the indoctrination they must endure and you have one crazed, determined dink. Incidentally, we have rows of concertina barbed wire and Claymore mines just below us spanning the perimeter. There is no way you'd talk me into penetrating this perimeter, doped-up or not!

The above is one of the few accounts of enemy action I wrote about in a letter home.

Doped up or not, most of the Vietcong and NVA were highly motivated. Most of us grunts held a grudging respect for our tenacious adversaries. In contrast, most of our forces lacked motivation. Sending young men to fight a war half way around the world in a small country which posed no real threat to America is not the ideal formula for rallying the troops. However, what our military machine may have lacked in motivating us grunts of the ground, it more than made up for with superior firepower. Helicopter gunships, Phantom jets, artillery, napalm, and other horrific weapons often saved our rear ends in battle.

One day our platoon patrolled through a village that had been pummeled by artillery the night before. I saw many horribly dismembered and burned bodies. For example, while walking near what was left of a hut, I caught a glimpse of a severed human head lying on the ground off to my right. The head belonged to a young male, probably a VC. I looked around and said to my fellow squad members, "Look, there's a head! Where is the rest of the body and how did it end up here all by itself?"

Gary replied with nonchalance; "Most likely shrapnel severed the gook's head and concussion sent it flying like a tetherball yanked off its cord."

Just as joking after a battle helps to boost soldier morale, offering sarcasm helps to temper witnessing the gruesome aftermath of battle.

About a month after the above incident, our company pulled bunker guard on another hilltop firebase. In the early morning hours of darkness we received fire from a village located in the flatlands below. We soldiers began firing back, and soon thereafter, our artillery shells came screaming in. From the clear view of a high vantage point, I saw bright flashes of light and heard thunderous roars as explosion after explosion pounded the small hamlet. The barrage, which lasted about twenty minutes, looked like a fireworks display run amok on the ground. *How could anyone survive such an onslaught?*

The following morning, my platoon entered to inspect what was left of the village. The scene looked like something out of one of those post-apocalyptic sci-fi movies. A smoky blue-gray haze clung close to the ground, and the odor of gunpowder and burnt vegetation filled my nostrils. The few trees left standing had been stripped to a skeleton of bare branches or shredded palm leaves, and only bits and pieces of what were once human dwellings lie scattered about like oversized matchsticks. I expected we would find dead bodies and pieces of bodies everywhere. Images of severed heads reverberated in my mind.

144

Much to my surprise, we didn't find anyone—alive or dead. The atmosphere felt creepy, like we had entered a ghost town. *Did the VC evacuate the civilians before attacking our hill? Were those who couldn't escape hidden in underground bunkers? How come none of the VC were killed? Where is everyone?* Members of our platoon searched for hidden tunnels and bunkers, but discovered none. I'll never know why we found the village deserted. All I know is despite the intense bombardment a few hours earlier, it was as if everyone just vanished into the *Twilight Zone.*

Bad-Ass Weapons
The Minigun

Fortunately for us grunts, the US military's arsenal of potent weapons vastly outmatched those of the VC and NVA. In addition to the array of small arms we infantry soldiers carried in the field, we sometimes called in artillery and airstrikes. The response was usually rapid, sometimes within a few minutes. I witnessed at close range the destructive power of some of these armaments.

The Cobra attack helicopter is equipped with two M134 Miniguns. This machine gun on steroids features six Gatling-style rotating barrels, and fires up to 4,000 rounds per minute. Its devastating firepower appeared at its most visually spectacular during the night. Every fifth round in the ammo belt is a tracer—a specialized bullet designed to leave a bright red-orange trail in flight, like the exhaust of a rocket. This enables the operator to see the direction of fire under conditions of darkness.

A comparison is in order here: The M60 machine gun we soldiers carried in the field is an ominous weapon, and it fires in rapid succession. However, the Minigun is orders of magnitude more potent. Tracer bullets discharged from the M60 appear as a series of dashes, and one can readily hear the rat-tat-tat sound as each round in the belt fires. In contrast, the Minigun fires so rapidly the trail of tracer light appears uninterrupted, almost like a laser beam, and its sound is a continuous loud, grinding drone.

One night a platoon in our company took fire from near a village. My platoon posted at their right flank awaiting instructions. Our captain called in a Cobra gunship, and it arrived within ten minutes. Hovering at about 200 feet altitude, the helicopter began firing its Minigun almost straight down at the enemy position located about 400 feet away from us. The tracer rounds rained down a curtain of red death. The light tinted the rising smoke pink, and the sounds of the chopper's engines and two Miniguns caused my skin to feel prickly. I turned to my machine gunner Ben and said, "This is scary as hell!"

Ben quickly replied, "Just be glad we aren't on the receiving end of that thing!"

"Yeah," I nodded, "We'd be coleslaw."

After ten minutes, the one-sided battle ended. Thanks to a prompt response by the Cobra and its overwhelming firepower, our company took no fatalities. Five VC were killed.

As our platoon moved out after dawn, Ken asked, "I wonder if we are going up there to check things out?"

I replied with a half grin, "I hope not. I'm not fond of coleslaw."

The Phantom

Not only did the Cobra helicopter bail US soldiers out of trouble on many occasions, but the F-4 Phantom jet was capable of massive destruction in a single strike. It carried under its wings and in its belly a large and varied array of powerful missiles and bombs. Only once during my seven months in the infantry did I observe from close range a Phantom drop one of its thousand-pounders. Once was enough!

On a bright, cloudless September day, our company went on patrol at the base of the Central Highlands. The gradually upward sloping terrain consisted of dense trees, low lying palms, and bamboo thickets interspersed with small, open meadows. It is difficult to spot the enemy in this highly vegetated environment. We could be within a hundred feet of a company of NVA soldiers in hiding, and not know it until they opened up on us.

My platoon followed behind the lead platoon and the entire company strung out like necklace beads along a trail heading northward. About midday, word came down an airstrike had been

146

called in because of a reported enemy presence at our forward area. Upon occasion and before our troops moved in, our leaders in the rear called in airstrikes to *soften up* locations suspected of harboring the enemy. *Soften up* is friendly sounding military-speak for *blast the hell out of 'em!*

Our squad leader reminded us to take cover or hunker down when the bomb dropped. After a few minutes, I heard the faint roar of a jet engine. I looked to the rear and spotted a reflective speck set against the bright blue sky. It was the Phantom, and it descended toward us like a peregrine falcon diving at prey. No sooner than you can snap your fingers, the machine appeared overhead. I felt like I could reach up and touch it, and the roar of its engines was so loud I thought my ear drums would explode. Someone in my squad yelled, "Holy shit! This is gonna be close." Then I saw one of the torpedo shaped bombs drop and tumble haphazardly in a downward arc.

A tremendous explosion rocked the ground like an eight-point earthquake. Although in a crouch, concussion caused me to fall to one side. As the jet banked away, a huge blaze of red-orange fire erupted above the tree line and ominous black smoke billowed skyward. Despite a distance of 400 feet from the blast, most soldiers shook their heads and pushed fingers onto ear flaps in an effort to recover from the sound and concussion.

"Damn, I can't stop the ringing in my ears," Andy complained.

Red grabbed his canteen, gulped some water, and then inflated his cheeks. Obviously uncomfortable, he swallowed and burbled, "Can't seem to clear my head."

Soon airborne debris and smoke drifted our way. The men inhaled a sickening combination of burnt vegetation, scorched earth, and gasoline. *It's napalm.* I intermittently covered my nose and mouth. Fifteen minutes later our company moved out and away from the blast area. Despite our growing distance, the nauseating stench still hung in the air, and fires continued to burn. The explosion generated so much heat that anyone located at ground zero would surely have been vaporized. If any NVA near the explosion survived, they dissolved into the bush undetected. We never made contact.

147

Hours later many of us still suffered with headaches, coughing spells, and congestion from inhaling residual napalm, smoke, and debris particles.

Hacking up goo from his throat and lungs, Larry sputtered, "I just can't get rid of this shit! My throat hurts."

"Me too," I replied.

Between the rubbing and blinking, Greg complained, "My eyes are still burning."

Our medic advised, "Rinse your eyes with canteen water, then I'll give you some drops."

Greg complied and it helped.

Most of our symptoms gradually diminished, and on the last day of our week long mission everyone felt almost normal again. Nonetheless, Red expressed the desire within all of us; "I don't ever want to be near one of those napalm drops again."

"Napalm is the most terrible pain you can imagine."
Kim Phuc; known from 1968 photographs and film footage showing the naked nine year old running away from a napalm attack.

Although our military deployed many chemical agents during the Vietnam War, napalm and Agent Orange have become part of the American lexicon—napalm for its widespread use and destructive power, and Agent Orange for its latent effects upon the health of US soldiers.

Napalm is a gasoline based compound, and its inflammatory components are bound by a gelling agent. The military deployed it both as a defoliant and weapon. A napalm explosion generates temperatures up to 2,100 degrees Fahrenheit. One of the agent's most insidious properties is the burning substance sticks to the skin, and is extremely difficult to remove. The graphic images of terrorized nine year old Kim Phuc, her naked body still burning from napalm, were widely distributed in the US and prompted public outrage. Her backside became permanently scarred. Between 1963 and 1973, 380,000 tons of the chemical fell on Vietnam.

Our company occasionally patrolled through terrain that weeks or months earlier had been napalmed. Often, large swaths of once densely vegetated land had been stripped to bare stubs. In some places I noticed that, like morning dew, almost every square inch of rock and remaining vegetation was coated with droplets of residual napalm gel. It looked like expectorated phlegm, or as we soldiers called it, hocked-up snot. Expecting a soft, gooey texture, I touched some of the *M & M* sized droplets and surprisingly, they felt like hard rubber. I assumed the substance had dried out under the hot sun.

Even after witnessing up close and inhaling debris from a napalm explosion, the thought it might adversely affect my future health never crossed my mind. I don't recall ever hearing recommended safety measures or warnings from our superiors about the dangers posed by the many chemical agents we soldiers encountered in the field. Also, some disease symptoms did not appear until long after soldiers returned home. More disturbing and according to documents, some American companies knew about the harmful effects of the chemical agents they produced, but denied or covered up the truth. For example, according to the Global Research Foundation, "A declassified letter by V.K. Rowe at Dow's Biochemical Research Library to Bioproducts Manager Ross Milholland dated June 24, 1965, clearly states the company knew the dioxin in their products, including Agent Orange, could hurt people."

Our military deployed Agent Orange as a defoliant, and dioxin is among the most dangerous chemicals on the planet. The Department of Veterans Affairs estimates over the long course of the Vietnam War, over two million US soldiers were potentially exposed to the toxic chemical. It is known to cause Diabetes, B-cell Leukemia, Hodgkin's disease, Ischlemic heart disease, Myeloma, non-Hodgkin's Lymphoma, Parkinson's disease, Peripheral Neuropathy, and other ailments. Stories about its negative health effects on Vietnam Veterans, public outcry, and calls for compensation made headlines after the war. In 1977, the VA began receiving claims, and in 1991, 18 years after the last US soldier left Vietnam, Congress passed the *Agent Orange Act*, which allowed veterans to apply for benefits.

I don't recall ever hearing the term *Agent Orange* during my time in the army, much less anything about its adverse effects. It wasn't until I investigated the matter at the Long Beach VA Hospital in 2012 that I learned for certain of my exposure—42 years after I left the war! So far, I have not seen any symptoms that can be directly linked to the chemical agent.

Although napalm and Agent Orange are well known, our military deployed several other nasty chemicals in Vietnam, for example, white phosphorous. Our planes dropped bombs containing the substance on enemy positions. Like a red hot drill bit, when the chemical makes contact with the skin, it continues to burn all the way to the bone. Even a small amount on one part of the body causes unbearable pain. In addition to its use in bombing raids, our soldiers tossed specialized grenades containing white phosphorous into Viet Cong tunnel complexes. The extreme combustion generated by the explosion sucked out the oxygen, thus suffocating enemy soldiers hiding inside. I can't imagine anything worse than enduring the excruciating pain of burning flesh while suffocating to death.

The A1 Skyraider is a vintage WW II propeller driven plane put to sporadic use in Vietnam. During daylight hours, I saw an A1 drop a white phosphorous bomb on an enemy location. The explosion is spectacular. Hundreds of irregular, white, tentacle-like rays spread out from the center. For a brief period, it looks like an enormous sea anemone. However, its outward beauty is only skin deep. Just as small fish are rendered helpless by the neurotoxins produced by an anemone, you don't want to be trapped in the searing tentacles of a white phosphorous explosion. I saw many mutilated and burned bodies in Vietnam, but this chemical is particularly nasty. Images of its effects—shredding flesh, splotchy skin, and disfigurement—can be found on the internet. They are not for the faint-hearted, and those depicting affected children are particularly disturbing.

During the long course of the war, US forces sprayed or dropped hundreds of thousands of tons of toxic chemicals on Vietnam. For many years following the signing of the Paris Peace Accords in 1973, and even up to this day in several places, the landscape of Vietnam remains contaminated by these noxious chemical agents. The negative effects upon the environment, agriculture, and populace have been catastrophic. For example, even today children are being born with physical deformities and mental disorders caused by lingering dioxin.

A war may end, but the suffering goes on.

CHAPTER 8

The Worst

Tossing a grenade into a bunker and killing three men and a teenage boy, described in Chapter 1, tops the list as my worst experience in Vietnam. In this chapter I share other terrible events, but I emphasize they are not included for the sake of exploiting the guts and gore aspects of war. Rather, I share the following stories because they contain what I believe is an important or thought provoking message.

"Show me a hero and I will write you a tragedy."
F. Scott Fitzgerald, American writer

Have you ever noticed that in many western and war movies, when the bad guys shoot at the good guys they always miss, but the hero always strikes his enemies down like dominoes? For example, in the Sylvester Stallone movie, *Rambo: First Blood, Part II,* Rambo, along with a female Vietnamese accomplice, attack a post war communist North Vietnamese Army base camp where American prisoners are still being held. In one scene, Rambo is standing in the open while blasting away in all directions with an M60 machine gun. Conveniently, the bad guys appear one at a time like pop-up targets, and Rambo always nails them an instant before they have a chance to kill him.

Like many Americans, I enjoy the Rambo movies and similar types of action-based escapism for their entertainment value. However, young people who are enraptured by romantic depictions of war need to know real combat is not like this. It is grueling, brutal, and unpredictable. Only a lunatic would attempt to penetrate and attack a well-armed and heavily-manned base camp practically alone, and expect to survive. Such a person, no matter how well trained, would likely be killed, wounded, or captured within a matter of minutes. In addition, there is no such thing as a successful one man army. Combat is a team effort.

Although the Rambo trilogy hit theaters after the Vietnam War, my baby boom generation saw its share of similar themed entertainment. Many comic books, novels, movies, and TV shows venerated battle and portrayed larger than life heroes as virtually invulnerable. However, I know of at least one wannabe hero who was not so fortunate.

Blonde Ambition

A cocky, gung ho young man named Tommy arrived at our platoon from another company. Short stature, wavy golden brown hair, and scattered freckles surrounding a pug nose made him appear even younger than his twenty years. Tommy's boyish appearance contrasted sharply with his type-A personality and combat experience. I don't know the reason for his transfer from another company, but it couldn't have been due to incompetence. Before joining our platoon, he had not only seen a lot of action, but obtained the rank of E5. Stateside, it might take 5 years to achieve sergeant, but Tommy earned it in just over a year—an impressive achievement for one so young. He planned to make a career out of the army, so some of us jokingly nicknamed him *Goldie*—for his hair color and the gold adornments worn by a General.

One day I overheard Larry ask, "Hey Goldie! When you get outta here are you gonna be chairman of the Joint Chiefs?"

153

He smiled, "You better believe it! And I'm gonna put your sorry ass on permanent KP."

In addition to joking around, Tommy enjoyed sharing his enthusiasm for stories about heroism and glory in combat. Among others, he idolized Audie Murphy and John Wayne—the former a real life WW II hero who later became an actor, and the latter a bigger than life actor who never served in the military.

Unlike most of us, Tommy not only volunteered to walk point, but seemed to relish it. Recall, the point man must be on his toes at all times. Although gung ho, in the brief time I knew Tommy I came to admire his high spiritedness, gregariousness, and sense of humor. Only his boyish looks and short stature could stand in the way of his being cast as a Rambo-like character in a movie.

Soldiers may have dreams of glory and set lofty goals, but the uncertainties of war are designed to undermine them. Reality can bite, and bite hard. After only three weeks in our company, Tommy was shot through the neck during a firefight. A dust-off arrived within 20 minutes and whisked him to the hospital at Chu Lai. We learned he survived the wound but would be paralyzed from the neck down for the rest of his life. The sad news shocked everyone in our platoon.

"He was one of the best of us," said squad leader Tyler.

Johnson, who towered over Tommy, added, "The kid had more guts in his little toe than most of us will ever have."

I thought, *that's certainly true of me.*

Goldie was universally liked and all the soldiers in our platoon felt bitterness over his misfortune. An anonymous bullet less than one inch in length not only shattered his neck vertebrae, but also his ambition for a career in the army—no more hash marks up his sleeve, no more opportunities for heroism in battle, and no more shiny medals to adorn his chest.

Tommy's tragic story stands in sobering contrast to the many movie and TV depictions in which the unpopular or unfit soldier always dies and the handsome, macho star rises to glory and survives intact. Real life potential heroes do not benefit from the protective armor provided by a script writer and production crew. Like so many incapacitated veterans returning home from the battlefield, I'm

154

sure Tommy struggled to cope with his new life in a wheelchair. I can't imagine how difficult it must have been for this formerly active and high-spirited young man. I can only hope somehow he managed to become a different kind of hero—one who, despite his limitations, moved forward to serve his country by becoming a good, productive citizen.

Clint and Cal

During his prime, actor Clint Walker stood six-feet-six and was built like a truck. He starred in the TV series *Cheyenne* and several films, including the acclaimed war movie, *The Dirty Dozen*. One of our platoon's M60 machine gunners bore a close resemblance to Mr. Walker. Cal sprouted a full head of jet black hair, a strong jaw, and stood over six feet tall. Although not as muscular as the actor, Cal carried the heavy M60 like a balsa wood toy. I envied his good looks coupled with physical stature.

Like the character often portrayed by Clint Walker, Cal was a soft spoken, no-nonsense young man who carried a confident demeanor. Unlike Tommy, he was not aggressive or gung ho, and did not hold ambitions of becoming a hero. Instead, he quietly went about his business and performed his job well. When I first joined the infantry unit, Cal had already earned his stripes as a seasoned combat veteran. He had less than two months left to serve in Vietnam.

One morning in July, our company heard the worst of possible news. Cal and a soldier from another platoon were killed the previous evening. A group of Viet Cong gunned down the two men as they rode in an open jeep through Ambush Pass. The aptly named section along Highway 1 ran alongside a lagoon on one side and a steep hill on the other. To make matters worse, the road curved sharply at one point, forcing drivers to substantially slow down. Although these conditions are ideally suited for a hillside ambush, our company saw very little enemy activity in this area. The majority of the civilian populace supported the South Vietnamese government. Even so, all soldiers knew the danger of being out at night—even in a pacified area and especially while driving through places that offer the VC a strategic advantage.

155

Our platoon learned that Cal and his companion had been on their way to a village, but not for official military business.

Gado commented, "I think they were going into the vil for some booze or hookers."

Johnson snapped, "Hey, man, so what? That don't mean they deserved what they—!"

Gado interrupted, "No, no, that's not what I'm sayin.' I'm sayin' that some of the guys sneak into the vils at night for booze and stuff, so this shit can happen to anyone of us."

Anticipating where this conversation might go, squad leader Tyler interjected, "Okay, enough already! Let it go. This is bad shit and there ain't nothin' any of us can do about it."

As often happens after a fellow soldier is killed, anger, frustration, hurt, and survival guilt emerge and fester.

Other soldiers had previously entered the local village after dark without any problems, so Cal and his companion likely decided the trip was worth the risk. Unfortunately, overconfidence resulted in tragedy. One could be seemingly in the safest of places in Vietnam and the next thing you know all hell could break loose.

Squad member Gary arrived in Vietnam after Cal, and the two became close friends. Some of the men called the pair Mutt and Jeff because of their size differences. Upon hearing the devastating news of his friend's death, Gary immediately lost his composure and fell to his knees.

While shedding rivers of tears, Gary confided, "He was my best friend. He didn't deserve to die. Not Cal."

Like so many soldiers who lost best friends in Vietnam, Gary was crushed.

Later, he lamented, "I should have been there with him."

This poignant expression was repeated so frequently in Vietnam it should have been engraved on a plaque and displayed as the infantry soldier's motto. Despite our best efforts to console our emotionally wounded comrade, Gary never recovered from the loss of his friend Cal. Anger and bitterness gnawed at his gut like a tapeworm. Not all casualties of war suffer solely from physical wounds.

The tragic circumstances causing serious injury to Tommy and the death of Cal, plus other experiences in Vietnam, caused me to

156

reconsider the images of heroes I saw in movies and on TV—images like those that inspired Tommy. Real heroes are not always the charismatic, tall, handsome, mostly white stereotypes depicted in popular entertainment. Rather, they come in all sizes, shapes, colors, and temperaments—and from different backgrounds.

Tommy and Cal dedicated themselves to the well-being of the unit and the men in it. In my mind they each personified what it means to be a true hero. Unfortunately, good soldiers like them are all too often cut down in combat, and their stories die with them. It is a cold hard fact of war that bullets, mortars, artillery, booby traps, and mines cannot distinguish between the popular and the disliked, the handsome and the homely, the exceptional soldier and the slacker, or the brave and the coward.

Unlike in a movie script, acts of heroism are seldom, if ever, planned in advance. They usually arise spontaneously out of the chaos and confusion of battle. Most Medal of Honor winners are unpretentious and feel uncomfortable being designated as heroes. Most say they were just doing their job and the situation demanded they act based upon their training and instinct—or pure adrenaline—along with the help of their fellow soldiers.

Not long ago as I write, our president placed America's highest award for bravery around the neck of a young man who served in Afghanistan. Instead of taking credit himself, the soldier chose to honor the courage of the nine men in his unit who were killed during the incident. He said, "The medal should go to them." Those magnanimous and humble words are typical of Medal of Honor winners, and reflect another kind of heroism—the qualities of good character and moral fiber.

I include the above observations on the subject of heroism in this chapter in honor of my two fallen comrades, Tommy and Cal. We must never forget that for every individual act of bravery, many soldiers who aspire to valor are cut down prematurely—and that acts of heroism emerge under the worst of circumstances—war.

Ankles and Elephants

Thanksgiving morning in the boonies arrived as just another damp, drizzly, gray November day. My thoughts soared home to family and the enjoyment of Mom's fabulous cooking. *Oh, what I wouldn't give to sink my teeth into her homemade sausage stuffing and finish the meal with a large piece of her carefully crafted pumpkin pie. Great, but here I am a million miles away in this miserable place. Will I ever get outta here?*

Our platoon learned that choppers would later bring turkey, stuffing, and other trimmings. Sure enough, our Thanksgiving feast arrived at 3 pm. Although not Mom's cooking, I relished this welcome treat. Everyone in the unit enjoyed the hot meal and spirits were raised—ah, but only temporarily.

After dinner and just as our morale had been lifted, our platoon lieutenant announced in a low, almost apologetic voice, "Orders just came in. Tomorrow morning at dawn, the company will be going on a combat assault mission into the mountains. Make sure your weapons are clean and get your gear ready."

Although not our lieutenant's choice, announcing this mission immediately after Thanksgiving dinner struck the men in the gut like salmonella from bad turkey.

I blurted in anger, "Are you kidding me?"

Reynolds added, "That's a chicken shit thing for those assholes in the rear to do to us on Thanksgiving."

Andy, who before joining the army taught high school English, expressed the feelings of the men in an uncharacteristically crude way, "First they feed our bellies, then they fuck us in the ass!"

Our infantry company spent the majority of its time in the rice paddy laden lowlands and coastline of Quang Ngai Provence. Our main enemy at these locations was the Viet Cong. We had to cope with their mortars, mines, booby traps, and punji stakes, but, thankfully, firefights usually didn't last long. Small groups of VC hit us hard and survivors scurried off—only to regroup to fight another day. However, the Central Highlands harbored the professionally trained and better armed North Vietnamese Army. They often attacked in great numbers and successive waves. Most of the battles with the highest casualty rates in the Vietnam War occurred between American forces and the NVA—for example, the five month battle at Khe Sanh which left 2,016 US Marines dead and 8,079 wounded.

Before a previous combat assault mission back in September, army intelligence informed us we would be dropped amidst a battalion of North Vietnamese soldiers, up to 800 men. Fortunately, during five days of humping through the mountains we saw no signs of the enemy. During two other previous operations, our company engaged in one brief firefight with a small group of NVA, and on one we captured two of their soldiers (Chapter 9). Other than this, we never engaged in the kind of fierce battle anticipated by army intelligence. Although our past missions proved relatively uneventful, on Thanksgiving Day I had one of those bad feelings—one's good luck can only run so far.

After hearing about the mission, my feelings of despair and impending doom sank to a new low. *I hate this dreary, damp weather. I hate this mission. I hate the infantry. I can't take this shit anymore. I'm going crazy.* I began thinking about a way to injure myself so I could be medevaced out. Previously on bad days I had thought about self-mutilation, but only in passing. This time I went so far as to remove my boots, look over my foot and attempt to figure out the right place to do the job with my M16—but without causing crippling damage. *What if I just shoot off my little toe? Maybe I should go for the left edge of my left foot. Yeah, this will do the trick, but with minimal damage—just enough to get me out.* When others weren't watching, I picked up my rifle and looked down the barrel toward my foot. I couldn't force myself to follow through. Survival instinct, fear, reason, distraction, or a combination of the above acted to restrain me. It is embarrassing to admit I seriously considered such dire action, and in such a methodical way. However, I feel an obligation to my readers to enter this shadowy corner of war because although it is not uncommon for soldiers to contemplate self-mutilation, it's seldom talked about openly.

Just after sunrise, our company moved out to the designated pick up location on a section of Highway 1. It's a busy thoroughfare, so I assume someone had previously ordered traffic held up at both ends of our temporary landing zone. By 6 am, our 90 man company stood under tall, erect palm trees lining both sides of the road. Air Cavalry was on the way to pick us up and transport us into some remote valley deep in the highlands. Minutes before we took off, our leaders

159

called in massive artillery strikes to kill, injure, or at least deter potential NVA soldiers lurking near our drop zone. However, the artillery barrage also serves as one gigantic neon sign announcing to those outside the targeted area that US troops are on the way. I am not an expert on military tactics, but I speculate sending advance artillery may have served another more ominous purpose—to *lure* any enemy in the area.

Meanwhile, over a dozen Huey's began moving in and forming up above the road.

Looking up at a nearby chopper about to make its decent, one of the men standing near me said, "He's not gonna try landing that thing between the trees, is he?"

The distance between the edges of the palm trees on either side of the highway appeared nearly identical to the circumference of the helicopter's spinning blades. Incredibly, the chopper descended vertically between the sixty-foot tall trees and landed on the road about 100 feet in front of us. The tips of the helicopter blades struck some of the palm fronds on the way down. Over the noise of helicopter engines and swirling debris, I yelled at my companions, "Now that's what I call a tree trimmer."

Greg yelled, "These chopper pilots are amazing."

Ask any infantry soldier who served in Vietnam about the chopper pilots, and you will receive similar responses. Flying a relatively slow moving, insufficiently armored aircraft into a combat zone takes great courage. One in two-hundred helicopter pilots were killed during the Vietnam War. Observing the impressive landing and the acknowledgement of their bravery gave me a temporary boost of confidence about the success of the mission.

Eight men from my platoon along with their bulky gear scrambled on to the awaiting Huey. In order to accommodate the soldiers plus their gear, and also ensure a quick escape in case the chopper takes on enemy fire while near the ground, the side doors and passenger seats are removed. The space between the cockpit area and tail boom is wide open. Even so, the only way to squash the group into such confined quarters is for some to sit at the edge of the flat floor with legs exposed outside and feet braced against the landing skid. These men hold on to straps or other objects secured inside. I was one of them. Hanging half-way out of a helicopter in flight sounds dangerous, but in truth it is not so scary. In fact, it's exhilarating. For one thing, when the chopper makes a turn the centrifugal force tends to hug you in.

One after another, the helicopters loaded with soldiers lifted off and headed west over an endless landscape checkered with rice paddies punctuated by small villages and scattered hills. Although I had seen sights like this from on high before, the artist and photographer in me once again became awestruck by the line of helicopters in flight and a landscape made more beautiful by long cast shadows and golden highlights created by the morning sun. I wanted to take pictures, but my cramped and precarious position encumbered access to my camera buried in the rucksack strapped to my back. *This damn mission—if only I could go up just to take photos.* Although the vast expanse of serene beauty provided a most welcome distraction, my mood changed as we approached the lushly vegetated Central Highlands. I couldn't shake my sense of foreboding. *Something bad is going to happen.* A lump the size of an apple began to form in my throat. My body shook in fear, and the vibration caused by the chopper motor didn't help matters. As we flew over the mountains, off in the distance I saw a large lime-green colored meadow nestled in a shallow valley.

Pointing ahead, someone yelled "There's our LZ!"

Meanwhile, two Cobra gunships had been circling the perimeter while strafing the tree line with heavy fire. As my chopper moved over the meadow, I looked down and noticed we were about to be dropped into a sea of elephant grass. *Oh, not that stuff.* At one time or another, all infantry soldiers experienced this aptly named plant. If we weren't tromping through it, we were landing in it. Elephant grass grows in thick masses reaching over ten feet in height, thus the name. The edges of the two-inch wide blades are razor sharp. Lacerations from this unwieldy plant had resulted in some of my previous staph infections.

The choppers began a gradual descent, but so far no enemy fire. Once arriving at the arena, they dropped to about one hundred feet and hovered briefly in order to coordinate the landings. At this point they become easy targets for the NVA. *Damn! My exposed body is an*

161

easy bullseye. My heart pounded and my legs felt like rubber. As we descended, I couldn't discern how far solid ground lay below the tops of the thick masses of grass. To complicate matters, choppers usually don't land during a combat assault. Instead, they hover a few feet off the ground while soldiers disembark.

Now about twenty feet above the top of the grass, I still couldn't see any solid ground through the swirling green grasses and debris stirred by chopper blade downdraft. *This will be a blind jump. No way to control my impact. Hey, maybe this is my way out! I know—I'll land stiff legged. Yeah, with luck I'll break my leg or ankle, especially if I hit a rock. Then I'll get a dust-off to a nice, cozy hospital.* The chopper descended to the tops of the tall grass. Our squad leader and helicopter machine gunners repeatedly yelled, "Disembark, now!" *Okay, I gotta keep my legs straight and stiff. This is your chance to get out Bob, so do it!* I tossed my rucksack, waited one second and jumped—*Geronimo!*

No way did I keep my legs stiff. I kept my legs loose and slightly bent so that I would land without injury. The grass cushioned my fall as I landed on my feet and then fell to my left side. *Well, no rocks, no broken bones.* I took a deep breath and stood up. The elephant grass caused a few small abrasions on my hands and arms, but none requiring treatment. Physically I felt fine, but my emotions vacillated. *Thank goodness I'm okay—damn, I couldn't manage to hurt myself!*

I felt like a Lilliputian in the forest of grass. *At least the NVA can't see us.* Visibility was limited to a few short feet, but three of us who landed next to each other knew roughly in which direction to head. We grabbed our rucksacks and moved off. Over the gradually diminishing noise of helicopters leaving the area, we heard a soldier yelling, "Third platoon, form up here—follow my voice!"

We pushed our way through the morass of grass toward the tree line and along the way caught up with other members of our platoon. In a few minutes our unit gathered with the rest of the company in the trees beyond the meadow. We learned via radio communication that none of the platoons had taken enemy fire.

Greg exclaimed, "Thank God that's over."

The men paused to catch their breath and calm their nerves.

Soon thereafter, my company formed up and headed off on patrol. The week-long operation passed without enemy contact.

Once back at Duc Pho base camp, I reflected on the previous week. *My fears were for nothing. At least I didn't hurt myself. No more going into the dark places of my mind.* I didn't know it at the time, but this was my last combat assault mission into the dreaded Central Highlands.

Shedding Light on the Dark Side

During the time I worked on this section of my book I had lunch with my friend Lenny, who I met during group therapy sessions at the VA Hospital. In 1969, Lenny served as a mortar platoon leader in the VC infested Mekong Delta. He saw a lot of action, including hand-to-hand combat. Curious about his views on the delicate subject of self-inflicted wounds, I waited for the right moment and asked, "While you were in Vietnam did you ever seriously consider shooting yourself in the foot to get out of the field?"

Immediately and almost enthusiastically, he replied, "Oh, hell yes! I thought about it many times, but obviously never went through with it." Lenny related that many other men in his unit had also contemplated self-mutilation. He elaborated, "During firefights some soldiers otherwise behind cover would raise their left hand up into the line of fire hoping it would be struck by an AK47 round so they could get out of there."

"That's a new one on me, but I suppose it would have done the job. It's hard to aim and fire a rifle with only one good hand. I feel better knowing I wasn't alone in my dark thoughts."

Lenny replied, "No, you weren't. It just goes to show you what a bitch it was over there."

According to US military records, 382 American soldiers died from self-inflicted wounds during the Vietnam War. However, the number who contemplated the act, not with suicidal intent but rather to be evacuated from a combat environment, is certainly substantially higher. I bet at one time or another most infantry soldiers pondered ways to harm themselves. However, a fog of uncertainty lies between contemplating such a drastic action and following through with it. Self-mutilation stands in direct conflict with our primal instinct of self-preservation. Circumstances must be grim before any otherwise rational person would carry it out.

163

Most recollections about unpleasant aspects of my life experiences tend to recede with the passage of time, while the more benign or joyful aspects tend to rise to the forefront. Believing this to be true, in writing the above story I found it difficult to accurately recreate my mindset during a mission that occurred over forty years earlier. How serious was I about shooting myself in the foot or breaking bones upon jumping out of the helicopter? It is tempting today to explain my contemplation of behavior as merely the venting of frustration. I could never have deliberately tried to harm myself just to get out of the field. However, the fact that the memory is so deeply engrained tells me otherwise.

Although I didn't carry out the act of harming myself, the fact I gave it serious consideration is disturbing enough. In the previous chapter I mentioned how movies and TV shows often romanticize soldiering and war. I include the above story as a counterpoint. The experiences a soldier endures in combat can be so horrific, grueling, and demoralizing that even otherwise mentally stable young men may seriously consider self-mutilation as a way out.

Ghosts of Children Past

I am still haunted by vivid nightmares from the war. These days, elements of my contemporary civilian life have become interwoven with episodes from Vietnam. These altered variations constitute a strange mix of two diverse cultures as well as past and present. The following nightmare, which I wrote down soon after it occurred, is a graphic example. As background, I live in a suburban neighborhood and almost every morning walk for exercise. Part of my walk encircles a small park, but no railroad tracks are located in the area.

I am walking on the sidewalk, the park is to my left, and upon turning a corner I see a patch of bright blue color next to some railroad tracks about 30 yards away on my right. *What is it?* On the right side of the tracks is what is left of a Vietnamese rice farming village. Through the haze of smoke from a recent US attack, I see broken trees and battered huts,

164

but I don't see any soldiers or Vietnamese. The area appears deserted.

I walk closer and am shocked to see two little American girls, each about five years old, lying side by side next to the tracks. One has a gaping hole in the middle of her stomach, and her intestines are spewed forth in a slimy mess of pinkish goo. Judging by its frilly shoulders and hem, she is wearing an Easter dress. The portions not scorched by whatever struck and killed her are sky blue, and her white socks and shiny black shoes with silver buckles look brand new.

The other girl is also wearing an Easter dress, except it gleams pearly white under the morning sun. Part of her shiny golden hair is caked with fresh blood. She is still alive, but barely. As her creamy white face turns toward me, the child's dry cracked lips seem to ask, "Why?"

Oh, no, I must do something. I must—

I awakened in a sweat with my heart pounding. I had to get out of bed and pace my living room to calm my electric nerves. Somehow, I managed to get back to sleep. That morning I felt apprehension, but determination motivated me to take my usual walk around the park. *I can't let the demons win—no way!* I completed my walk and carried on with the day. However, flashbacks of the nightmare haunted me for weeks, and occur upon occasion to this day.

"I dream of giving birth to a child who will ask, *mother, what was war?*"
Eve Marriam, American poet and playwright

Our platoon occasionally bivouacked at a base camp we called ARVN Hill. Originally built for our forces, they eventually turned over the facility to the South Vietnamese Army. The soldiers, along with their families, lived just off base in a hodgepodge of hooches. One day, while most of my platoon went on light patrol, one of our medics and I remained on base. I guarded the gear left behind by our soldiers, and the medic, along with two Vietnamese helpers, set up a

165

makeshift indoor clinic to check up on some of the civilians. In order to take shelter from the blazing sun, I set up a temporary lean-to attached to the side of a building next to my fellow soldier's rucksacks. My temporary abode faced the perimeter, and the building blocked my view of the main compound.

At midday while relaxing in the shade under my lean-to, suddenly, a loud explosion rocked the area. Jumping up, I shouted, "Shit—mortars!" I expected more explosions, but none came. Instead, I heard people yelling and screaming. *What the...?* I rounded the corner to see what was happening.

Surrounded by a group of agitated civilians and ARVN soldiers, a young Vietnamese woman staggered toward the middle of the compound. She carried an infant boy, about three years old, in her arms. Both were drenched in blood. The shiny wet blood soaking into her black shirt turned it a nauseating deep maroon color. *What happened to her?* Sadly, the blood belonged to her child. Our medic arrived, placed the boy on a blanket on the ground and attempted a frenzied resuscitation. The infant's pale and expressionless face reminded me of a manikin, and his breathing appeared shallow. Meanwhile, the boy's mother, her face twisted in agony, screamed hysterically. Several people struggled to hold her back.

Approaching to a few feet away, I noticed a hole the size of a nickel near the center of the child's chest, just above his tiny heart. I watched helplessly as deep red blood oozed out in ever weaker pulses, his lips turned blue, his eyes glazed over, and his life ebbed away. Although our medic worked feverishly, nothing could have been done to save this child. He lost too much blood too rapidly. Someone wrapped the dead child in the blanket, and friends and ARVN soldiers escorted him and his mother away.

So, what caused this terrible tragedy? Apparently, two South Vietnamese soldiers became embroiled in a heated argument. In a fit of rage, one threw a hand grenade at the other and it detonated at his midsection. The explosion splattered his guts in a thirty foot radius—a horrific sight. In a terrible stroke of irony, a single piece of shrapnel less than one-inch long struck the infant in the center of his chest and pierced his tiny heart. In disbelief, I thought, *If only it had struck an arm, leg, his stomach, or almost anywhere else, he would have made it.*

I don't have words to describe how this freakish spectacle made me feel.

I saw the ARVN perpetrator, hands bound, being hauled off. I wanted to grab my M16 rifle and blow him away, but then it struck me I would be reacting out of impulse and anger—just like him. I have no idea what happened to the soldier, but no amount of punishment could mitigate for this totally unnecessary tragedy.

Something happened that I didn't anticipate. I had always assumed a clear line of distinction separated life from death. As the infant's life faded away, I expected to pinpoint an instant in time, for example, a last gasp of breath, marking the end of his life. My expectations proved wrong. I perceived no instant in time I could point to and say, *at this moment he is alive, but at this moment he is gone.* Instead, the process occurred gradually and subtlety—as if the child's life whispered its way toward death. In a most surreal and profound way, I discovered life and death are sometimes tied together by the thinnest of threads. This unsettling insight has always remained with me.

The incident occurred in late October, 1969. By then I had experienced and witnessed many terrible things in Vietnam—fine young American men killed or wounded, bodies torn to pieces, the unbelievably putrid stench of rotting corpses, Vietnamese villages destroyed—and some close calls in combat. However, with the exception of the incident I described in Chapter 1, the death of this child impacted my psyche more deeply than all the others. Up until that day I had never observed close up a human being in the process of dying, much less a child. It was a horrific experience, and the unnecessary and freakish circumstances of his death made it all the worse.

To have witnessed the life of one so young snuffed out like a candle by an act of stupid rage on the part of an adult is a dreadful memory that I carry to this day. I still have vivid nightmares in which I see the nickel-sized hole in the child's chest and watch his blood seep out in successively weaker pulses. I see his dull, lifeless brown eyes. I hear the mother's horrific screams. I see her bloodied shirt and twisted face, and rivers of tears. I feel her anguish as she watches powerlessly, the life drain from her baby.

167

In Chapter 3, I related that after one intense firefight, squad member Gary appeared extremely stressed. He claimed that during the enemy encounter, bullets were flying all around him and only a miracle prevented him from being killed. He sincerely believed God intervened to save his life. Some of my other fellow soldiers had related similar stories, but not being religious, I regarded them as emotional, gut reactions.

Whenever I hear personal claims of miraculous survival, the vision of the Vietnamese child's death instantly comes to mind, and my blood begins to boil. I feel compelled to ask of anyone who claims to be the recipient of a miracle: *Why are you deserving of Gods' divine intervention, and not that three year old boy? Do you believe your life is of greater value than his? What kind of God would weigh the life of one person against the other, especially that of a child, in such a capricious and cruel a manner?* I've never heard cogent answers to these questions. That is why I feel compelled to always speak up for one dead child of war who never had a chance...or a miracle.

The young Vietnamese mother and her child will always serve as symbols of the terrible chaos, wastefulness, irony, and unfairness of war. I will never forget what I saw on that day. As emotionally disturbing as it is to remember, I don't want to forget. It profoundly impacted my outlook on life, children, war, justice, and religion.

CHAPTER 9

Hearts and Minds

"We must be ready to fight in Vietnam, but the ultimate victory will depend on the hearts and minds of the people who actually live out there."
President Lyndon Baines Johnson, May 4, 1965

In order to win the "hearts and minds" of the South Vietnamese people, in 1967 the Johnson administration initiated a policy called the Pacification Program. US civilian and military advisors would work with the South Vietnamese government to establish a secure environment for civilians in cities and rural areas. The administration believed the effort would reduce infiltration and harassment by the Viet Cong, which, in turn, would ease civilian fears of retribution. In addition, they designed supplementary programs to instill confidence among the public about the ability of their government to deliver future stability and prosperity.

This strategy worked fairly well among those Vietnamese who benefitted the most from US presence—for example, the educated and relatively prosperous residents living in or near Saigon. However, reaching and retaining interest and trust among the majority rural population would become a far more difficult problem.

Winning the hearts and minds of the Vietnamese people, a daunting task in itself, constituted only half the battle. The success of the program also depended upon US soldiers respecting the civilian populace and showing compassion for their condition and welfare.

Dehumanization of the enemy is a psychological tactic employed by our government to foster an atmosphere in which killing the enemy is sanctified. Often, dehumanization has been directed not only toward the military forces of the country at which a nation is at war, but also toward the entire population. For example, during WW II, not just US soldiers in the field, but also the media and most American civilians commonly referred to the Japanese people as Japs, nips, and slants. Artists created unflattering, exaggerated caricatures of them, and the drawings appeared in mainstream newspapers. Our government confiscated the businesses and properties of Americans of Japanese descent and moved them into internment camps.

Dehumanization tactics didn't end with the Second World War. Soldiers in the Mideast wars referred to native peoples as "towel heads" because of the turbans commonly worn by men. During stateside training, our drill instructors made us sing as we marched or ran. One song lyric we often repeated went, "I want to go to Vietnam. I want to kill a Charlie Cong." Although not as blatantly condescending as the examples cited above, obviously *Charlie* is not a Vietnamese name. The term is based upon the International Radiotelephony Spelling Alphabet (ICAO), a phonetic means of clearly communicating the single letter designations frequently used by our military. For example, the letter A designates Alpha, B, Bravo, C, Charlie, etc.

The term *Charlie* became a convenient label used to lump all Viet Cong and North Vietnamese Army soldiers into one impersonal, cartoon-like category. In addition, the majority of US soldiers, including line officers, referred to all Vietnamese—civilians, South Vietnamese Army soldiers and enemy alike—as *gooks* or *dinks*. We soldiers frequently expressed disgust or amusement at the appearance and behavior of the Vietnamese people, who we believed were primitive and inferior. Use of such demeaning terminology encouraged negative attitudes and uncivil behavior by American forces.

Unlike most American wars, a military map of Vietnam shows no clear-cut battle lines. During WW II, and under most circumstances, soldiers knew in advance when and where they would go into combat. This provided time for them to psychologically prepare. In addition, sometimes soldiers were provided down time between battles. In contrast, any place in Vietnam—jungle, rice field, village, or our own bases—could become a battlefield. Thus, we infantry soldiers had to be constantly at the ready and aware we could be attacked at any time, even in relatively safe areas. This pressure cooker environment is extremely stressful, and people under severe stress sometimes do stupid and bad things—like abusing the civilian populace.

"To a Vietnamese peasant whose home means a lifetime of back-breaking labor, it will take more than presidential promises to convince him that we are on his side."
Morley Safer, CBS News war correspondent in Vietnam, 1965-6

Routine duties of the infantry included entering rural villages unannounced, conducting thorough searches, and interrogating the residents. Imagine this situation from their perspective. For one thing, most US soldiers stood several inches taller than their Vietnamese counterparts. Foreign soldiers, intimidating in appearance and draped with lethal weapons, intruded into their space, pointed weapons toward them, ordered them around, restricted their movement, and treated them with suspicion and often hostility. The large gap between our two cultures and languages exacerbated the problem.

Such circumstances placed American soldiers and Vietnamese civilians in an awkward position. We grunts entered villages with trepidation because we never knew if some or all of the inhabitants supported the Viet Cong. The civilian villagers felt edgy because they feared our intentions might be aggressive or hostile. The inevitable resulting tension on both sides not only undermined trust, but often morphed into animosity and sometimes fervent hatred. It's a small step from harboring hatred to committing acts of violence, and acts of violence sometimes scale up to become atrocities.

171

It's not hard to understand why rural villagers feared and mistrusted US soldiers, but what about those civilians who worked with us? During the last three months of my tour in Vietnam, I served at an artillery base camp called Arty Hill (Chapter 11). I pulled guard throughout the night inside a perimeter bunker. Each morning at sunrise, I left the bunker for the comfort of my hooch. I tried sleeping until noon, but this didn't always happen. Three local Vietnamese girls in their late teens arrived most mornings to perform daily domestic chores in and around our building. The water trailer and large tubs used for washing clothes happened to be located outside about 20 feet away from where I slept. Twice a week around 9 AM the three girls gathered together to do laundry for nearby base soldiers. Like young girls everywhere, they liked to talk and their constant native jabber often woke me up.

One morning their conversation and laughter became particularly raucous, and kept me awake. Frustrated and cranky, I rose up, put my face to the window screen and lashed out in anger, "Damn it— shut the fuck up! I was up on guard all night and I'm trying to sleep. Get the hell out of here!" Normally, the locals didn't express hostility or seriously challenge us soldiers, but not this time.

One of the girls struck back with venom; "This our home. You not welcome here. You go home. We no want you here in Vietnam!"

The girl's comments hit me like a pie in the face. Her response seemed to confirm one of my persistent questions; *what are we fighting for?* A therapist friend once advised that words uttered in anger often reveal a person's true feelings. These girls depended upon the US for a relatively prosperous livelihood and the villages in which they lived were supposedly among the most loyal to the American and South Vietnamese cause. If the young woman and her friends really felt as expressed that morning, what about the Vietnamese who were not dependent upon the US for support and, at best, indifferent to our cause—the majority rural population?

Adding Fuel to the Flames

172

General William Westmoreland commanded US military operations in Vietnam from 1964 to 1968 and served as U.S. Army Chief of Staff from 1968 to 1972. His strategy, called *War of Attrition*, committed our soldiers to engage the enemy in combat and utilize superior US weaponry to wear them down. Gruesome as it seems, victory in battle was determined not by territory gained, but by counting the numbers of dead enemy bodies. The military never overtly acknowledged it, but Westmoreland's tactic often translated down the line to, *kill as many gooks as you can*. Some of us grunts nicknamed him General *Waste-more-land*, but *Waste-more-lives* would have been more appropriate.

In addition to encouraging more killing than necessary, the attrition strategy served to motivate already frustrated and embittered soldiers to commit acts of abuse and sometimes atrocities toward noncombatants. All soldiers knew that randomly shooting civilians, especially the elderly, women, and children is a war crime, not to mention morally reprehensible. We learned about the rules of engagement during stateside training. However, the Viet Cong didn't wear nicely starched uniforms with shiny brass buttons. They dressed in civilian attire and blended in with the locals.

How is a soldier supposed to distinguish the good guys from the bad under these circumstances? Motivated by self-preservation, most of us soldiers regarded all Vietnamese, except children, with suspicion. However, it's one thing to be suspicious, it's quite another to assume guilt. My experience is that most of the civilians whose villages we entered just wanted to eke out a living from the land or sea without outside interference. Sadly, some soldiers, including some senior officers, hated the *gooks* and painted all of them with a broad brush—as the enemy.

I never understood how following Westmorland's policy of body counts—the ongoing practice of dehumanization of the enemy—the large gap between US and Vietnamese cultures—our continual intrusion into their space and lives—and the ambiguity about who is civilian and who is VC—could possibly square with the goals of President Johnson's Pacification Program.

The My Lai Massacre

On March 16, 1968, elements of the 11th Brigade, Americal Division—the Division and Brigade to which I would be assigned one year and three months later—attacked My Lai village, in Quang Ngai Province. According to Wikipedia, American soldiers, led by Lieutenant William Calley in the field, committed the mass murder of 504 Vietnamese civilians, including elders, women, and children. Some of the victims had been previously beaten or tortured, young women were subjected to sexual abuse, and bodies were mutilated. Who has not been horrified upon seeing the famous photographs showing the dead Vietnamese piled together like cordwood?

"We weren't in Mylai (sic) to kill human beings, really. We were there to kill ideology that is carried by, I don't know— pawns—blobs—pieces of flesh…"
Lieutenant Calley: His Own Story, **by Lieutenant William L. Calley**

"War makes murderers out of otherwise decent people."
Ben Ferencz, US Army prosecutor, Einsatzgruppen Trial, Nuremburg, Germany, 1947-8

I heard Ferencz make the above comment during an interview on *60 Minutes*. Its profound truth should be etched on a monument.

Letter to my Family - December 26, 1969
Disgust

I read with disgust the article in the November Time Magazine about the My Lai incident. What kind of person would fire a magazine of 16 rounds into a little child? I've seen guys, who after seeing their buddies get blown away, feel like shooting at anyone with slanted eyes, but they didn't because their reason dispelled their emotions.

During the day, the farmers we see plowing their fields are innocent civilians. At night, however, some of them are out setting booby traps. But, we cannot hold an entire village, especially children, responsible for those among them who are VC. Many of the civilians we believe are VC sympathizers may just be scared civilians who pay taxes to and are harassed by the VC who come at night to the villages. Most of these people are loyal only to themselves and their families. They live in fear of destruction by VC and GI.

The My Lai incident became public knowledge around March, 1969, one year after it occurred. During my time in the infantry I heard only sketchy stories. I first learned the details upon reading the above mentioned Time Magazine article shortly before sending home my December 26th letter. What I find unnerving is had I been through the kinds of frequent and sustained combat that drove some young men toward acting out their hatred of the Vietnamese people, I might be among them.

Most Vietnam combat veterans will tell you that although the numbers of dead at My Lai were exceptionally high, it was not an isolated incident. In his book, *Kill Anything that Moves*, journalist and historian Nick Turse documents numerous examples of atrocities committed by US soldiers. In Vietnam, the line between killing the enemy and committing murder became blurred. Although I did not witness any atrocities, I did see post-mortem mutilated enemy soldiers—for example, ears and genitals cut off. Some soldiers displayed these and other body parts on their helmets or kept them as trophies. Unfortunately, atrocities and uncivil behavior occur in all wars, but because civilian and enemy could not be readily discerned, this behavior occurred more frequently in Vietnam than in conventional wars.

Shades of Gray

The military provides rules and guidelines for soldier behavior in combat situations, but between those lines lie shades of gray. In terms of violating military codes of conduct as well as American values and common decency, the My Lai incident is at the *black*—meaning extremely morally wrong and blatantly illegal—end of the spectrum. However, what about lesser acts of abuse and cruelty aimed toward civilians that lie in the gray areas between the *white*, meaning exceptional moral behavior, and *black* ends of the spectrum? Which non-lethal acts committed by soldiers are worthy of punishment and which are not? Which are deemed immoral and which are not? How should the military ensure the security of its forces while respecting the rights and dignity of a civilian populace in which the enemy is imbedded? I don't have ultimate answers to these lofty questions. Instead, I offer perspective from the ground.

In the following section I provide observations and insights about acts of aggression and abuse conducted by American soldiers toward Vietnamese civilians that don't fall under the category of atrocities. They represent the shades of gray leaning toward the darker end of the moral spectrum. I believe the gray section of the scale is worthy of more attention because:

The incidents occurred far more frequently than outright atrocities.

In terms of morality, they are more nuanced and ambiguous.

They provide insight into the mindset of a significant percentage of soldiers who served in Vietnam, rather than a minority.

The greater frequency of soldiers behaving badly in the gray range toward Vietnamese civilians significantly undermined the goals of President Johnson's Pacification Program.

Relatively minor acts of aggression and abuse by soldiers in war are not brought to the attention of the public because they are overshadowed by more sensational examples of cruelty, like My Lai.

In the rest of this chapter I delve into the mindset and behavior of US soldiers set against the backdrop of two widely different cultures clashing within a war of moral uncertainties and murky ambiguities.

Shell Game

One day my platoon accompanied a track vehicle unit riding through a Vietnamese fishing village located along Highway 1. We soldiers usually rode on top of the tanks and armored personnel carriers (APC) because inside was hot and if the vehicle struck a landmine we would be thrown off rather than face injury or death inside by shrapnel or concussion. One of the three-man track crew drove, and I accompanied the other two, who I didn't know, on the APC's flat top. Large crowds of Vietnamese villagers milled about alongside the road conducting commerce and carrying on with routine affairs.

The muscular soldier sitting across from me began bad-mouthing the Vietnamese; "Look at these filthy dinks squatting in the dirt. They're fucking disgusting." As the caravan moved through the heart of the village, he grabbed a handful of discharged 50mm shell casings that were lying around. Poised in a crouch, he began throwing them indiscriminately into the crowd, which included women, children, and old people. Each solid brass 50mm shell casing is four inches long, and heavy for its size. In the hands of an angry, disgruntled young man with a strong throwing arm, the unwieldy object can inflict considerable pain and injury. However, none of this even slightly concerned this bad-ass soldier. Laughing like a child skipping stones across a pond, he smirked; "I'm gonna make these dinks scramble."

The Vietnamese who noticed the soldier tried dodging his incoming missiles, but sooner rather than later one would find its mark. Sure enough, one shell struck an elderly man in his exposed right calf. His deeply tanned and wrinkled skin revealed a lifetime of long hours toiling outdoors. The old man stumbled, grabbed his leg, and winced in pain. Although he said nothing, his expression spoke volumes. He rose up and glared at us with a pinched face and tight frown as if he had just swallowed the juice of an entire lemon. It was a look of pain and frustration induced rage I will never forget.

As our convoy moved down the road I couldn't help but wonder, *will this resident of a village friendly toward US forces now be motivated to go out at night and plant booby traps and mines, or grab an AK47 and seek revenge on American soldiers?* Military records indicate that acts of abuse by US soldiers incited many Vietnamese civilians to convert to the VC cause, or to independently carry out acts of aggression toward our forces.

I considered speaking out against the soldier's irresponsible behavior, but feared retribution from him and his crew. Besides, I doubt a lecture from me would have made a dent in this soldier's hostile disposition. Ironically, because those of us in the infantry spent much of our time exposed to danger in the field, we were most likely to suffer the wrath of revengeful civilians.

In his rage, I'm sure the old man wanted to pick up the shell casing and hurl it back at the soldier. Wouldn't you? However, during my one year tour I never saw a Vietnamese civilian attempt to strike back physically when an American soldier became abusive. They dared not. Imagine the fear, frustration, and anger seething underneath the surface of the Vietnamese people subjected to frequent acts of abuse by American soldiers. This is not the way to win the hearts and minds of a people whose native land you occupy.

Burn Baby Burn!

In early August I was still adjusting to life in the field and learning the ropes of the infantry. Our company entered a village the day after the Viet Cong attacked elements of our forces. We found the village deserted—no living souls and no dead bodies. Most likely the elderly and children had been forewarned by the VC to evacuate. Although the attack emanated from the village, it didn't mean all its residents were Viet Cong. Often, groups of VC bullied their way into villages at night so they could stash weapons and supplies, or use the facility as a temporary base camp.

Our company captain ordered my platoon to burn down all of the dwellings, storage hooches, along with their caches of rice, and every other structure in the village. All of the huts, constructed from mostly bamboo, palm, and straw-like material, burned readily. I felt relief that no one asked me to participate. I didn't have to—several of my fellow soldiers eagerly set the blazes. Their behavior reminded me of kids playing with fireworks on the 4th of July. I photographed one of the small storage huts just as a soldier put his match to its thatched roof. The fire consumed the dry material in seconds.

Turner, a tired, embittered soldier with ten months in country, needed to shed some frustration. While lighting up one of the hooches he yelled to the others with relish, "Let's burn this stinking vil to the ground."

Meanwhile, in the distance I overheard another soldier shout, "We're gonna smoke out the fuckin' dinks!"

178

Much to his displeasure, it didn't work. If any "dinks" were present and hiding, they escaped discovery.

In no time, what had previously been a thriving rice farming village became a mish-mash of smoldering cinders. The common Vietnamese farmer worked hard to construct and maintain his scratch-built dwellings. I'm sure our gung ho captain justified burning down the hamlet as an act of military necessity—to deter the VC and cripple their food supply. However, I suspect his decision was primarily motivated by revenge and/or conducted just for sport. By the time I arrived in Vietnam in 1969, burning down Vietnamese villages, even upon the slightest rumor they might be occupied by VC, had become a common practice.

After the incident, disturbing thoughts entered my mind. *Will this be me in a few weeks? Will combat harden my heart and cause me to want to lash out toward all Vietnamese villagers? Am I really all that different from these men?*

Captain T

Sometimes field lieutenants and captains, commissioned officers who should have known better, also abused civilians. During my first three months in the infantry, our company was under the leadership of an aggressive, gung ho captain who held utter contempt for the Vietnamese people, civilian and enemy alike. His dark, cold eyes, although shadowed under protruding brows, seemed to pierce right through my own. I feared him, felt uncomfortable in his presence, and tried my best to stay out of his way. You would think I would remember his name, but after leaving Vietnam he was one member of the outfit whose name I wanted to forget. For purposes in relating the following stories, Captain T—for *Too much Testosterone*—seems an apt designation.

Kids in the Crosshairs

Before I relate my next story, I must review our rotating assignment along Highway 1. Each of the four platoons in our company set up several hundred feet apart along the highway in order

179

to provide road security. The majority of the locals supported the South Vietnamese government and showed reasonable tolerance of our presence. As noted earlier, the kids enjoyed visiting our bivouac. Sometimes we played games and gave them food items. The children always wore simple attire—a long or short sleeved silk shirt or T-shirt, and shorts. Some wore flip flops or sandals, and some went barefoot. One or two pairs of clothing items probably represented the extent of their wardrobe. Despite living in poverty, like kids everywhere they loved to laugh and play. The company of these happy and energetic children boosted our morale.

On one of those welcome days on road security, our platoon set up next to Highway 1 a quarter mile from a fishing village. Two dozen children and teenagers had gathered about 200 feet away from our location. The area consisted mostly of open terrain scattered with palm trees and granite rocks ranging in size from a suitcase to a car. For some reason, the kids did not approach our bivouac area. I guess they were busy doing what kids do on their own. Apparently the tranquility of the morning bored our leader, so he sought entertainment, Captain T style. Noticing the teenagers and children off in the distance, he decided to grab his M16 rifle. I thought, *Oh no, what is this moron going to do now?*

The captain boasted to soldiers nearby, "I'm gonna have some fun scaring the shit out of those gooks."

With hate-filled glee, he began firing a few short bursts at the rocks and trees near the kids. The youngsters became aroused by the sound of the M16 and the clacking of rounds striking nearby rocks, which caused bits of stone to fly off. For a few seconds, some of them seemed confused and didn't know how to react. Disappointed, Captain T began firing a succession of rapid bursts to egg them on. This did the trick. The kids screamed while scurrying away in a panic. Laughing all the way, Captain T moved toward them and kept firing his M16 until they escaped out of sight. Rifle pointed skyward and body posed like a statue of some Roman conqueror, he shouted, "Get outta here you fuckin' gooks!"

Our captain treated the entire matter with frivolity, but I'm certain the kids didn't see it his way. They ran away terrified. Some soldiers in our platoon seemed dismayed by Captain T's childish behavior, some seemed indifferent, and a few seemed to enjoy it. I was pissed. Our captain acted outrageously and irresponsibly for a person in a position of leadership. Never mind that ricocheting rounds or flying pieces of rock might strike a child. Never mind his actions caused confusion and panic. Never mind the kids undoubtedly went home to tell their parents and fellow villagers about the incident. Never mind some adults in this pacified village might choose to take matters into their own hands and seek revenge on us. Captain T didn't give a damn. He hated the Vietnamese and found great pleasure at intimidating them—even the children. My frustration is that I was in no position to question the authority of a *superior*.

The Fisherman

All Vietnamese civilians living within our assigned territory were subjected to a nightly curfew. They could not be outside after dusk, except within a few select villages near our home base at Chu Lai. One late afternoon, our platoon set up bivouac on a hillside overlooking a two-mile long, shallow lagoon located just northwest of a coastal fishing village. Good visibility provided a clear view of placid waters mirroring the sun as it began its descent toward distant hills to the west. We noticed a lone fisherman sitting inside a Sampan floating idly in the middle of the lagoon. At an estimated distance of 1,000 feet and with the sun behind him, we could only make out his silhouette and the shape of his vessel. At this time of day he should have been heading in to shore. Perhaps busyness at reeling in fish hand over fist caused him to lose track of time. Although I didn't know why he chose to remain outside at dusk, I did know fishing wasn't just leisurely activity to these poor people—it provided their livelihood.

Upon seeing the man violating curfew and not caring why, Captain T ordered the M60 machine gunner to load a belt of tracer rounds. Every fifth round in this specialized belt is a tracer, and each leaves a bright red-orange trail in flight, like the exhaust of a rocket. Successive firing of the machine gun initiates a stream of red-orange dashes, thus enabling the gunner to better hone in on a target under conditions of low light. You do not want to be on the receiving end of the M60. In a matter of seconds it can shred a human body into a pile of mincemeat.

Captain T extended the gun's two front legs and set it on top of a knoll curving slightly downward toward the distant lagoon. So as to ensure for steady aim, he lay down behind it in a prone position. Right eye gazing down the barrel of the gun, he began shooting toward the man in his boat. Hitting a human target at a distance of 1,000 feet with the M60 posed a difficult challenge. It's just the kind of challenge that appeals to a wannabe John Wayne who is drunk on ego. I watched the tracer rounds eventually zero in on the defenseless angler. Although I couldn't make out details, for a few moments I saw him furiously moving about inside the boat.

Our captain laughed, "Look at that stupid gook squirm!"

I lost sight of the man just after seeing the machine gun rounds causing splashing around his Sampan. *Did he jump out?* I could only hope he found shelter from the fiery hail of bullets by wading in the water on the other side of his wooden vessel. After five minutes and encroaching darkness, Captain T finally let up. I have no idea if the machine guns rounds killed or wounded the fisherman, or if he managed to eventually find his way safely to shore. As darkness settled in, the last thing I saw was his empty boat sitting motionless in the middle of now stilled waters.

The fisherman did not pose an imminent threat to us. After all, no way could he set booby traps or plant landmines in the middle of a lagoon. Although he shouldn't have been out at the cusp of curfew, our captain could have chosen the humane option of shooting near the man just to scare him off. Then our platoon might have enjoyed some comic relief while watching him grab the oars and make haste for shore. No real harm done. Of course, this was not about to happen. Instead, Captain T got his nuts off by terrorizing and possibly killing the man.

Ironically, while showing off his keen-eyed aim, he was most certainly blinded to the wider circumstances before him. The distance to his target provided a shield for his ego and what remained of his conscience. From 1,000 feet away, Captain T couldn't see the anguish on the man's face. He couldn't envision the possibility of his having children, brown eyes heavy with uncertainty, or the attempts of his wife to camouflage from them her anxiety about the lateness of the hour and absence of her husband. He couldn't care less that the livelihood of the villagers is dependent upon the skills and reliability of their fisherman. No! From Captain T's perspective, the distant target was merely an abstraction, like the cardboard silhouettes we shot at during stateside training.

A wise, judicious leader would have set a good example for his men by letting the fisherman off the hook. Instead, Captain T behaved like a kid at a carnival shooting gallery—only his was a live target. Ardent hatred and inflated ego prevented him from showing compassion. I wanted to stop him. I wanted to speak up, to plead, *sir, this is just a poor fisherman trying to eke out a living. He is no threat to us. Why not cut him some slack?* However, challenging his authority would likely backfire. His unpredictable and aggressive behavior might be turned against me. Out of fear and futility I said nothing and did nothing—nor did any of the other men in the platoon. Looking back with the distance of time and the wisdom of years, I feel regret I chose to remain silent. Wartime guilt is not always associated with a soldier's *actions* in combat situations. Sometimes, it is about his *inactions*.

P.O.W

Under the leadership of Captain T, our company set out on patrol in the Central Highlands. Sergeant Sawyer informed us one of the other platoons had captured two North Vietnamese Army soldiers. All four platoons in the company soon joined up. I knew some NVA soldiers were women and teenagers, but seeing these two prisoners up close caused me to do a double take. Each appeared only 15 or 16 years old. Typical of NVA soldiers, the hair around their ears was cropped almost to the scalp. Stripped of their uniforms down to their shorts and sandals, our captain had them tied up back to back and seated on the ground.

Captain T assigned me, along with another soldier, to guard the two boys. We stood a few feet away with our rifles pointed at them at all times. The older NVA soldier showed fear and avoided eye contact with us. However, the younger soldier did not appear to be afraid. Instead, he displayed a goofy, open-mouthed expression, and his eyes appeared glazed over. His manner seemed detached, like one of my stateside friends who had inhaled copious amounts of marijuana. As a courage booster, sometimes the NVA provided their soldiers with drugs. Sometimes they became shell-shocked from concussion—a result of countless B52 bombings along the Ho Chi Minh trail, and sometimes they felt relief upon capture. Perhaps this boy was just too young and naïve to grasp the gravity of his situation. Whatever the reason, I felt a degree of pity for him. *What does this poor, dumb kid know about anything, much less the complex geopolitics resulting in his being here?*

Intense midday heat caused salty sweat to stream down the prisoner's foreheads and into their eyes, and this attracted flies. With hands tied all they could do to alleviate the discomfort is blink excessively and shake their heads. Despite their misery, the two boys never broke down into tears. While I felt empathy, I had to remind myself that they could be responsible for the deaths of American soldiers.

I said to my fellow guard, "I sure as hell wouldn't want to trade places with these guys."

Martinez, who had been in country for two months, asked, "What are they gonna do with them?"

"They'll probably call in a chopper to pick 'em up."

My response was a half-truth. I concealed from Martinez my very real fear Captain T might order us to shoot them. It would save him the hassle of calling in a Huey to pick them up. I had no doubt Captain T was crazy enough to give such a blatantly illegal order. All too often in Vietnam, the international rules of warfare existed only on paper. For example, many a would-be prisoner ended up thrown out of a helicopter in flight—just for the *fun* of watching the *gook* fall to his death. Martinez and I faced a potential direct order from a superior officer to kill the prisoners, and I suspected several of the aggressive platoon members would back him up. Over and over in my mind I kept begging, *please don't order us to shoot these guys. I don't think I can find it in me to kill a young man again, especially in cold blood.*

Martinez and I stood guard over the two prisoners for about thirty minutes, the longest thirty minutes of my young life. Throughout the tense ordeal I tried to conceal my anxiety. Yes, I had the right, at least on paper, to refuse an illegal order, and I'm sure Captain T could have easily found another volunteer. However, by refusing I likely would be deemed a traitor, not just by our captain, but also by other aggressive members of our unit. *Would I be looking over my shoulder for the rest of my tour?* On the other hand, were I to comply I couldn't live with myself. *Am I capable of shooting these two young men while they are tied up and sitting on the ground? It is one thing to shoot at an unseen enemy in a firefight, but this would be an execution conducted at close range.* My thoughts turned to the earlier episode in which my grenade killed the 14 year old boy hiding with his comrades in an underground bunker. They never had a chance to fight back, and I reeked with guilt over that horrible day.

Thankfully, the order to kill never came. *Was it because they are so young, or is he in a good mood? No use speculating about the motives of this lunatic. I'm just relieved he did the right thing.* The chopper finally arrived to pick up the prisoners. Along with two other soldiers, Martinez and I escorted the boys to the Huey and I watched it take off. What happened to them after that…?

I am often haunted by the following question: How would I, 22 years young at the time, have reacted had the captain given the dreadful order—an order in defiance of military codes of conduct? I like to believe I would have declined. However, I cannot say with certainty that I could have mustered the courage. Confusing situations that test a soldier's moral character are inevitable consequences of war, and peer pressure within a combat unit can be intense. Fortunately, I didn't have to face this agonizing wartime dilemma—and live with the inevitable resulting guilt and nightmares.

Letter to my Family - August 27, 1969
New C.O.

Our new CO is a nice guy, not a conceited ass like the other one (Captain T). He speaks Vietnamese and instead of shooting at people, he talks to them.

185

The sarcasm expressed in my letter home doesn't capture my feelings adequately. I felt exuberance over Captain T's departure. With middle finger extended toward the outgoing helicopter, I stated in a muted voice only my nearby buddies could hear; "Good riddance asshole." Andy and Larry nodded in agreement.

Andy said, "It's great he's gone, but what if this new guy is as bad or worse?"

Larry came back, "How could anybody be worse than that jerk?"

Fortunately, it turned out our new boss, Captain Hartman, wasn't reckless and bigoted like his predecessor. I don't recall any negative incidents resulting because of his behavior. He conducted himself in a professional manner at all times.

Two months after our new CO arrived, Sawyer, our highly respected platoon sergeant, went home. We learned a Second Lieutenant fresh out of Officer Candidate School would soon arrive to command our platoon.

"I wonder what this new guy is going to be like," Larry speculated. "I hope he's not some crazy maniac looking to earn medals."

During the first few days after his arrival, Lieutenant Fredericks seemed reserved. He didn't say much and appeared unsure of himself.

I said to the soldiers nearby, "Isn't his behavior unusual? He doesn't seem assertive enough for an officer."

Blake replied, "Maybe he's just feeling us out."

Greg added, "Well, I sure hope he doesn't turn out to be another gung ho asshole like you-know-who!"

A few minutes later, Lieutenant Frederick's approached our group. Squad leader Bryant asked, "Is everything okay, sir?"

Fredericks confided, "During stateside training, rumors ran wild about soldiers fragging their superior officers, especially Second Lieutenants. We were all worried about our safety in Vietnam—not from the enemy, but from our own men. We heard morale was low, and discipline was nonexistent. So, I thought is best to remain low-key until I got to know the men under my command."

Fragging is an expression used to describe an act in which a disgruntled soldier kills a despised officer. The classic example is by tossing a grenade into his sleeping area. Our new platoon leader

186

seemed like a nice guy, nothing like Captain T, so some of us sought to ease his conscience.

I said to Fredericks, "Like most rumors, these are exaggerated. As far as I know, perhaps one or two fragging incidents happened in our battalion (1200 men) since I've been here."

Seth added, "Richert is right. I've been here ten months and I only heard about those two and maybe one other. So, don't sweat it, sir—you'll be okay here."

Fredericks seemed reassured.

Bryant added, "Some Second Lieutenants arrive in Vietnam breathing fire. They want to prove themselves in battle, earn medals, and become the next George Patton—"

I interrupted, "Yeah, this gung ho shit doesn't sit well with most of us tired grunts."

Seth said, "Missions conducted by officers just so they can earn medals, but end up causing unnecessary casualties, are probably the main reason for the fragging stories you heard about."

Larry added, "None of us want to get into action if we don't have to. This is not like WW II where our country fought for its survival. This is...hell, we don't know what we're fighting for. We grunts just want to stay away from danger and bide our time until that happy day comes when we get to go home."

The lieutenant responded, "I'm not into the gung ho mentality. I was drafted and because I had some college, they offered me OCS. Like you guys, I just want to do my job, keep you all safe, not get into too much shit if we don't have to, and then go home. I don't give a damn about earning medals."

Music to my ears! It didn't take long for Second Lieutenant Fredericks to relax and fit in well with the platoon. As time went by, he earned our admiration and respect. Ben commented, "He's a good guy." We nodded in agreement.

I feel empathy toward the draftees who were dragged kicking and screaming into the Vietnam War and for the enlisted men and officers, like Lieutenant Fredericks, who were not gung ho, but whose main concern was with the safety of their men. I feel empathy for those who underwent terrible and prolonged battles, and for those who lost close friends and had to live with the resultant anger,

187

despair, bitterness, and survivor's guilt. I understand how such experiences can turn otherwise *normal* young men into killing machines. On the other hand, I cannot feel the same degree of empathy for those soldiers who yearned to engage in battle, yet showed contempt for the very people for whose country they fought to protect—soldiers like Captain T.

Military leaders in Vietnam were obligated to maintain a high standard of ethical conduct and instill those values in the draftees and enlisted men under their command. Sadly, all too often this didn't happen. Furthermore, others more knowledgeable than me have stated publicly that General Westmoreland's *War of Attrition* strategy contributed toward countless unnecessary abuses and deaths directed toward Vietnamese civilians.

To this day I retain little respect for him. History does not usually honor generals who lose wars. In my opinion, history should not look favorably upon Westmoreland—not because of the unsuccessful end to the Vietnam War, which was not entirely his fault—but because of his misguided policy of measuring success in combat by the accumulated numbers of piled up bodies.

I end this chapter with the following question for your consideration: When young men are sent into a controversial war with the many strategic and moral ambiguities of Vietnam, how can we expect them to behave honorably?

CHAPTER 10

Attitudes and ARVN's

"War is not only a matter of equipment, artillery, group troops or air force—it is largely a matter of spirit, or morale."
Chiang Kai-Shek, Chinese Military and Nationalist Leader, 1928-75

During WW II, my uncle served for over two years as an infantryman in the sweltering, mosquito infested jungles of the Philippine Islands. I spent one year in Vietnam, and only seven months serving in the infantry. I can't imagine having to endure two years of it. One crucial difference distinguished the WWII conflict from that of Vietnam, and this difference greatly impacted the morale of the common soldier. During WW II, our entire nation fought for its survival.

As bad as things may have become, every soldier knew the preservation of the American way of life—and on a personal level the well-being of his family and friends—was at stake. In addition, the American civilian population, including its women, sacrificed greatly to assist the war effort. Our country became united like never before. However, despite the widespread support of the American people and exigency of winning WW II, our military still struggled to maintain the morale of those soldiers who served in combat zones. Combat stresses a soldier's emotional well-being and morale to its breaking point.

During 1969, support for the Domino Theory continued to erode among the American public and many soldiers serving in Vietnam. To many of us it didn't seem credible that a small, poor country like Vietnam constituted a threat to the most powerful nation on earth. We frequently uttered sarcastic comments like; *they say we are fighting for our country. How will the Vietnamese accomplish this, by attacking America in their Sampans?* This flat bottomed Asian skiff, the principle Vietnamese fishing vessel, served as a colorful metaphor for the backward nature of Vietnamese technology.

The Moon Landing

Although morale among US soldiers remained low most of the time, sometimes bright spots filtered through the gloom. On July 20, 1969, America landed a man on the moon. With all of the domestic turbulence occurring at the time, the festering war in Vietnam, the Cold War, and previous Soviet dominance of space technology, this monumental accomplishment greatly boosted the spirits of the American people—and those of us serving overseas.

Letter to my Family - July 21, 1969

How about those astronauts? I have only received pieces of information on the landing, but so far, all is perfect. I wish I could see it on TV. Doesn't it make you sort of shiver with pride and joy to know it's our country and science doing it?

Letter to my Family - August 5, 1969
Not a creature was stirring…

I wish I could have been home to experience the togetherness that the world must have felt when the TV cameras showed Armstrong step onto the moon. Joanne wrote there wasn't a car moving on her busy street that day.

190

While one of the most momentous technological achievements in human history took place, my unit patrolled and bivouacked somewhere in the middle of nowhere in Vietnam. We might as well have been on the moon. During the night following the Apollo 11 landing, I sat up on guard with legs crosses and M16 rifle nestled in my lap. As I gazed up at the magnificent moonless night sky full of stars, the irony of my situation stared me in the face; *the same species capable of landing a man on the moon is also capable of conducting the most horrific acts of warfare. I wonder which side of these two faces of our species will win out in the long run.*

A couple of weeks after the landing, my platoon provided road security near Highway 1. As I mentioned earlier, I never saw any schools among villages in the area. I often wondered; *where do these children receive an education, if any?* One morning I sat reading a recent copy of Time Magazine featuring a story about the moon landing. Numerous color photographs accompanied the text. One featured a breathtaking view of the earth taken by Apollo 10 astronauts from deep space. The image showed the entire globe frontally lit and centered among the blackness of space filling out the rectangle. Before the Apollo mission, no one had ever seen this awe inspiring, yet humbling full-earth view in a photograph.

Full of pride about our nation's accomplishment, I wanted to share my enthusiasm with the kids hanging around our bivouac. I called over a nearby boy who appeared about ten years of age. Typical of local youth, he wore a T-shirt, shorts, and flip flops. I asked his name and invited him to sit next to me so that I could show him the Time Magazine photos. Huy's alert demeanor conveyed eager anticipation. I readily perceived he typified bright kids his age—curious and anxious to learn.

I pointed to the picture while patiently trying to explain; "Look, this is a photograph of the earth—the whole planet earth—the whole world—taken by our astronauts from outer space!"

Gazing back and forth between me and the picture, Huy's curious expression indicated the wheels in his head were turning. I passed him the magazine. He held it up close to his face, moved it back, turned it sideways, looked at a few other pages, and then went back to ponder the picture of the earth. After a couple of minutes, the young man's wide-eyed expression began to change. His furled brows and frown conveyed confusion. I kept trying various ways to make him understand the picture depicted the earth as seen from space, but couldn't connect. Although most of the local Vietnamese kids spoke English fairly well, I became frustrated at my inability to communicate. Just then his eyebrows raised, his brown eyes opened wide, and his head rose. *Is this a Eureka moment?*

Huy placed his index finger on the black area surrounding the earth in the photo and in a cautious voice, looked at me and asked, "Ocean?" I will never forget that remark. It dawned on me this poor, uneducated young man might not understand the earth is a globe in orbit around a star within the vastness of space. From his limited perspective, the two dimensional image depicted the circular earth as an island floating in a vast sea. Realizing nothing more could be accomplished, I smiled, patted his shoulder and waved him on.

As Huy walked away, I felt simultaneously fortunate and heartsick. Fortunate because I lived in a wealthy country that had provided me with a good education, and saddened because only by accident of his place of birth, this bright, enthusiastic boy did not have access to the basic societal amenities I took for granted. My fervent wish is that Huy's intelligence and curiosity propelled him toward further inquiry and education. It would be wonderful to learn he grew up to become an astronaut or astronomer.

The moon sets on Japan

In early April, 1970, I took my scheduled R & R to Japan. I had planned well ahead to spend two days at the World's Fair, called *Expo 70*. Soon after arrival in Tokyo, I rode the new bullet train to Osaka. I enjoyed the luxury ride and seeing the countryside, which in parts reminded me of Northern California. The theme of *Expo 70* expressed noble aspirations—*Progress and Harmony for Mankind*. The magnificent and futuristic mini-city sprawled over 900 acres.

Dozens of nations were represented at the fair, including South Vietnam, and each built a unique pavilion designed to showcase their culture. Everything everywhere appeared new, clean, and fresh. The futuristic architecture dazzled my eyes. *So much to see, hear, and taste— it's overwhelming!* As if on autopilot, my camera clicked at everything everywhere during my two day visit. Camera secured to a tripod, I even photographed the colorfully lit grounds and structures at night.

America's Cold War rival, the Soviet Union, constructed the tallest pavilion at the fair—300 feet in height. The façade of the asymmetrical structure blazed bright *communist red.* The right side rose in a sweeping curving arc culminating in a thin spire at the top left— as if reaching for the moon. Chuckling, I thought, *this atheist-communist design reminds me of a cathedral.*

In distinct contrast, the US pavilion, an unassuming one-story oval shaped structure, clung to the ground like an abalone. However, unlike any other pavilion at the fair, long lines of people encircled the building all day and into the night. Why? Because on display was a rock picked up on the surface of the moon by the Apollo 12 astronauts in November, 1969—just four months after Apollo 11 astronaut Neil Armstrong stepped down off the Eagle and made history. Like everyone else, I felt excitement at seeing up close an extraterrestrial object plucked from the surface of earth's nearest neighbor.

Outside the entrance to the room containing the precious rock sat a full-size mock up of the Apollo 11 lunar lander, along with a model of Neil Armstrong stepping onto the surface of the moon—an inspiring sight in its own right. I grinned so broadly with pride my cheeks ached. After waiting for what seemed like hours, I finally entered the jam-packed room. Trying to obtain a good view, hordes of people buzzed about like bees inside a crowded hive.

The display containing the rock had been placed above eye level along one wall of the large room which was devoid of all but a few accompanying signs and secondary exhibits. *Tastefully done.* I muscled my way toward it, but couldn't edge any closer than 15 feet. To my untrained eyes, the softball sized, light gray object appeared indistinguishable from the rocks I picked up alongside streams in the San Gabriel Mountains. For security purposes, the priceless object had been sealed inside a Plexiglas or glass container about one-foot square which in turn had been placed inside a metal and glass structure about five feet square. A concealed source just above spotlighted the rock like some precious crown of jewels.

Sounding like strings of firecrackers going off, cameras clicked away as people pushed and shoved to obtain good pictures. Fortunately, my height advantage over the mostly Asian onlookers provided a clear view. Knowing the light of my flash would bounce off the glass and back into the lens causing glare, I decided against using it. However, the otherwise dimly lit room meant I had to set the exposure time at a low level, thus risking camera shake resulting in a blurred image. Despite being jostled by onlookers, I held the camera as steady as possible and managed to click three shots.

Once processed, I excitedly held each slide up to the sky for viewing, but just as I suspected, the images of Expo 70's major attraction came out blurred. *What a bummer.* Notwithstanding, I had stood among the first group of people on earth to view and photograph a moon rock up close. My reaction can best be expressed in the vernacular of the time—*far out!*

During the height of the Vietnam quagmire, the image of the US around the world had become strained. Considering the circumstances, architects of the US pavilion could easily have given in to the temptation of outdoing the Russians by creating an even larger, splashier statement. However, it would likely have been perceived as boastful and ostentatious. Instead, I thought the designers displayed wisdom by going in the opposite direction. The humble structure demonstrated to the entire world a country confident in itself and its achievements. We didn't have to go bigger to show up the Soviets— we had been to the moon.

Sometime in the distant future the Vietnam War will be largely forgotten, but not so July 20th, 1969. The moon landing will be remembered as one of humanities greatest achievements, and stand as a prime example of the best in us as a species. Although about as removed from civilization as one could be when this colossal achievement took place, I nonetheless felt like part of it.

Crushed Hope

Letter to my Family - August 28, 1969

194

Nixon announces a delay in troop withdrawals

So, Dickey Baby isn't going to pull troops out for a while, eh? I'll bet a lot of hell is raised now—I hope so! The North could keep these bi-monthly offenses going forever. Does that mean we have to stay here forever also? Once again Nixon has put himself into a bind by opening his big mouth—saying 100,000 troops could be pulled out by January—and getting the nation's hopes up. Now this!

Unfortunately, the excitement I felt over the moon landing couldn't long suppress the hard and harsh realities of serving as a grunt on the terra firma of Vietnam. My bitterness is reflected in the above and following two letters. Any scrap of news about potential troop withdrawals always raised my hopes. However, in Vietnam hope was as fragile as a candle flame fluttering in the wind.

In 1967, several news organizations quoted General Westmoreland as saying that in terms of an end to the war, he saw a, "light at the end of the tunnel." Although the general denied saying it, other military leaders and Johnson administration officials made similar confident, but non-specific predictions. In a most dramatic way, the bloody Tet Offensive of February, 1968, shattered the crystal balls of optimism. After Tet, and for most of the American people, the *tunnel* now seemed to extend forward into a dark abyss.

Letter to my Family - September 11, 1969
Change in Attitude

I just wrote to Jim saying that this war is a big farce and he shouldn't be a hawk. Nixon might as well say, "My fellow Americans, we will have world peace if we have to kill everyone on earth to achieve it!"

I pointed out to Jim that it is ridiculous to believe we are here to stop the spread of communism. To think I actually believed that Domino Theory garbage once too.

Letter to my Family - November 14, 1969

Nixon's Speech

Nixon's speech was nothing. His policy is too slow for me, I want out now! Why don't we just pack up our gear, go home, and say we won? Very simple. Seriously, I thought it ridiculous when Nixon said there would be more war if we pulled out suddenly. He thinks that Berlin would flare up—any place where there are U.S. troops overseas. The longer we stay the more honor we lose, as far as I'm concerned. This war is not helping inflation and definitely keeping us away from our domestic problems. That is enough reason for us to pull out right there. Is Vietnam more important than America, which is being torn by dissent and crumbling from within?

Throughout his campaign for the presidency in 1968, one of Nixon's often repeated slogans boasted that the US would achieve "Peace with Honor" in Vietnam. He claimed to have developed a "secret plan" for ending the war. Despite persistent efforts by the press to elicit specifics, Nixon and his surrogates remained closed-mouthed about the details until after the election.

The Nixon administration took office in January, 1969, two weeks after I entered the army. One key element of Nixon's secret plan, called *Vietnamization*, would place increasing responsibility upon the South Vietnamese Army to take over the bulk of the war as our troops gradually withdrew. Although the potential for pullouts lifted my hopes, the new policy contained a hitch. The Nixon administration believed that for Vietnamization to be effective, it must be backed by strengthening US military muscle. Increasing military pressure against the North would allow more time for the South Vietnamese Army to prepare for taking over the bulk of the war. In addition, the administration believed their aggressive policy would force the North Vietnamese into offering more concessions at the peace talks, and perhaps stimulate a settlement agreement.

By the time I entered the war in June, 1969, President Nixon had dramatically escalated the bombing campaign on the Ho Chi Minh Trial, including inside Cambodia. The Cambodia operation began in March, 1969, and lasted until April, 1970, a month and a half before my scheduled departure from Vietnam. During this 14 month period, over 3,500 B52 missions dropped 110,000 tons of munitions over Cambodia alone.

From my perspective on the ground, it seemed like, *this war isn't winding down, it's gearing up.*

Bombs a-wasted

Nixon's secret plan met with many setbacks. For example, despite countless B52 bombing runs, including inside Cambodia and Laos, the Ho Chi Minh trail, the main supply route used by the North to enter the South, was never destroyed, only temporarily disrupted. It is no wonder. A network of countless underground tunnels and bunkers accompanied the lifeline and most of the trail meandered through dense jungle or thickly vegetated forest. When US forces destroyed sections, the NVA busily rebuilt or rerouted the trail. In addition, like the individual strands woven together to make up a rope, the trail was comprised of multiple complimentary or sub-routes. Dense vegetation not only provided the Ho Chi Minh trail with cover and protection from bombing runs, but inhibited detection of troops movements by surveillance aircraft.

B52 bombers dropped hundreds of thousands of munitions on the Ho Chi Minh trail during the Vietnam War, but ultimately with minimal effect. I saw firsthand one reason why this is true. One day under gray skies shedding misty rain, our unit patrolled through the dense jungle of the Central Highlands. We came upon a B52 crater, and its size awed me—about fifty feet in diameter and twelve feet deep. It had to have been the result of a relatively recent drop because the depression had gathered only a small amount of water. Although nearby trees had been stripped bare, the dense vegetation greatly hampered the bomb's effective radius. Many trees beyond the epicenter remained mostly intact.

Water flinging off the rim of his bush hat as he shook his head, Larry commented, "So many bombs dropped for so little results. What a helluva way to wage war."

Spec 4 Blake, nodding in agreement, added, "Yeah—no wonder it just keeps going on and on."

The train of North Vietnamese soldiers and supplies moving along the Ho Chi Minh trail throughout the war is analogous of the lines of ants relentlessly invading your kitchen searching for food or water. You can slow down and disrupt them with powerful chemicals, but it is nearly impossible to get rid of the tenacious pests completely. The maintenance of the Ho Chi Minh trail throughout the war is an incredible story and a tribute to the ingenuity and persistence of the Vietnamese people.

One *hill* of a mess!

Most people have heard the famous battle cry, "Take the hill!" An elevated perspective provides an occupying military with the advantage of greater visibility and deters accessibility. Hills are associated with some of the most famous battles in every American war, for example, Bunker Hill, San Juan Hill, and Mount Suribachi, to name a few. These famous battles are known for great acts of heroism and shaping the direction of their wars. However, we must never forget about their brutality and resultant heavy loss of life.

The siege of Hamburger Hill stands as one of the most controversial military decisions in recent American history. Between May 10th and 20th, 1969, two weeks before my arrival in Vietnam, American troops fought against heavily fortified North Vietnamese forces occupying Doi A Bia Mountain in the dense jungle near the Laotian border. Hamburger Hill acquired its culinary moniker from the resemblance of its soil to ground beef as well as for the numerous ravaged bodies strewn about. The NVA had spent weeks digging in, making rooting them out extremely difficult and dangerous. The arduous ten day battle resulted in 72 US soldiers killed and 372 wounded. Incredibly, soon after capturing the mountain, military leaders ordered the troops to abandon it. It turned out Hamburger Hill held little strategic value.

The incident made headlines across the US and caused outrage among the public as well as criticism by many of our military and political leaders. Imagine the affect this pointless battle inflicted on the morale of the soldiers who fought so hard there and lost friends, as well as the families of the soldiers who ended up wounded or dead. Word of the episode spread like monsoon rains throughout the infantry, and, to say the least, it didn't serve to boost spirits. Further adding to soldier frustration, many other hard fought missions to take hills, like the prolonged siege of a marine base at Khe San in 1968, resulted in their later abandonment.

"You can kill ten of our men for every one we kill of yours. But even at those odds, you will lose and we will win."
Ho Chi Minh, Popular Nationalist Leader of North Vietnam

Most of the Allied military missions during WW II consisted of re-taking territory formerly captured by the Axis powers. Our leaders set clear-cut goals and made detailed plans to carry them out. Allied ground forces fought hard to re-take the land, and once secured, they usually held it. General George Patton's rapid advance across Nazi held France stands as a notable example. So it went until the Allies eventually encircled Berlin, and in the Pacific, closed in on Japan.

In most situations in South Vietnam, the strategy wasn't about gaining ground, holding it, and then moving on to take more. Clear cut boundaries between enemy and friendly territories could not always be drawn because the VC blended with the civilian population. They hid themselves and their supplies effectively, and didn't remain in one place for long. One day they were here, the next day they moved on. Trying to nail down the location of the VC was like trying to snatch a slippery bar of soap from the shower floor while your eyes are stinging from suds.

To compound matters, throughout the war the North Vietnamese Army took refuge in Laos and Cambodia. Thus, instead of taking and occupying land, the American infantry hoofed it through various territories in search of the enemy, and tried to root them out and destroy them—Westmoreland's War of Attrition. Although we killed the enemy when and where we found them, replacements continued to filter down from the north, or emerge out of the civilian population. Under these circumstances, our military leaders couldn't present us grunts on the ground with immediate, clear cut, and enduring objectives.

I've mentioned before that identifying villages in rural areas as friend or foe posed a huge problem for our forces. In many situations, it was not even a meaningful effort. For example, some locals welcomed and accommodated our forces during the day when we visited, but after we left they became loyal or subjected to the VC who infiltrated at night. For some villages, cooperating with both sides wasn't so much a matter of choice, but a practical necessity. The main concern of the average peasant farmer in Vietnam was more down to earth than politics—the arduous work of eking out a meager living from the soil. After many visitations to rural villages, I came to believe most residents seemed far removed from and unconcerned about greater political issues. Judging by their body language and behavior, I could almost hear them saying to both GI and VC, "Go away! We just want to be left alone to farm our fields."

As our units patrolled near or through rural areas, the villagers often greeted us with smiles and welcoming gestures, but unless they cooperated in some way, we could not ascertain their sincerity. Rarely, and at great risk, some gave us information about the Viet Cong. Once we left a village it might be weeks or months before our return, if at all. This gave the VC the opportunity to swoop in and take advantage. They coerced neutral locals to stash weapons, give them rice, and in some situations, join the fight against the South.

Even if their hearts were not really in it, many villagers had little choice but to cooperate with whichever side dominated the area. Resisting cooperation with our forces could result in harassment and occasional aggressive treatment. Resisting the VC often resulted in severe physical abuse and sometimes death. Throughout the long war, many of the poor villagers in Vietnam found themselves stuck between this rock and hard place.

For US soldiers to greatly diminish or destroy a slippery enemy under such conditions seemed a fruitless endeavor. After one grueling mission, Spec 4 Johnson expressed our pent up frustration; "What's the point of doin' this shit? The dinks are just gonna come back after we leave. Hell, it don't make me no difference. I'm outta here in 26 days."

It seemed to me the mission of the infantry in Vietnam is analogous to the Greek myth of Sisyphus. As punishment for trickery, this king of Ephyra was forced over and over—ad infinitum—to push an enormous rock up a steep hill, only to have it roll back down...again and again.

Lack of Intelligence Reports

We grunts placed little confidence in the reliability of intelligence reports. This is not intended to be a knock on our military. Trying to gather accurate data about VC and NVA activities had to be a logistical and source gathering nightmare. Information about when and where we grunts on the ground might face danger often turned out to be inaccurate. On several occasions the brass in the rear warned our company about an impending heavy enemy presence in a given area. Even if the intelligence seemed questionable, we soldiers felt compelled to take it seriously—better to be safe than sorry. We had to be better prepared than on average—for example, to make double sure our weapons were thoroughly cleaned and functioning properly, carry extra ammo, and remain hyper-hyper-alert.

One rainy day our company embarked on a mission into an area supposedly infested with NVA and VC. The terrain consisted of highly vegetated hills punctuated with expansive flatlands of rice paddies interspersed with villages. The four platoons in our company split up, but always remained less than 2,000 feet apart. Avoiding the nearly impenetrable hills, each platoon patrolled through the flatlands in search of the enemy. Everyone was on edge. As usual, I followed just behind and to the left of Ben, our squad machine gunner. Safety demanded that when possible, the men stay off roads, trails, and rice paddy dikes—favored places for Charlie to plant mines and booby traps. Our progress became impeded by having to tromp through muddy rice paddies six inches deep in water. To make matters worse, intermittent downpours soaked us through.

Blake complained, "Damn, this is a bitch. I hope my new camera doesn't get wet."

I asked, "Did you put in double plastic bags?"

"Yeah, you think it will be okay?"

"Should be fine." I responded politely, but my inner reaction was one of puzzlement. *We're humping through goopy mud, we're soaked to the bone, we could be attacked by hordes of NVA at any time, and this guy is worried about his stupid camera.*

I felt badly for my buddy Ben. He carried the M60 machine gun for miles. The extra weight sank his boots deeper into the glop than the rest of us. Pulling each foot out time after time had to be fatiguing. However, the big cornhusker never complained. *He's a rock! I envy his toughness.*

We occasionally encountered groups of farmers plowing behind their water buffalo through muddy fields. Some offered a half-hearted wave, but most avoided eye contact and tried to ignore our presence. *Do they have something to hide, or are they just afraid of us?* We slogged our way through rice paddy after rice paddy until evening finally arrived. Exhausted from a stressful and rough, miserable journey, we soldiers welcomed the end of the day. Time to rest and take inventory of ourselves.

I said, "The good news is, the rain has let up. The bad news is, here come the clouds of mosquitoes."

"Yeah, you just can't win out here," quipped Andy.

My legs ached from trudging through the muck all day. I took my boots off and scraped off the caked-on mud. Next, and while swooshing mosquitoes away, I cleaned my bare feet as best I could and gave them a massage.

"My fatigues are soggy as hell," Reynolds complained. "I wish we could build a fire so we could dry our clothes out."

Squad leader Tyler interjected, "Yeah, the dinks would love to see that!"

"I know, I'm just venting."

Tyler told the men, "Ring out your clothes as best you can, especially your socks. We got a long day ahead tomorrow. We've been lucky so far, but keep quiet and be extra alert on guard tonight. Oh yeah, and make sure to check your weapons. The dinks must be out there somewhere."

In order to deter the enemy from spotting our bivouac, as usual the company moved to set up after dark. About one hour after sunset, my group noticed a soft orange glow breaking the blackness of night about 30 feet away.

Reynolds commented, "Damn, that's Gary lighting a cigarette under his poncho liner. He must think it blocks the light. As long as he's been in country, he should know better!"

Andy said, "Great! If Charlie is nearby, they may now know where we are."

Squad leader Tyler confronted Gary; "Do you know we can see the light from your cigarette through your poncho liner? It makes the inside glow. You might have compromised our position."

"Really, you could see my cigarette? Oh, shit, I'm sorry!"

Our squad leader advised, "Double up the liner when you light up and go behind those bushes to smoke."

Gary replied, "Okay, got it. It won't happen again."

I stayed alert throughout my two shifts on guard, and didn't sleep well in between. Fortunately, Gary's temporary *lantern* produced only soft light, so it didn't give away our position.

Next day, more of the same—trudging our way through muddy rice paddies and getting soaked through. By day's end we hauled our exhausted bodies and wet gear onto waiting trucks.

Speaking for everyone, Tyler stated in a tired voice, "I'm glad that mission is over."

Always one to speak his mind, Johnson added, "All this shit, and no dinks anywhere. Where was all the dinks? Why is it every time we is s'posed to be neck deep in shit, nothin' happens?

Tyler came back, "So, would you be happy if we'd run into a regiment of the bastards? Mission's over—just be happy we're going back to Duc Pho for a couple days rest."

Expecting an enemy presence in a given area and finding none is one side of the coin. Unexpectedly coming under attack in a pacified area is the other. Either situation will tie a soldier's stomachs in knots.

Letter to my Family - July 12, 1969
2nd Platoon sees action

When I was in the hospital, our second platoon got hit at night. They were on a hill across the road from my platoon and at night parachute grenades—something new—started coming in. One guy was killed, 14 wounded. My buddy Sanchez got some shrapnel and earned a purple heart. He was just scratched really—was only out of the field for one day for his wound. I didn't know the guy who was killed.

The incident was partly the fault of their platoon leader. They stayed in that one spot for seven days straight, something they should never have done. During the day, Charlie surely watched where the trip flares and claymore mines were set up because just before the attack they avoided the flares and cut the wires leading to the claymores. In addition, the side of the road they set up on has some high, densely vegetated areas about one mile away. The NVA probably have base camps located there. Our artillery is forever pounding that area.

Sanchez and I met during basic training at Fort Ord and quickly became friends. He hailed from Santa Maria, California, then known for strawberry farms and today also for vineyards. I enjoyed his easy going manner and sense of humor. Although with the same company in Vietnam, from day one we served in different platoons. The four platoons worked separately most of the time, so I saw Sanchez infrequently. Coincidently, he was brought to the hospital at Duc Pho for treatment of his shrapnel wounds at the same time I had been recovering from heat exhaustion. He came to my bedside and the first thing I asked was, "Hey, how ya' feeling?" Sanchez joked about his wounds, and showed me his bandaged leg.

"Just a scratch, really. I feel funny being given a Purple Heart for this."

Humor and humility aside, I'm sure the tragic loss of a life and numerous injuries inflicted upon his buddies weighed heavily on his mind. After a few minutes of light conversation, I asked Sanchez about the attack and his expression suddenly changed from one of frivolity to one of sobriety.

He said, "When our lieutenant told us we would be staying at the same spot for a few days, it made me very nervous. I assumed he had a reason for his decision—trying to draw out the dinks, maybe?"

"Damn, that's dangerous business. Our platoon always moves and sets up after dark. What was he thinking?"

"I don't know, but what could I do about it? Just do whatever I could to protect myself in case we got hit."

I queried, "You must have been pissed after the—"

"Pissed, I'm beyond pissed! When I go back to my platoon, I don't know how I'm going to keep from decking the son of a bitch!"

"I feel for you buddy, but you know how it is—you're just going to have to suck it up."

Shaking his head, Sanchez said, "I guess you're right, but man, this sucks."

I replied, "Well, the good news is you're okay my friend."

We raised our hands in a high five.

In addition to moving each night, most infantry companies worked a variety of territories. This keeps Charlie off guard. My platoon visited three or four locations on a regular basis, but not in a consistent pattern—for example, always visiting the same place the last week of the month. In the infantry, variety *is* the spice of life. Upon those occasions when we remained in the same area for a week or so, such as providing road security along Highway 1, we never stayed more than one day and night at the *exact* same place. The following day we would move a few hundred yards and set up after dark. Setting up each evening after dark in a different location is a pain in the ass, but, it sure beats being a sitting duck. It's hard to train mortars on a ghost. As an exception to the rule, we often stayed at Bridge 104 for days. Bridges and other structures of strategic value must be guarded at all times because they are prone to enemy sabotage. Fortunately, 104 happened to be located in a pacified area. During the three times my platoon pulled security there, we never came under attack.

Letter to my Family - August 8, 1969
Carelessness

B Company lost 18 men the other day due to carelessness. One of the guys was playing with a grenade, pin out, and dropped it. A buddy picked it up and threw it, but it exploded just after leaving his hand. Both men were killed, three others, including the commanding officer, were critically wounded, and the remaining 15 were injured. I tell you this not to scare you, but to point out that many casualties are caused by similar carelessness. Our company has its act together—our leaders are cautious. I've learned many little things from the old-timers that can mean the difference between life and death.

Most soldiers carried the M16 rifle and three or four hand grenades. Usually two men carried the M60 machine gun, two the M79 grenade launcher, and two to four men carried claymore mines. During stateside training, the instructors drummed safety procedures into our heads—same in Vietnam. Nonetheless, young people tend to be reckless. It is a sad fact of war that with such powerful weapons at our disposal, one young man's over zealousness coupled with carelessness may result in numerous casualties.

"It is well known that in war, the first casualty is truth—that during any war truth is forsaken for propaganda."
Harry Browne, American writer, politician, and investment advisor

So many things negatively affected the attitudes of infantry soldiers toward the ongoing war in Vietnam you would think they would spill over to negative attitudes toward our country. Sure, many of us soldiers questioned the decision making of our military and political leaders, but serving in rural Vietnam motivated most of us to become all the more appreciative of the many benefits our country provides.

On a steamy September day, our company patrolled through a broad valley checkered with rice paddies, bamboo thickets, palm trees, and villages. While walking along a narrow trail, I noticed a piece of paper with printed words nestled against the base of some bamboo. *This is odd. I've never seen pieces of paper lying around in the boonies.* I picked up the leaflet, about the size of an index card. It had to have been left recently because the harsh elements hadn't yet turned it into oatmeal. I noticed the type appeared rather crudely and unevenly printed, like that produced by the ancient Chinese art of woodblock. The message is shown below.

206

CROSS TO THE LIBERATION
ARMY'S SIDE,YOU WILL BE
WELCOMED AN HELPED TO
GO HOME OR TO WHATE-
VER COUNTRY YOU LIKE.

I'll be damned. This is a VC propaganda leaflet—never saw one of these before. I laughed out loud at its obviously crude, unsophisticated literary style, and equally crude, unsophisticated message, which strained credulity.

"Hey guys, look at this!" While showing it around, I asked, "Anyone convinced to Chieu Hoi?" Recall, Chieu Hoi is a Vietnamese term used by enemy soldiers to indicate their desire to surrender to our forces.

Seth smirked, "I'll pass. I don't like Asian food."

Andy, my English teacher friend, said, "Whoever wrote this would definitely fail my class."

We all had a few laughs, and no one took the message even remotely seriously. Instead of undermining our morale, this pathetic attempt by the VC actually boosted it.

Like me, none of the other men in the platoon had ever before come across a North Vietnamese propaganda leaflet. Looking around for more, but finding none, I decided to keep my unique discovery as a souvenir. *Maybe it will be valuable some day.* Slightly torn with some ragged edges, the document otherwise appeared in good shape. To protect it from the elements, I gently folded it in half and placed it in one of my plastic bags. Today, it, along with a few other souvenirs from the war, is framed and hangs in my bedroom. It reminds me never to take for granted the comfortable lifestyle my country provides.

One of those hunches

In terms of the overall war effort, the minimally consequential patrols and missions to which the army subjected us not only impacted our morale, but also our attitudes toward engagement with the enemy. Most of us didn't want to take unnecessary risks. We just wanted to do what it takes to survive and then go home. After Captain T's departure, my unit adopted a more defensive than offensive posture. Even most of the gung ho soldiers in my platoon showed more interest in harassing civilians or taking aggressive action when we were attacked than going out of the way to make contact with the enemy.

One morning our platoon leader, Lieutenant Fredericks, prepared to lead us on a trail winding through a narrow gap between two steep sloping hills—the ideal configuration of terrain for the worst kind of ambush. Enemy troops firing down on your unit from elevated positions on both sides of a trail is not a place any soldier wants to be. It's a potential slaughterhouse.

Looking toward the gap, squad leader Bryant said, "I don't like this. I got one of those strange feelings the dinks are out there waiting for us."

Seth added, "Yeah, a couple of months ago first platoon got hit in this area, and a guy got killed. I don't know if it was in this valley, but the dinks are likely still around here."

"So, what are we gonna do?" asked Greg. "Fredericks is new, so maybe he doesn't know going through there could be bad news."

Bryant explained, "He knows. He's following Hartman's orders, but the captain hasn't been here to check out this area for himself. He probably gave the order by looking at his map, which isn't the same as being here. I'll go check things out."

Bryant summoned our platoon's other two squad leaders and they joined with Lieutenant Fredericks to discuss the matter. Ten minutes later, our platoon leader ordered us to move out. We moved out all right, but thankfully, in a direction away from ambush alley.

Andy said; "Whew, we dodged a bullet on this one!"

With a slight smile, Greg quipped, "Maybe a few grenades and a machine gun too."

Andy came back, "As soon as those words came out I figured one of you guys would jump on 'em."

Bryant interrupted, "Listen up squad! By circumventing the valley, our platoon will have to take a longer route around the hills. Get ready to move out."

No one complained, including me. We made our way through flatlands of rice paddies with scattered villages. We saw no signs of Charlie. That evening, we joined up with the rest of the company.

While munching some C-rations, Greg asked our squad leader, "By avoiding the valley did our platoon leader defy a direct order?

Bryant replied, "No. After meeting with us, Fredericks got on the horn with Hartman, explained the situation, and got permission to alter the route."

I said to my buddies, "Thankfully, Hartman is no Captain T. That bozo would have been anxious to plunge us into an ambush."

Andy added, "Yeah, and for what?"

Larry answered, "For a medal earned over our dead bodies."

Rather than blindly following orders from the outset, Lieutenant Fredericks showed respect for the knowledge and experience of his squad leaders. Listening to and acting on their concerns gained him additional admiration among members of the platoon. It's unlikely his decision altered the course of the war one inch, but it might have saved several lives.

THE ARVN

The South Vietnamese government formed the Army of the Republic of Vietnam (ARVN) in 1955. Like their government, the South Vietnamese military became besieged with problems such as poor administration and widespread corruption. In addition, the ARVN experienced difficulty recruiting highly motivated young men. All of these problems negatively impacted their effectiveness in battle—despite the fact that for much of the war, ARVN forces outnumbered and were better armed than their counterparts in the north. According to Vietnam historian Kevin Boylan (N.Y. Times, Aug. 22, 2017), South Vietnam's military, "was reluctant to fight." Conversely, under the leadership of popular Nationalist Ho Chi

209

Minh, the highly motivated, well-organized North Vietnamese Army fought aggressively. The South Vietnamese Army contained some well-motivated and trained units, but their small numbers could not alone effectively conduct the bulk of the war effort. These are some of the reasons why, in 1965, the Johnson administration decided to send increasing numbers of US troops to take up the slack.

Audiotape - February 9, 1970
C-ration Robbers

One day the kids came crying, "You know C-rations you give us? We go into village and ARVN's take!"

The ARVN's saw the kids dragging the boxes of C's and grabbed them. They stole them right away from the kids. It's a shame. We can't stand the ARVN's anyway, much less having to feed them.

Everyone in my platoon regarded the ARVN we encountered and worked with as unreliable, untrustworthy, and incompetent. In addition, we felt resentment and anger about our having to perform the blood and guts jobs that should have been assigned to them.

Letter to my Family - August 27, 1969
Sittin' on their Asses

I'm irked because there is at least a company of ARVN's near Charlie Brown (one of our base camps) and they just sit there all day. Some of them guard Sa Huynh, the pacified village there, and rarely do they work with us. They should be out humping the hills where we know the NVA are located. The ARVN's could really help by combing the hills, setting ambush at night, searching villages, etc.—especially searching villages—they are a lot better at it than we are.

Vietnamese men my age, who should be in their army, instead ride the soda girls up and down the road all day on the back of their motorcycles. That's all they do every day. So why do they need me over here?

210

Long before Nixon implemented his Vietnamization program in 1969, our military advisors had been working to develop and train the South Vietnamese Army to gradually assume responsibility for the war effort. Before I arrived and after I left Vietnam, our government provided a pat answer to my question, *so why do they need me over here?* Our military claimed that because the ARVN lacked sufficient numbers and adequate training, the gap had to be filled by US troops. I found the army's justification puzzling because I never fired a weapon in my life before joining the army and I received only four months of training before arriving in Vietnam—not to mention the added problem of the culture and language gap. *So, why is it taking so long to prepare the Vietnamese to fight their own battles?* I'm sure the government offered a pat answer to that question as well.

Many, if not most, ARVN soldiers our unit encountered lacked enthusiasm and dedication to the cause. I doubt most of these uneducated farmers and fisherman understood the differences between communism and capitalism. For many, the decision to join the South Vietnamese Army was a practical, not political decision— to provide a steady source of income. It sure beat plowing through mud behind a water buffalo or bending over all day under the hot sun plucking rice in soggy fields.

Within our main area of operations near the coast, the majority of villages supported the South Vietnamese government. However, patrolling the 11th Brigade's vast and less visited territory to the west posed greater potential danger. Few pacified villages existed there, and many harbored VC. The language barrier made our attempts at communication nearly impossible, so sometimes ARVN scouts and interpreters assisted our units. On a few occasions I witnessed them in action.

One day my company inspected a remote rice farming village a dozen or so miles inland from the coast. An ARVN interpreter, age about 30, joined us. His close cropped hair and neat, orderly uniform reflected a sense of pride. About forty residents had been rounded up and ordered to sit down in a tight knit group outdoors in front of a hut. The kids had been separated and gathered off to the side. The interpreter ordered the adults to remove their conical coolie hats. To

211

avoid being singled out, most tried to keep their heads down or otherwise avoid eye contact.

Throughout the interrogation, the ARVN displayed an aggressive demeanor and the atmosphere turned electric. With a menacing glare on his face and forceful gestures, he shouted at the group and then began singling out suspicious looking individuals. Sometimes he just stared into their eyes for what seemed like minutes before saying anything. *Is he trying to read their minds?* Although speaking in his native tongue, I could discern the gist of his query; "Where is the VC? Are you VC?"

Turning to Ben, I said, "This guy is bad news. He reminds me of the drill sergeants back in basic."

Ben replied, "I guess he has to scare them to pry out information."

Once in a while the ARVN interrogator grabbed the arms or shoulders of his victims and shook them while screaming in their faces. Heads moving side to side quickly and nervously, they pleaded in Vietnamese, "No VC, no VC!" Their harried expressions and body language indicated fear, and I could sense anger seething under the surface.

The interrogator's red-faced rant went on for about twenty minutes, but the residents continued to defy him—or perhaps they merely told the truth. No VC and no evidence of their presence came forth—although it's possible some remained hidden underground or in the bush outside the village. Ferreting out the VC from rural villages, even with the help of ARVN interpreters, was like trying to scrape paint off an old weathered barn.

I told some of the men, "Perhaps an approach modeled after that expression about catching more flies with honey than vinegar would have produced better results."

Gung ho Billy Caleb overheard my words; "What are you, Richert, some kind of gook lover?"

Ben intervened, "Ease off Billy. He's—"

I interrupted, "It's not about loving anyone. It's about doing what works best. Did you ever stop to think these harsh tactics will turn some of these civilians into VC?"

Caleb came back, "Fuck 'em! There all VC as far as I'm concerned."

212

I decided to discontinue the discussion. Nothing I could say would make a dent in Caleb's hostile, black and white attitude.

It appeared to me our interrogator put on the show of force mostly to impress our unit, but he also seemed to relish it. Perhaps fear also motivated his actions—fear of being perceived as weak by our forces, his ARVN superiors, and the villagers. It is safe to assume that before joining the military, he eked out a meager living from the sea or soil. All Vietnamese knew we Americans enjoyed a much higher standard of living than theirs, and many aspired to improve their own. The interrogator's association with powerful American forces, wearing an impressive uniform, and carrying lethal weapons—along with the power and authority associated with the job—had probably gone to his head.

Upon observing many times the way our troops conducted themselves in villages and the harsh techniques employed by Vietnamese interrogators, I couldn't help but wonder, *is this any way to win or sustain the loyalty of rural people to the South Vietnamese government?*

Bridge 104

The 150 foot long wooden structure that our military named Bridge 104 spanned a shallow meandering river, and supported a road leading to Highway 1 three miles east near the coast. A unit of ARVN soldiers provided permanent security. Occasionally our company rotated platoons to assist. Bridges served as vital transportation and supply routes for our forces and the ARVN, so naturally many attracted VC insurgents. Repairing damage caused by planted explosive charges requires expenditure of time, money, and manpower, so keeping the structures secure is an important military objective.

Letter to my Family - October 1, 1969
Living with the Vietnamese

We stayed at an ARVN location just off the road last night. The ARVN's have bunkers and concertina wire for protection as they guard the bridge here. There are ARVN outposts like

213

this one on all bridges because *Charles* would love to plant a charge under the structure and blow it up. I'm hoping we can stay here all twelve days of the mission, the squad leaders think this would be the safest place to be. It would be nice to be in one place for a while so I can build a make-shift hooch instead of having to tear down each day and move each night.

Some of the ARVN's have their wives and kids living here with them. Now I can say I actually lived with the Vietnamese, not many can claim that. Yesterday, I saw the damnedest thing. A young girl had her baby sitting in a C-ration box. The baby had urinated in the box, so I pointed this out to the baby's sister. She removed the baby, dumped the box over, then took a cloth and wiped the inside. A little later on, the sister wrapped the same cloth around the baby's head—yech!

I always wondered why the babysans are always nude from the waist down. They have a shirt on, but no pants. Now, I realize that mamasan doesn't want to go through the trouble of cleaning the baby's soiled clothing.

I notice, however, the kids eagerly grab at the soap we sometimes give away when we can spare it. Most of the people are fairly clean, considering the conditions.

Our platoon sergeant informed us our assignment at the bridge would last four days, not the twelve we had hoped for. He said, "I guess one-third of something is better than all of nothing."

Gary replied, "All is good except for one thing—we have to spend time with the worthless ARVN!"

"They make me nervous. Their behavior is erratic," Larry added.

I agreed, "Yeah—sometimes they act like bratty kids!"

Larry came back, "Only these brats have lethal weapons at their disposal!"

Audiotape - February 9, 1970
VC attack?

A funny incident happened at Bridge 104. It happened in early October the day before I went into Duc Pho to see the doctor about my sores. I stayed back at the bridge instead of going out along the road with the rest of the guys. About 1 PM I saw ARVN's dragging some of their guys back here to the bridge. I wondered what was going on. As they dragged them closer I saw that two guys were shot. One guy was shot in the leg and the other was shot in the arm and chest. The guy shot in the chest was hurt pretty bad. Someone immediately called a dust off to get them off the bridge and to a hospital.

The ARVN's dragging their men were saying, "VC, VC!" I thought, *gee, I wonder what's going on.* Only to find out later—our guys were down the road near the ARVN's. Our guys saw these ARVN's clowning around, gesturing, and pointing their weapons at each other. VC shot them? S-u-r-e the VC shot those two guys (meant to be sarcastic). It goes to show you— and I'm speaking of the ARVN's we worked with, not all of them—many were very immature. It's like giving a ten year old a weapon.

No one in our platoon held the slightest doubt the injuries to the two ARVN's were caused by their own childish behavior, not a VC attack. Earlier in the day I saw a group of them on the bridge shooting at the numerous discarded soda cans cluttering the stream bed below. It appeared they were engaged in some sort of competition because throughout twenty minutes of this tomfoolery they laughed and strutted about like teenagers—sometimes firing their weapons into the air. Although their reckless behavior at the bridge didn't result in any injuries, I kept my distance. Soldiers are supposed to be trained to act professionally, not cavalierly, with deadly weapons. The accidental shooting later that afternoon caused injury, and it's possible the soldier hit in the chest later died. Sadly, it is not the only example of ARVN incompetence I witnessed in Vietnam.

Our company set up for the night on a hillside overlooking a broad, flat valley of rice paddies. The two-foot high dikes separating the paddies provided the only available protection from enemy small arms fire. The next morning and from a long distance, my unit observed a column of soldiers moving through the valley. A platoon of American soldiers from another company formed the lead, while a group of ARVN soldiers followed behind.

Suddenly, the column came under attack from their forward position, but exactly where we couldn't discern because the hillside blocked our view. Shockingly, the ARVN's scurried off toward the rear and out of our sight—leaving the American troops to fend for themselves in the middle of the rice paddies. Our troops took cover behind dikes and began firing their weapons toward the enemy. Less than five minutes later the shooting stopped—a typical hit and run attack. I don't recall hearing about injuries or deaths to the Americans.

The ARVN's should have remained to fight and assist our soldiers, but they took off like a flock of frightened ducks caught in a buckshot barrage. It's a good thing large distance separated our platoon from the ARVN. Otherwise, an ugly situation may have ensued. All of the men in my platoon were furious, and some expressed eagerness to retaliate.

Face red with rage, Gary said, "If I was down there I'd waste those fucking ARVN gooks."

"I hate the worthless bastards," Johnson came back.

I added, "Those guys don't give a shit about fighting for their country, so why should we? This is nuts!"

As if we infantry soldiers didn't have enough stress in the field, we surely didn't need to be confronted with the incompetence and cowardice of our so-called allies. I never learned the ARVN's fate, but most of the experienced soldiers in my platoon suspected they never paid a heavy price for what we perceived as desertion under fire. They were, after all, Vietnamese, and their army suffered from a shortage of forces. Yet more grist for the low morale mill.

ARVN Hill

I mentioned previously that the South Vietnamese Army occupied a small American built base camp we called ARVN Hill. They, along with their families, lived in simple huts located just outside the base. The platoons in our company rotated at providing supplementary security, and we usually stayed between three and five days.

216

Potable water arrived at ARVN Hill via US tanker trucks. Local girls hand-washed American and Vietnamese clothing outdoors the old fashioned way in large, round metal tubs. Civilian clothes and military uniforms hung to dry on rows of lines between buildings, and this picturesque display stirred imagery from home. Throughout her life, Mom never used an indoor dryer, just a series of clothes lines strung between two poles Dad planted in our backyard. No mechanical dryer and chemical softener can come close to duplicating the tactile feeling and fresh scent of bed sheets dried by Southern California sun and kissed by clean Pacific sea breezes. If you have never slept on bedding dried in this manner, you have missed one of life's small, but gratifying pleasures. *Oh, how I miss those fresh smelling sheets and the comfort of my own bed.*

Already crowded ARVN Hill didn't provide adequate indoor sleeping quarters for everyone in our platoon. Some of the guys packed together inside the only plywood building on base with a few square feet of open floor space. I didn't care for this claustrophobic environment so, using my poncho, I set up a makeshift lean-to attached to the outside of the building. Underneath, I stacked a group of empty wooden ammo boxes about two feet high, and placed my air mattress on top. *It's not like sleeping on sun dried sheets, but this is a cozy arrangement.* The bottom edge of my lean-to, about three feet off the ground, allowed me a view of the perimeter while lying down inside. However, someone standing outside and facing my poncho couldn't see me unless they bent over.

In Chapter 4, I described how the local prostitutes, who we called boom-boom girls, tried to act in a sophisticated manner, but their crude rural roots always penetrated through caked-on layers of mascara. One morning while relaxing under my lean-to, I heard someone walking nearby. All outward signs indicated she was one of the base prostitutes. She couldn't see me. Stopping just outside my hooch, she raised her flimsy, flower-patterned dress, and while facing away from my peering eyes, squatted to take a piss in the dirt.

Disgusted, I shouted, "Ugh, number 10, number 10!"

The young girl turned and noticed me, but acted nonchalantly as she continued about her business. "No big deal, GI. You no see nothing."

I had seen enough. As she finished up, I scolded, "Next time go pee somewhere else. It's gross!" Flapping her arms in dismissive gestures, she muttered something unintelligible and scurried away. While cussing under my breath, I got up and kicked dirt over her remnant puddle. Then I thought, *why didn't she use the shitter? Was it because the locals shunned their prostitutes? Maybe, or maybe she just couldn't hold it any longer.*

The base provided four lavatories to accommodate its 150 or so residents. Each plywood outhouse-like shack held three toilet seats secured over holes cut through the base. The waste fell through the openings into metal tubs filled half-way with kerosene. At the end of each day, an elderly Vietnamese worker pulled out the tubs and set fire to their contents. We callously referred to him as, "the old shit burner." During evening hours, the stench of kerosene and burning human waste did not exactly enhance a soldier's dinner appetite. Incidentally, two shithouses were designated exclusively for American use, and the other two were for the Vietnamese. *Heaven forbid Americans and Vietnamese share the same toilet seats.* Sadly, segregation was alive and well in Vietnam.

Camera Caper

When we soldiers went out on half-day patrols, we left our heavy rucksacks back at ARVN Hill, along with one or two men to keep guard. One afternoon I returned hungry and in need of some C-rations. Browsing through my rucksack, I noticed something was missing. It suddenly dawned on me, "Hey, someone stole my camera!" I sought the two men who stayed back to guard our gear and asked, "My Yashika camera is missing—either of you guys seen it?"

Almost simultaneously, each said "No."

Trying to maintain my cool, I asked, "Come on, you guys were supposed to be watching our stuff, didn't you see anything?"

Collins said, "We were here all day, but I didn't see any gooks come near your stuff. I mean, I can't be sure 'cause we weren't watching the stuff every second."

I replied with sarcasm, "Great, thanks a lot!"

218

Collins said, "Sorry, but it's not our fault. Some gook probably snuck over here and grabbed it. You know how sneaky they are and they steal like crazy."

Walking away frustrated, I thought, *those Bozos were probably napping most of the day*. It is a virtual certainty one of the ARVN on base copped my camera. Almost all of our guys possessed one, and because we were together most of the time, it would be nearly impossible to keep a stolen object that size hidden. The clincher is that all but the two men left behind to guard our gear had been with me on patrol that morning.

In addition to losing my new Yashika, included with it were three completed and one nearly full roll of film—one inside and three attached to the strap. I lost about 140 precious images. At the time, my brother Jim served in the Air Force in northern Thailand (Chapter 13). We had met in Bangkok, and I took several pictures with the camera during our one day together. I looked forward to later sharing them with Jim and the rest of my family.

During the remaining days on base I persisted in asking around about my missing items, including interviewing the locals who spoke English; "If you know who took my camera, just have them return all the film and it will be okay." I reiterated, "They can keep the camera—all I want is the film." My desperate pleas went unanswered. None of the items were recovered and my heart ached at the loss. *A camera can be replaced, but not my once-in-a-lifetime pictures from Vietnam and Thailand. Damn, all those happy moments with my brother will now only survive in my memory.*

This experience initiated an artist's palette of emotions—first the *red* rage of anger, then the *blue* melancholy of loss, and, when I thought things through, the bright *yellows* of acquired wisdom. I realized that from the perspective of the average Vietnamese peasant, American soldiers are rich. They saw helicopters bringing us everything we needed, including abundant food, clothing, and other supplies. We didn't have to toil to obtain these items—they seemed to arrive like welcome spring rains. Thus, when the thief stole my camera I could imagine him thinking, *no problem, helicopter bring him new one.* I muttered sarcastically to my buddies, "The sticky-fingered burglar probably sold it on the black market. I hope he obtained a good price."

We soldiers spent very little time actually mingling with the ARVN—mostly by choice. We called them gooks and our attitude and behavior most certainly conveyed superiority. When stationed at Bridge 104 and ARVN Hill, we made no overtures toward befriending or acknowledging the Vietnamese as our allies. When our units worked with ARVN in the field, the soldiers of both armies did not amalgamate. All of the aforementioned difficulties contributed to mutual feelings of alienation between American and South Vietnamese forces. Lack of trust and uneasy cooperation between allies is not the optimal way to win a war.

CHAPTER 11

LZ Gator and Arty Hill

During most of my early months in the infantry, rumors abounded about the impending breakup of the 11th Brigade and its soldiers being sent home. I wanted badly for them to be true, but rumors being what they are, I remained skeptical. Well, as Gomer Pyle might say, "Surprise, surprise, surprise!" In early December, 1969, a report came down through the chain of command announcing the disbursement of several 11th Brigade units, including mine. *Great news...I think?* It turned out most affected soldiers would not be sent home, just reassigned. *But, where? Will I be sent to another infantry company, one that sees a lot more action?*

Two weeks before Christmas I received orders transferring me to an artillery base camp near Chu Lai. My happiness meter went off the chart. *This means I'll have a permanent indoor place to sleep—yes! No more humping mile after mile in over 90 degree heat—no more entering villages in search of Charlie—no more combat assault missions into the Central Highlands—no more surviving on C-rations—no more sleeping in the open and in the rain—no more tormenting bugs—no more living in the filth of the field.* Like a wolf howling at the moon, I shouted, "Good riddance infantry!" A huge weight would soon be lifted from my shoulders—in addition to a 70 pound rucksack.

After kissing the order form, I turned to Ben and Andy to announce the good news. "Hey guys, in four days I'm outta here—going to an artillery base called LZ Gator. Where are you guys going?"

"Don't know yet," Ben replied. "I'll find out in a day or two."

Andy said, "I'm assigned to a desk job in Chu Lai. I guess my college background and teaching experience had something to do with it."

Excited for my friend, I said, "Lucky you! Chu Lai never sees action."

Ben added, "And you have all those nice benefits, like the beach and maybe even an air conditioned trailer. Good for you Andy!"

Andy replied, "Yeah, but I don't want to gloat about it in front of the others. Who knows what hellhole some of these guys may be sent to?"

Andy's expression of humility impressed me, but then I became overcome by a feeling of melancholy. "As much as I want to get the hell outta here, I'll miss you guys. I don't know what I would have done without you. When things got rough you kept me going. Ben, you carry the 60 like it's made of Styrofoam. Unlike me, you hardly ever gripe and you're strong as an ox!

Ben replied, "Thanks. You and me made a good team."

I continued, "Andy, despite all the bad stuff we've been through, we've had some good times. I'll never forget the night you were outside the perimeter taking a shit when the trip flare went off. Your pale bare butt could be seen for miles." Ben and I laughed.

With a forced smile, Andy barked, "Don't remind me. You guys will never let me live that one down. But, it's been great serving with you. Maybe we'll all make it out of here in one piece after all."

Always the stoic pragmatist, Ben said, "Well, we aren't out of here yet, so let's not get careless these last few days."

Asking around the platoon, I discovered none of my comrades had been assigned to Gator. Like Ben and Andy, I assumed they would be scattered throughout the Americal Division.

My last day in the infantry—can't believe it's over. I said my final goodbyes to friends at Duc Pho and boarded a jeep to my new

222

assignment. *What will life on an artillery base be like, and what will I do there?*

"A wise man adapts himself to circumstances, as water shapes itself to the vessel that contains it."
Chinese Proverb

The jeep dropped me off at LZ Gator, a large artillery base spanning about 200 acres, and located a few miles south of Chu Lai Airbase. The facility sat upon two hills of unequal size and height joined together in a pear shape. The majority of the plywood constructed, corrugated, tin-roofed buildings as well as two chopper pads were located on the broader lower hill. My new quarters were located on the smaller but taller upper hill, which rose about 350 feet above the surrounding flatlands of rice paddies.

I learned my new job would be pulling observation duty throughout the night in a 40 foot high wooden observation tower located on the highest point of the upper hill. Like a lighthouse projecting from a peninsula, the tower dominated the surrounding landscape. A ten-by-ten foot plywood observation cubicle, unprotected by sandbags, stood atop a latticework of beams. A long, wooden ladder ran inside the support structure, and soldiers entered the cubicle through a small, square opening in the floor. *I'm going to feel vulnerable sitting high up in that tower unprotected by sandbags, but it'll be gravy duty compared to pulling guard at night in the infantry.*

Letter to my Family - December 16, 1969
My new job

I work in a tower at night looking for possible enemy incoming mortars and rockets. There is a tremendous view of many miles around the tower, so enemy rocket trails are easily visible at night. Should we see this or the flash that occurs when a mortar is fired, we sight in on it using a funny looking periscope-like instrument. We call in on the radio the direction. Artillery is called in on the bad guys, thus thwarting their efforts—at least this is how it's done in theory.

If only one location sees the flashes they must estimate the distance to the target—it's not as accurate as two separate sightings. I'm told things have been quiet for a while and it is likely I will not have the opportunity to use the device. However, TET is coming up and you never know what the little devils are up to.

Soon after arrival at Gator, I met my fellow observers, Stan Webster and Carl Washington. The job required that two men be up in the tower throughout the night, and we rotated shifts. Washington and I bunked in a twelve-foot long plywood hooch located near the tower. Stan quartered separately. Like me, Washington didn't smoke cigarettes or pot. He was a tall, lean, but muscular black man with a gentle, warm demeanor and carefree, giggly laugh. *I think we'll get along well.*

Two rows of sandbags, stacked three feet high, encircled the plywood hooch in which Washington and I would sleep, and only a handful of scattered, torn bags topped its corrugated tin roof. Obviously, maintenance had been neglected for months. The roof offered little protection from potential incoming mortars or rockets. However, adjacent to our quarters sat a small, waist high bunker well protected with sandbags.

Washington informed me, "The two of us will crawl into it if we're attacked. I wouldn't worry too much. I've been here five months and have never had to use it. Charlie's main targets are the two chopper pads, the main buildings, and artillery down below us."

"Okay, that's good news. But, being fresh out of the infantry, I'm very cautious. I always want to know my ass is covered, so I'm glad the bunker is here."

I slept on an air mattress placed on an elevated plywood base, and a poncho liner served as both sheet and blanket. *It's crude but cozy. Sure beats sleeping in the open on wet ground.* Located just outside, a simple plywood structure with a twenty-five gallon metal water container, supported overhead by two-by-fours, served as our shower. A series of five-gallon cans brought up weekly by jeep from the chopper pad below provided our drinking water.

Daytime high temperature during 1970's monsoon season averaged in the low seventies—well below normal compared to previous years. Although it had to be quick and cool, I delighted in the opportunity to shower regularly. In addition, three times each day I took a leisurely walk down to the mess hall. *Just to be able to sit at a table and eat freshly prepared hot meals—it's great! Compared to life in the field, this place feels like the Hilton.*

Hope Pays a Visit

At the end of my first week at Gator I was afforded the opportunity of a lifetime—to see the Bob Hope USO show. On Christmas Eve I hitched a jeep ride to Chu Lai Airbase.

Letter to my Family - December 24, 1969
Thanks for the Memories

Because I'm off during the day, I got to go by myself to the Bob Hope USO show in Chu Lai today. I sat close enough to smell his breath. The show was great! Also featured was astronaut Neil Armstrong, The Gold Diggers, Connie Stevens, the negro girl on Laugh-In (Teresa Graves), a juggling act, some star from a Broadway show, Miss World from Australia—what a doll! A really big *shew*—Ed Sullivan couldn't do it better. Neil Armstrong received a standing ovation.

I used my noggin—I waited until the vast majority was seated then looked for a spot up front. I sat on the ground in front of the first row of seats about 30 feet from center stage. I think I may have been on camera at least once—I was the guy without a hat on. I brought my slightly dirty Kodak camera, but I only had six pictures left and the PX was out of film. Unfortunately, the stupid camera broke after I shot only one picture. I only got one picture, but it is of Bob Hope—I hope it turns out okay. One chance in a million to get close up pictures of famous people and my camera breaks—damn!

225

Sadly, my one and only picture from the show did not turn out. Previously, I found Hope's humor too cornball for my taste. However, on this occasion I laughed until my sides ached. I will always remember Bob Hope fondly for those many years he entertained American troops overseas.

Morbid Fascination

Two weeks after arriving at LZ Gator and off duty for the night, a commotion awakened me at 2 am. *What the hell?* Groggy, I grabbed my M16 rifle and ran out of the hooch to investigate. Parachute flares lit up the lower section of the hill about 500 feet away. The flares are launched high into the sky via mortar tubes, and burn for about two minutes. I yelled up at the tower, "Hey guys, what's happening?"

Washington shouted, "The base is under attack."

"Damn, I just got here and already this shit! Shouldn't you guys come down? You're sitting ducks up there."

"We're okay. There's no incoming here."

I didn't hear any small arms fire or feel rounds zipping by, but just in case of incoming mortars and rockets, I stood close by our little bunker. Other soldiers scrambled about and many asked questions. It soon became obvious our section of the hill was not the object of the attack. Washington waited for instruction via the tower radio, but none came. At our distance from the activity, all we could do is remain on alert and in place. Twenty minutes later, things quieted down and I went back to sleep.

After sunup, I learned a group of VC tried to penetrate the fortified perimeter below one of the chopper pads on the lower hill. They inflicted minor damage to a Huey and other items on the pad. Five of the insurgents were killed. None of our soldiers ended up killed or wounded, and my section of the base never came under serious threat.

On my way to breakfast, I decided to walk down to the location of the night raid to check it out. The five VC bodies, all dressed in black pajamas for cover under darkness, were lined up on the ground near the perimeter. Each showed multiple wounds, mostly from small arms fire. I couldn't help but feel a degree of respect toward the enemy insurgents. *Those guys showed a lot of guts to face such overwhelming numbers and firepower. It's a suicide mission.*

A half-dozen artillery soldiers had gathered to take pictures of the corpses. While I stood at a distance, some of them, seemingly with ghoulish pleasure, snapped close up photos from several angles. I overheard one young man say to his buddy, "I can't wait to send these pictures home so my folks and girlfriend can see we killed these fuckin' gooks." His comment made me cringe. Although many opportunities became available in the infantry, I don't recall seeing any of my former comrades taking pictures of dead bodies. *Why would anyone in his right mind want to share such ugliness with his family back home? Maybe these guys are new in country or haven't seen much action.* Whatever their motivation, capturing a photographic record of the incident, or more precisely its aftermath, became tangible proof they had been involved in a combat situation. I suppose for them the images represented a badge of honor—trophies of sorts. Shaking my head in bewilderment, I walked away.

Washington and Webster

Carl Washington and I called our fellow guard *Old Man Webster* because of his age, early thirties, and balding head. Despite ten years in the army, he remained an E-4. During that length of time most soldiers earn 6 stripes or more.

When I asked him about his rank, Stan admitted, "I've been busted a couple of times."

With a curious smile, I came back, "A couple of times?"

Stan didn't elaborate on what had to be a checkered military history, and quickly changed the subject. His mostly negative attitude showed all the hallmarks of a lazy *Sad Sack* drifting aimlessly through the army. In addition, he smoked two packs of cigarettes a day. Although I didn't dislike Webster, I was grateful he quartered separately from the hooch Washington and I shared. During the month and a half I knew Stan, he managed to stay out of trouble. I had a feeling this might have set a personal record.

227

Although I lived among black soldiers in the infantry, it was mostly outdoors within the context of our communal 23 man platoon. Washington and I spent much of our time together either confined in the observation tower or our hooch.

One day I told Carl, "Do you realize many married couples aren't together as much as us?"

He smiled, "Yeah, but don't get no ideas."

"Don't flatter yourself. You're no bikini clad beauty like I see at the beach back home."

We laughed.

Despite many hours within close contact, Carl and I got along well. He laughed at my silly impressions of various celebrities and characters, and I greatly admired his dedication to family.

Washington and I frequently wrote letters home and he made weekly tape recordings for his wife and baby daughter back home in Maryland. A devoted father, his frequent audiotape messages always conveyed love and caring. Carl was the real deal, American as apple pie. I liked and admired him.

Letter to my Family - January 8, 1970
Weirdo

Today we were sent a new guy, so now there are four of us here at the tower. But this new guy is a weirdo! Take last night for instance—we were discussing the fact that the gate we use to go to the head was now locked with a padlock and the guy who locked it lost the key. This means we have to walk out of our way to use the toilet. We said we wanted to bust the lock open. So this doofus grabs his M16 and starts to put a loaded magazine into it while saying, "I'll use my M16 lock opener." I don't know how serious he was, but I barked at him to get the magazine out of the weapon, and he did. I don't like anybody playing with this weapon—it's too damn deadly.

This guy is like Jack Lemon in the Odd Couple. No kidding, right now he's up in the tower scooping sand off the floor. Ever since he got here he says, "We need this..." or "We should

228

do that..." Also, he doesn't hesitate to mess around with someone else's stuff.

I don't mind the guy that much, but one of the other guys who has been here for a few months cannot stand this character. Tomorrow he's going to Chu Lai to tell the CO we don't want him here. In fact, the supply driver who brings us our mail says we got him because his other outfit got tired of him. I think he would drive me nuts after a while. He is very immature and I don't want to be near when he has a weapon and ammo near him. He has already demonstrated to me he cannot be trusted with an M16.

I'm glad this weirdo wasn't part of my infantry unit. His strange behavior could have led to disaster in the field. I don't remember many personal details about him, including his name. Thankfully, he left after serving with us less than two weeks. I'll never know if he was wacko before joining the army or something happened in Vietnam to set him off. The former possibility is unnerving. In the army's haste to draft more fighting bodies, I wonder how many emotionally unstable young men slipped through the cracks and ended up in combat units?

Adjustment

Once events on LZ Gator quieted down and I learned my job, it didn't take me long to settle in. For one thing, the stability of a day-to-day routine brought a refreshing change from the chaos of the infantry. I spent most of my idle hours writing letters home, reading, listening to Armed Forces Radio, visiting the mess hall three times a day, and chewing the fat with my fellow observers and other soldiers situated nearby. On the days following all night duty in the tower, I usually slept until around noon. Sometimes the booming artillery disrupted my morning sleep, but eventually I managed to acclimate to the noise. Fortunately, the big guns were located on the lower hill and active mostly during the night.

After three weeks on the job, none of us in the tower observed any enemy activity—not a single mortar or rocket flash. After discussion, Webster, Washington, and I decided one man at a time up in the tower would be sufficient. We didn't ask or receive permission to make the change, but decided to take the risk. Officers never came around after dark.

During my months in the field, I became accustomed to pulling two separate one hour guard shifts per night. Despite being exhausted much of the time and having my sleep interrupted, fear that Charlie might be sneaking around always motivated me to remain alert. However, the situation up in the tower posed a different challenge—staying awake throughout the night and coping with boredom. For one thing, the structure's location on top of a hill and away from the guarded perimeter meant I need not worry about an immediate attack directed my way. *Thank goodness no RPG's can reach me here.*

Under the circumstances, I tried my best to remain awake while staring into the dark landscape below. I nodded off episodically, but usually only briefly. In order to help keep myself occupied, I usually brought snacks and munched on them periodically throughout the wee hours. *Although this duty is boring, it sure as hell beats serving those seven hyper-alert months in the infantry.*

Top Secret

One day in late January and just after Webster went home, Washington and I received notification that some high ranking officers would soon meet with us. Their purpose remained hush-hush. My curiosity was aroused, but I also felt nervous because I didn't want some big shots with scrambled eggs on their hats messing with my cushy new job. A few days later, Washington and I joined two officers waiting at the base of the tower. A captain and lieutenant informed us about a new military instrument that had been set up in the cubicle that morning.

In a firm voice, the captain told us, "For reasons of security, do not talk openly about the device, write home about it, or take any photographs. Only select military personnel on Gator are to know about this, and that's an order. Is that clear?"

We both responded simultaneously, "Yes sir!"

230

The captain left. Carl and I, along with the lieutenant, climbed the ladder to check out the piece of equipment. It looked like an ordinary thirty-inch long telescope. Disappointed, I asked, "Sir, what is so special about this thing?"

In a prideful voice, the lieutenant informed us, "This is a very sophisticated piece of equipment. It's an advanced high resolution light amplification device—an improved version of the starlight scope. Even in almost total darkness, the instrument is capable of displaying the nighttime landscape below in incredible detail, almost like daylight."

I had never heard of the starlight scope, so the lieutenant's description aroused my interest.

Before I could ask a question, Carl asked eagerly, "Can we look through it now?"

The lieutenant replied, "Not unless you want to go blind. It's way too sensitive for daytime use. You will be using it during the night to scan the surrounding terrain for enemy movements. A technician will come by tonight at twenty-one hundred hours to show you how to operate it."

The technician arrived on time, and Washington and I couldn't wait to peek through this high-tech thing-a-ma-jig which seemed like a prop from a science fiction movie. Mounted on a sturdy tripod, the scope easily swiveled in all directions. Our instructor went over the details about its operation and invited us to look through the eyepiece. While peering through, I exclaimed, "Wow, the view is amazing! It's like daylight out there, but it looks unnatural. Why is everything tinted green?"

The technician replied, "The device works by amplifying light, and the human eye is more sensitive to and comfortable with the green end of the spectrum."

With childlike enthusiasm, Washington said, "It's my turn." Upon gazing through the lens at the landscape below the base, he commented, "As long as we look through this scope there's no way Charlie can move around out there without us seein' him. I can see everything. I could even see a small animal moving around. This thing could win us the war—it's great!"

Our military didn't keep the device secret exclusively because of its new technology. Night vision scopes had been around for several years, although they were designed primarily to be mounted on rifles. Secrecy on Gator had to be maintained so the enemy would not know our forces had acquired the capability of seeing them move about at night. All Vietnamese villagers surrounding our base were required to remain indoors after dark or they would be considered hostiles.

The technician informed Carl and I to log and report any human movements we detected through the scope so immediate action could be taken—usually by calling in an artillery strike. After the instructor left, Carl and I spent the rest of the night alternating peering through the scope at the terrain outside of the base. The night passed quietly, as did those of the following week.

I enjoy relating this story because it is emblematic of the tremendous technological advances that have transpired since 1970. Our military still uses night vision, but the quality of illumination required of the 30 inch long, bulky scope Carl and I used in Vietnam now comes in the form of goggles. Today, you can purchase a night vision device online and at numerous retail outlets. I saw one advertised that fits into a shirt pocket—incredible!

Wouldn't you know it, just as Washington and I became accustomed to operating the night vision scope, another form of new technology arrived to make our job obsolete.

Letter to my Family - February 9, 1970
More High Tech

Up in the tower is this $56,000 dollar radar set up and it's really something. It's got an antenna on top that rotates about 120 degrees and it has an instrument with a small screen that shows little dots. If there is any movement out there they can see it on the screen and also hear it through earphones because the device also has a sonar apparatus. The instruments are able to distinguish between the movements of bushes and humans. When they pick up human movement the operators push some buttons and it automatically tells them the distance to the blip and the azimuth—the angle from the observer to the target. Then they call in artillery and in another ten minutes or so the artillery hones in on the target. It's unbelievable! So our job is essentially useless because the radar does the job better and faster. In fact, the army is getting rid of these Observation Posts.

The new radar device needed to be manned by a well-trained operator, so Washington and I were now out of a job. Like all good things, Carl and I knew our *vacation* had to end, and soon we would be reassigned—but where?

I told Carl, "My worst nightmare is I'll be sent back to the field."

"Keep the faith, my man. I doubt they'll send you back to that shit."

"Thanks, but I still have over three months left in country. Who knows where they'll send me."

Carl's optimistic prediction came true. In mid-February, I received orders to transfer from LZ Gator to another artillery base located closer to Chu Lai. Upon hearing the news I told my buddy, "Good news—no going back to the field. I've been assigned to another artillery base."

"Told ya', Carl replied. "What are you gonna do there?"

"I don't know—probably pull guard. Where are you going?"

"My orders haven't come down yet, but I'll probably be sent to another artillery base."

One week later we said our goodbyes. I didn't find out where Carl ended up, and never heard from him again. So it goes within the ebb and flow of the army.

Base Camp Arty Hill (Artillery Hill)

In late February and with duffle bag in hand, I boarded a jeep for the short journey along Highway 1 from LZ Gator to a base called Arty Hill. It was smaller in acreage than LZ Gator, and perched on top of a much shallower hill. The highest point rose only about 150 feet above the surrounding countryside. The view to the east overlooked the highway and flat lands of rice paddies extending to the coast about three miles away. To the west and northwest, rice farms and scattered villages extended less than a mile toward densely vegetated hills which increased in size with distance.

Most of the buildings on base were plywood structures with A-framed, corrugated tin covered roofs, but better constructed than those at Gator. Three layers of stacked sandbags or rows of fifty gallon drums filled with sand surrounded their sides. However, the angled roofs could not support the heavy layers of sandbags necessary for protection from incoming rockets and mortars.

If my former dwellings at LZ Gator compared to the Hilton, my new accommodations at Arty Hill seemed like an upgrade to the Waldorf Astoria. Screened and louvered windows ran the lengths of both sides of the hooch. For safety reasons, glass is nowhere to be found on firebases. The A-framed shape of the structure allowed hot air to rise and dissipate through openings on both upper ends, and this kept the temperature relatively tolerable inside. I shared the hooch with three other men who worked in artillery.

Upon first noticing my new sleeping accommodations, I thought, *Wow, this is nice—a real twin size bed complete with metal frame and even a mattress!* After seven months sleeping on the ground in the infantry and then at Gator on an air mattress, the pleasure of lying on a real bed seemed too good to be true.

New Friends

I met new friends on Arty Hill. Before Uncle Sam caught him in a draft, Terry Gibbons had lived the hippie lifestyle in upstate New York. Considering his background, you would think Terry was a pothead, but he imbibed relatively mildly for Vietnam—a joint or two here and there. I liked him. Intelligent and college educated, he enjoyed discussing philosophical and esoteric subjects like whether life exists on other worlds, psychic phenomenon, religion, and geopolitics. Like me, Terry felt embittered at having to serve in war he believed to be misguided and wasteful of human life. The attitudes of many soldiers serving in Vietnam leaned toward cynicism, but with Terry it seemed like an integral part of his personality.

234

Sometimes I found it annoying because in my new and improved surroundings I tended to see the glass as half-full.

When we first met, Terry managed to maintain a vestige of his former hippie lifestyle by wearing a mustache. Strict army regulations demanded they be neatly trimmed and not extend even a fraction below the corners of the mouth. However, in keeping with the civilian style of the time and as a mild act of rebellion, the ends of Terry's mustache drooped into the forbidden zone.

He commented, "I just gotta express my contempt for the establishment when and where I can and try to get away with it. It keeps me sane."

I replied, "Yeah, but you'll have to stay away from the lifers or keep your hand over your mouth. Good luck with that."

Terry's overt act of disrespect lasted less than one week. A lieutenant noticed the one-quarter inch long violations and ordered they be trimmed—or else! A couple of days later I noticed Terry's pride and joy no longer occupied his upper lip.

I said, "Jeez, you shaved off your whole caterpillar. I thought you'd just trim it."

"Fuck no. Those military mustaches look stupid. I hate 'em. If I can't have it my way, the hell with it!"

In an attempt to offer some comfort, I replied, "I'm sure you'll find another way to express your contempt for the army."

He did. During idle hours, Terry often sat outside playing an old, beat-up guitar left by a previous Arty Hill resident. He enjoyed singing popular anti-war folk songs. He wasn't much of a singer or musician, but strumming away helped to keep up morale—his, not the rest of us. A couple of days before leaving Vietnam, Terry asked me and a couple of other friends to join him outside and behind one of the hooches.

I asked, "What's this all about?"

Terry replied, "You'll find out."

"Okay, see you then." *What the hell is this crazy hippie up to?*

Five of us gathered behind the hooch in anticipation of Terry's ad hoc meeting. He greeted us and said, "I wanna get some things out of my system before I go home, and I need an audience."

235

Before any of us could ask a question, Terry began bashing his precious guitar against a three-foot high metal post while blurting several choice expletives about the army and war. *Whoa!* Once the initial shock abated, our group enjoyed watching him behave like some drugged-out rock star on stage. In less than two minutes his guitar became reduced to a pile of splinters. Our little group applauded the spectacle.

None of us had to ask our friend why he chose to rebel by destroying his former musical companion. We knew it was a symbolic gesture to show disdain for having to serve in a war he didn't support. Terry left Arty Hill in early April, two months before my departure date. I never heard from him again.

Guitar smashing Terry Gibbons and Harvey Milton couldn't have been more different. Well groomed and disciplined, Harvey didn't come close to fitting the hippie stereotype. He also seemed out of place within the grit and grime of an artillery base. Unlike most soldiers on Arty Hill, including me, he always appeared in well-pressed, spotless fatigues, along with neatly combed and trimmed military-style hair. Harvey worked at an administrative job at base headquarters, and seemed to come and go as he pleased. No doubt his orderly appearance and diplomatic personality enabled him to nurture clout with the base brass.

Harvey and I became buddies. Like me, he expressed an optimistic outlook on life. Despite an aristocratic Boston heritage, Harvey could never be typecast as an east coast snob. He was down to earth, personable, and loved to laugh. Harvey didn't care to talk about politics and philosophy. Instead, we shared stories about our lives on opposite sides of the USA. He expressed interest in visiting Southern California and taking in its many attractions, and I expressed interest in visiting Boston with all its history.

Harvey and I enjoyed trying to outdo each other with jokes. He seemed to have an endless repertoire and in fitting with his personality type, most came out clean. My terrible puns often elicited groans. The coup de grâce of our attempts at humor had to be my impression of comic Stan Laurel of Laurel and Hardy fame. I didn't have to say a word. All I had to do is imitate Stan's goofy smile or squeaky cry, and Harvey keeled over with laughter. Once he started,

236

we fed off of each other like two giggly teenagers. Harvey and I shared many happy moments during off hours.

Smitten

I didn't see much of the other three men who occupied our hooch because they worked days and I pulled guard throughout the nights. None became friends. However, one of them, Wayne, stands out in my memory. I don't recall his job on base, but he went to work early in the afternoon. Wayne was a handsome young man of average height with angular, chiseled features, and a good build. A full head of wavy, reddish-blonde hair and fair skin scattered with freckles suggested Scottish ancestry. Unfortunately, his good looks didn't match up to his dreary personality. I never saw him laugh out loud, and he rarely smiled. Understandably, most soldiers experienced periods of sadness and loneliness, but with Wayne it seemed like a permanent condition.

I remember Wayne well not so much because of his melancholy mood, but because of his obsession with a local village girl named Kim, age 18. She arrived almost daily to work around our hooch. Like so many young Vietnamese girls, Kim was cute as hell—petite, pug-nosed, and perky. Always ready to laugh, she exuded wide-eyed, youthful energy. Kim's personality couldn't have been more different than that of her admirer.

When I arose around noon after pulling guard duty all night, I usually saw Kim busily cleaning the hooch or ironing soldier fatigues. Almost daily, Wayne sat on his bunk sweet talking her. This routine went on for over a month. Although I couldn't hear everything said and didn't feel comfortable listening in on their conversations, his intentions came through loud and clear.

One morning while lying in bed, I overheard him confess, "I love you Kim. I want to marry you."

Kim responded audibly, "I no love you and you no love me. You just horny GI."

If not tactful, Kim's response was forthright. Although shrugged off, Wayne kept persisting. As days went by he went on about how wonderful their lives would be together in the USA. Many

237

Vietnamese believed America to be *number one*, and many local girls became swept off their feet by American soldiers. Starry-eyed, young and naive, they longed for a romantic and better life away from the hardships of Vietnam with its seemingly endless war. According to Wikipedia, between 1964 and 1975, over 8,000 Vietnamese women married American GI's and came to live in the US.

Wayne seemed to be a troubled, lonely young man searching desperately for love, but as we all know, love often blinds our reason. In truth, he really didn't know Kim very well. Speaking with her a few hours a week within less than a two month period is hardly adequate time to build an enduring relationship. Add in the enormous gap between cultures. Maybe I should have butted out, but when Wayne wasn't around I encouraged Kim to keep standing her ground. I advised, "You might not be happy in America. Yes, it's a great country, but life there is much different than here, and what about your friends and family? Could you leave them behind? Plus, you really don't know Wayne. He's just a lonely GI who is homesick."

Kim confessed, "He make me feel not comfortable. No want to be with him."

With a thumb up, I said, "Good for you, girl!"

To her credit, Kim perceived the unattractive qualities lurking underneath Wayne's handsome skin and lofty promises, and knew she wouldn't be happy hooked up with a Sad Sack. Conversely, a relationship with a young Vietnamese girl certainly wouldn't be the solution to Wayne's emotional problems. People like him usually bring others down with them. Kim stood firm and never bought into his fantasies. I gained enormous respect for this young girl wise beyond her 18 years. By late March, Wayne finally left Arty Hill empty handed—and empty hearted.

Letter to my Family - March 7, 1970
Art and Pot

It always amazes me how so many people are indifferent to things like art and music. By art I mean anything that is beautiful, be it a Cezanne or a sunset. I'm thinking of this right at the moment because there is a really nice sunset tonight. These *marijuana-holics*, so plentiful in Vietnam, should learn to turn on to the world as it is.

The language is preachy, but the above letter is an honest expression of how I felt, and not just at the time. Since childhood I had always been *turned on* to art and the beauty of nature. Although I tried pot before entering the army, no cannabis induced high could compete with the feelings I derived from my esthetic interests and pursuits. Even during days in the infantry when my morale sank low, I sought to find beauty in my surroundings. Some of the photographs I took from Arty Hill of the Vietnamese countryside are breathtaking.

The leaders of my former infantry unit did not tolerate drug usage, and rightly so. Surviving in the bush requires a clear, acute mind. I never saw any of my fellow soldiers in possession of pot or any other drugs in the field, much less using them. In contrast, marijuana usage on rear bases reached epidemic levels. I saw joints almost as big as cigars. Soldiers obtained the drugs from local Vietnamese, and rumors abounded that the suppliers had laced them with heroin or other mind altering chemicals. On LZ Gator and Arty Hill I saw my share of soldiers high on Vietnamese pot, but to me their demeanor appeared no different than those of my indulgent friends stateside. Perhaps our military deliberately exaggerated the dangers in an effort to frighten soldiers away from using drugs as well as doing business with Vietnamese black marketers. If so, it didn't work well.

For most soldiers, drugs and alcohol helped to suppress the stress and discomfort of the war, and the loneliness of being so far away from loved ones. I cannot relate any experiences where drug use caused casualties, but I can relate one story in which a soldier's excessive indulgence negatively impacted my new job.

Santos

Specialist 4 Felix Santos and I pulled guard throughout the night in a perimeter bunker on Arty Hill. A first generation American of Philippine descent, Santos stood below average American male height. His straight black hair, espresso colored eyes, and olive skin typified those of his native countrymen. Conversation helps to alleviate the boredom of having to spend every night pulling guard together in the bunker. Unfortunately, Santos showed no interest in worldly things. In fact, before joining the army, he had dropped out of high school. Except for the mundane day to day life on Arty Hill, Santos and I shared little in common. Although he occasionally displayed a sense of humor and pleasant smile, most of the time his demeanor seemed distant and sometimes gloomy.

Occasionally I asked, "Is everything okay?"

He muttered incoherently or just said, "Yeah," and changed the subject.

I found Santos' moodiness puzzling until one day I overheard a soldier I didn't know refer to him as, "that little gook." Considering the negative attitude most US soldiers held toward the Vietnamese, this was more than just a casual unkind remark. Although not present at the time, Santos had no doubt overheard similar prejudicial snipes before. This, and his superficial resemblance to the Vietnamese, may have been the primary reason for his bouts of introspection, depression, and frequent drug use. He must have felt uncomfortable in his own skin.

Virtually every night beginning around 8 PM, Santos and a couple of his friends smoked pot inside the bunker. During our first week on duty, one of his buddies asked, "Come on, take a drag, Richert. This is good shit. Don't you want to get high with us?"

I replied with a polite, "No thanks. Not while I'm up on guard. Besides, aren't you afraid someone will come by and bust you guys?"

Santos said, "Nah. We've been doing this for three months and no one ever comes by to check on us."

Santos paid little attention to observing the perimeter. When I asked what would happen in the event of an attack, he said, "This base ain't been hit for forever. There's nothing to look for out there. This is gravy duty." I had the feeling he would have found any excuse to justify his pot habit and shirk his responsibilities. On the other hand, my experience in the infantry compelled me to never take anything for granted.

Santos' friends usually left the bunker by 10 pm. Having spent the last two hours escaping Vietnam in a drug induced stupor, my fellow guard curled up on the bench next to the back wall and fell fast asleep. Our job was to stay awake all night and observe the terrain beyond the base perimeter for possible enemy activity. I cannot recall a single occasion when Santos stayed up throughout the night. Thus, night after night I kept watch alone.

On numerous occasions I complained about his behavior, but to no avail. He repeated the lame assertion about the base never coming under attack, so why bother. I could have reported his drug usage and dereliction of duty to our base leaders, but it would have resulted in serious consequences, probably a court marshal. More trouble for an already troubled young man. So, feeling empathy for his situation, I bit the bullet and kept my mouth shut.

It didn't bother me greatly to stay up all night while Santos slept. I had become accustomed to long nights alone on guard at Gator. However, I felt uneasy during the two hours he and his friends smoked pot in the bunker. I worried a superior would come by. One part of me hoped Santos and his buddies would be busted, and one part didn't. Knowing that many senior enlisted men and officers categorized ex-grunts like me as libertine potheads—and despite my innocence—I probably would have been busted along with them.

Letter to my Family - March 19, 1970
Appetite

Lately my appetite has been voracious. I have been eating a lot at chow time. The food is good here on the hill. Today they had hot dogs, raspberry Jell-O, pork and beans, potato chips, and other goodies. Really, I have been eating well since I left the infantry. I have to make up for those many days when all I had were C-rations.

I never saw any fat or even slightly overweight Vietnamese. Their rice based diet is sparse in sugars and glycerides, plus the hot, humid climate causes fat to sweat out like water squeezed from of a sponge. Although already thin upon entering the army, I lost about ten pounds in Vietnam. This translated to almost seven percent of my total body mass. Weight loss among soldiers who served in the infantry represented the rule, not the exception, and it wasn't all due to a decrease in caloric intake. In addition to diet and climate, it's unlikely a foot soldier will add pounds when he is subjected to elevated stress levels, trekking over long distances, light meals, and occasional lack of sufficient hydration.

Despite Vietnam's mitigating factors inhibiting weight gain, several of the older career soldiers in rear areas bore bulging beer guts. Many sat on their asses all day, didn't exercise, and during off hours drank large amounts of alcohol. One of the senior sergeants on base consumed at least a six-pack of beer almost nightly. Military protocol demands that all personnel maintain fitness, so why did commissioned officers allow senior enlisted men off the hook? High ranking sergeants held enormous clout within the army. Based upon their body language and the tone of their voices, some officers, especially lieutenants, seemed intimidated by enlisted men with ranks exceeding E7. It has often been said that senior sergeants really run the army. Bulging beer bellies provided demonstrable evidence that the claim might be true.

"Once upon a time, there was a generation of parents who were certain that Elvis Presley's unashamed hip swiveling was most certainly the end of society."
Charlie Caruso, Puggle FM, an online radio and podcasting station created especially for parents and children

Terms and expressions emblematic of the sixties included—*the times, they are a changin'—the generation gap—don't trust anyone over 30—counter culture—hippies—marijuana—LSD—tune in, turn on, drop out—burn your bra—the pill—free love—all you need is love—make love, not war—hell no, I won't go*. If parents in the fifties worried about moral decline among our nation's youth, parents in the sixties must have thought the apocalypse was upon us. The gulf between generations during the turbulent sixties may have been the greatest in recent American history. Despite the highly disciplined nature of the military, the generation gap nonetheless seethed under the surface in Vietnam.

Letter to my Family - March 19, 1970
Busted

Yesterday, I was caught without my hat on (heaven forbid!) by our illustrious first sergeant. He claimed this was not the first time he caught me without my hat. I claim otherwise, but it is futile to argue with him. He has harassed me before about not having the bottoms of my pants properly bloused or a few buttons not buttoned—so, he gave me an *Article 15* for being out of uniform. Coincidently, my orders for Specialist 4 just came down and he is annulling them as punishment. So, I'll remain a PFC for at least two more months. The nerve of these lifers—they really get uptight over things like this. I wouldn't mind so much except I should have been Spec 4 at least two months ago. Do you think it's fair of them to take away my promotion for something so trivial?

This is nothing, though—I know a guy who was given an *Article 15* for yelling, "Short" (I'm going home soon). Some gung-ho captain didn't like it. The soldier was probably punished for insubordination, but really. What right does some officer have to tell someone he can't yell short? This is the kind of crap we have to put up with in the service.

Most of us draftees described older career officers and enlisted personnel with the disparaging term, *lifer*. Almost every soldier serving in the infantry was young and of low rank. We seldom saw lifers in the field, so out there the *generation gap* didn't exist, nor did *spit and polish* rules. My wallet and I had to learn the hard way that this was not the case on rear base camps like Arty Hill.

Letter to my Family - April 9, 1970
The Light at the End of the Tunnel, Racism, Hypocrisy

Vice President Spiro Agnew says he sees "the light at the end of the tunnel" in regards to the end of the war. Humphrey saw the same light before Agnew and whoever follows Agnew

243

will probably also see the same light. My intellectual friends here on Arty Hill and me always get into deep discussions. Unfortunately, we are all disgusted and bitter about so many things—it is very difficult to be optimistic about the future.

Last night the mail clerk got drunk and threatened Santos, the Philippine guy who pulls bunker guard with me at night. The drunk called him a *spic* and other such names. The mail clerk, a Texan, is prejudiced against Negroes as well. Yet while in their company, he's very friendly with them. So many people, lifers especially, have this George Wallace philosophy— it makes me want to puke! Such people are full of hate. These same people seem to be the biggest alcoholics. They also hate the so-called potheads. I'm by no means defending pot, but it strikes me odd to see some alcoholic lifer staggering around drunk every night like an idiot, then accusing young people of, "blowing their minds" on pot.

Most senior officers and enlisted men—lifers—favored US involvement in Vietnam. Many considered soldiers who expressed skepticism about the war effort as at best unpatriotic and at worst outright traitors. Many openly expressed animosity toward the hippies and anti-war protesters back home. "They outta line the bastards up and shoot 'em," I overheard one senior sergeant say.

Our company first sergeant fit the mold to the letter. He knew I had transferred from the infantry, and he knew I associated with young men he considered anti-war, libertine potheads masquerading as soldiers. Therefore, I had to be one as well. It's called guilt by association.

Knowing the first sergeant's attitude toward me and my associates, one evening in the bunker I asked Santos, "I wonder why he never stops by here at night. He would easily catch you and your buddies smoking pot."

Santos chuckled, "Every night after he's off duty he goes straight to the EM Club. He's a worthless drunk. That's why we don't worry about him coming up here."

Still, I thought Santos and his buddies took a *high* risk by doing drugs while on duty. For one thing, the smell of pot drifted outside

244

the bunker. They didn't seem to care. Whether correct about the first sergeant or just plain lucky, during my three and a half months on Arty Hill, Santos and company were never busted.

Why did so many young soldiers and lifers abuse drugs and alcohol? Some of the answers are obvious—fear of the possibility of injury or death, missing loved ones and life back home, suffering from boredom, living in unpleasant conditions, and enduring intense heat and humidity. However, I think another explanation lies deeper under the surface—the ambiguities about our nation's ultimate objectives in Vietnam and the stagnancy of the war effort.

It's likely some senior officers and enlisted men harbored doubts about the US mission in Vietnam, but fearing retribution, dared not disclose it openly. Some must have felt uncomfortable about sending young men into battle without clear-cut objectives. Such internal conflict had to weigh heavily on their morale. On the other side of the coin, many of the hawkish, hardened senior officers and enlisted personnel felt frustrated by anti-war politicians back home who they believed thwarted the military's effort to go all out and achieve victory. I once overheard a colonel say, "God damn politicians! If it weren't for them, we could win this war in a few months."

It seems almost no one was satisfied about the conduct of the Vietnam War, left or right, young or old.

The Bunker

Before I move forward to the next story, I must provide some details about the perimeter bunker in which Santos and I pulled guard. Built with heavy lumber, including one-inch thick plywood walls, the solid structure sat five-feet off the ground on a latticework of cross-beams. The increased elevation provided improved visibility toward the sloping hillside below. Sandbags and expended artillery shell casings filled with sand provided two feet of protection over our heads—enough to impede a vertically descending mortar or rocket. In sharp contrast, the side walls of our elevated bunker had been left unprotected. Although the thick plywood might slow down rifle rounds, Santos and I were vulnerable to a laterally launched rocket or explosion at or near ground level.

The bunker's forward viewing area, an opening about sixteen inches in height that spanned the front and sides, allowed us to sit comfortably and observe the perimeter without exposing our bodies to potential enemy rifle fire. Santos and I had each been issued an M16 rifle and two bandoliers, which contained sixteen magazines of ammo. Two wall-mounted telephones and a battery operated radio provided us with excellent communication between surrounding bunkers and base headquarters.

We seemed well equipped in the event of an attack, except during my first week at Arty Hill I perceived one problem. I expressed concern to Santos; "Look at the distance between the floodlight to our right and the one to our left. This leaves the sloping hillside below us very dark. The VC could move around there undetected."

Unimpressed, Santos smirked, "The dinks never come around here, so don't sweat it."

I figured that since he had been at Arty Hill for several months and I had recently arrived, my fellow guard knew what he was talking about.

The villages surrounding the base had long ago become pacified—so much so the locals were allowed outside after dark until 10 pm. Not only could they move about within their villages, but between those nearby. Arty Hill had not seen a ground attack for at least a year before my arrival. However, my caution meter, still at a high mark from the previous seven months in the infantry, aroused skepticism; *all this sounds too good to be true.*

Room with a View

Gazing beyond the perimeter during day and evening hours, you would never believe the peaceful appearing countryside below sat amidst a war. I took many interesting and aesthetically pleasing photographs. Basking in evening light, the mosaic pattern of rice paddies dotted with village huts presented a pastoral setting. Rounded stacks of ochre-colored harvested rice reminded me of the haystacks depicted by French Impressionist Claude Monet. Placid waters flooding rice paddies mirrored warm sunset hues. The flatlands below our base eventually gave way to the dark greens of

246

densely vegetated hills, which with distance transitioned into mountains. I even observed a change of seasons. Winter's lime-green rice fields turned gold in the drier months of spring.

Before sunset, I often observed the local inhabitants toiling in the fields. Planting and harvesting rice is tedious, back-breaking work, and I couldn't help but be impressed by the industriousness and tenacity of the people.

Looking out evening after evening over this peaceful agrarian setting, I thought, *I feel safe here.*

Tranquility Interrupted

While up on guard one night in late February, I noticed a dim orange colored light on top of a distant hill. *What is it, a campfire?* I didn't bother to roust my slumbering companion. Not knowing whether our guys or Charlie was out there, I decided to call in and report the light. I provided the map coordinates and about ten minutes later, three or four artillery bursts struck the area. Afterward, the light disappeared and the rest of the night passed quietly. Later I inquired about the incident, but nothing came of it. It looked like Santos was right about Arty Hill being safe after all.

"All things are ready, if our mind be so."
William Shakespeare, from his play, Henry V

By the third week in March, all of the goodies I received from home for my birthday on the 6th had been devoured. Snacking at night helped to keep me awake. After sitting through night after night of calm, my former concerns about the blind spots on the perimeter had become a faded memory. I felt tempted to sleep on guard, but just couldn't do it. The tiger from the infantry still clawed at the back of my mind. I sat in my folding chair looking into the darkness on a moonless March night while Santos slept curled up on the rear bench. At 2 am, all remained quiet as usual.

All of a sudden I saw a short, but bright yellow-orange streak of light aimed in my direction, and immediately another. Both came from the dark area down the hillside to my left. *What...?* I waited for

247

a split second. "Shit—someone is firing at us!" My heart raced as I grabbed my M16 and starting shooting toward the source. I fired alternate bursts for about thirty seconds, but didn't receive any incoming—*weird*. Meanwhile, Santos practically exploded out of his slumber.

"What's happening—are we taking fire—what's happening?"

Pointing, I yelled, "I saw two flashes of light come at me from down there."

The phones started ringing like fire alarms. Confusion reigned and everyone asked questions. I tried frantically to explain what had happened while keeping my M16 and eyes on the perimeter. None of the other nearby bunkers had begun firing weapons because they didn't receive any incoming. I'm sure some of the men thought Santos and I went off half-cocked over nothing.

Someone from base headquarters called and again I explained what happened. They informed me an officer would come by in the morning to question Santos and me. After ten minutes or so, things settled down, but everyone on perimeter guard remained on high alert until dawn. Happily, the rest of the morning passed without further incident.

Just after sunrise, Santos and I, still at the bunker, were subjected to an interview by a lieutenant and my nemesis, the company first sergeant. The sergeant asked most of the questions. Unsurprisingly, his tone conveyed skepticism.

"Richert, why didn't you see this coming? Were you asleep on guard?

I could barely contain my anger, and blurted loudly, "I saw the flashes of light! They looked like meteor trails. That's why I started firing. If I was asleep I wouldn't have seen the flashes." I wanted to add, "...you fucking lifer moron!"

I don't remember what lame excuse Santos gave for his inaction when the shit hit the fan, but the focus of the first sergeant's interrogation remained on me. I stated firmly, "I did my job as best I could. Whoever hit us didn't succeed. Maybe I scared them off." In an effort to buttress my rationale for taking action, I added, "You know, the section of the perimeter where I saw the flashes is poorly lit at night." Pointing, I added, "Maybe someone should add another light over there."

Just then an artillery soldier motioned the group to come down and join him on the hillside. Santos and I accompanied the lieutenant and first sergeant to a six-foot high chain link fence located about thirty feet below our bunker. Astonishingly, we saw two rocket propelled grenades lying harmlessly on the ground at the base of the fence. They lay directly in line with our bunker and the area in which I saw the flashes. The RPG is a thirty-six inch long Russian made shoulder launched anti-tank weapon in common use by the NVA and VC. The twenty-inch long projectile consists of two main parts—a cylinder containing propellant, located at the back end, and a bullet-shaped housing in front containing the explosive.

Analyzing the situation, the lieutenant and first sergeant concluded what likely happened. Making use of the blind spot between floodlights, at least two VC, each carrying an RPG, crawled up the hillside and through a layer of concertina wire to a spot where they could take aim at our bunker. They fired the two rockets in rapid succession, and then made haste to escape. In the darkness, all I saw was the rocket's fiery exhaust.

Santos asked, "Why didn't the two RPG's detonate?"

The lieutenant explained, "It's not likely both were defective, but I think I know why. The detonator is at the tip. Each tip must have penetrated through the openings between the fence wires, but the wider section behind got caught up, and the entire device fell to the ground without exploding. It was a fluke."

The soldier standing nearby pointed and said, "Wow! But sir, aren't these still active?"

The lieutenant replied, "Yes. For now, don't anyone touch them. I'll get a crew to come and pick them up immediately. Meanwhile, you stay here and keep everyone away until they arrive."

The lieutenant and first sergeant, satisfied with my explanation and the evidence, left. Meanwhile, I felt frustrated because I never received as much as a whisper of recognition for my alertness and dedication to duty that night. *They give me an Article 15 for not having my hat on, but not even a thank you for maybe saving lives—bastards!*

Later I told Santos, "Do you realize how lucky we are? What are the odds of those tips not striking the fence wire, and what if the chain link fence had not been there? Jeez, we would have been killed or hurt bad!" I gave up a half-hearted laugh, but it wasn't out of humor. What emotional response or gesture is appropriate when one is confronted with such blind good fortune?

Santos didn't say much, probably because he felt guilty about his night-after-night negligence in the bunker. About twenty minutes after our interview, two soldiers arrived to collect the unexploded grenades, and they were taken to an ammo dump for safe detonation. Meanwhile, Santos and I left for our hooches to try and grab some sleep. I couldn't. My nerves kept vibrating like clashing cymbals and images of the flashes coming toward me reverberated through my mind. Later in the day a soldier I didn't know came to me and said he saw blood on the ground near the source of the attack.

"You must have winged one of them. Good work!"

"Thanks." I didn't go down to check it out. I didn't want to.

The following night, Santos and I went back to our routine of pulling guard in the bunker. In a firm, but diplomatic tone, I said, "Maybe it's time to take this job more seriously. You never know when the shit is gonna hit the fan."

All Santos could muster is a weak, "Yeah."

He managed to stay up throughout the night, but I couldn't help wonder, *how long is this going to last?* Sure enough, after a few days Santos glided back to his normal routine of smoking pot just after dark and then crashing by 10 pm. Frustrated, I thought, *this guy is worthless.*

During the remaining long nights in the bunker, I often pondered recent events and my previous ten months in Vietnam. *I faced several close calls in the field. Yet, here in one of the safest places I could be I come close to being killed only two months before it's time to go home. This is nuts!*

CHAPTER 12

Freedom's Flight

Letter to my Family - April 9, 1970
Short and Nervous

There is too much action going on lately. I'm too short for all this jazz. There has been some kind of enemy offensive going on, but, I think it's close to over now. I guess it's only natural for me to get nervous my last few days.

Like most short-timers, I worried about surviving intact as the end of my one year tour drew near. Stories abounded about soldiers being killed just a few days before or on the day of their scheduled departure. However, I refused to allow negative thoughts to overwhelm the joy I felt at managing to make it through the day to day grit and grind of the infantry, combat, and recent rocket propelled grenades launched in my direction.

It's May 31st, Mom's birthday. I can't wish her happy birthday in person, but soon I'll be hugging the stuffing out of her. I can almost hear her saying, "Your being here is the best birthday present I ever had." *It doesn't seem real. I can't get my head around the fact that in just three days I'll be on my way home.*

On the evening before departure, I said my goodbyes to our housekeeper Kim, my buddy Harvey, and the other young men I befriended over the last few months. Harvey insisted upon seeing my Stan Laurel impression one more time, and I eagerly obliged. I performed his goofy smile and squeaky cry. We laughed ourselves silly. Then a feeling of melancholy came over me. *It's unlikely I would ever see these fine young men again.* I wished them well. *Goodbye friends— goodbye Arty Hill!*

On the morning of June 1st, I, along with my duffle bag, caught a jeep for the brief ride to Chu Lai Airbase. On the way, a series of images from the previous year raced through my mind like the individual frames of film through a movie projector—the close calls, the physical hardships, but also the good things. As the jeep approached the gate at Chu Lai, my thoughts drew back to the present. *I can't believe I'm actually leaving. I'm so excited I feel like I'm gonna pee in my pants!* I boarded a Chinook helicopter for Cam Ranh Bay, my last stop in Vietnam.

Before the war, Cam Ranh Bay earned a reputation as one of the country's premier resort destinations. Incongruously, its deep water bay and geographical configuration served as an ideal military port— one with a long and colorful history. Upon viewing its emerald shallows, azure depths, and snowy white sands, I understood why this former resort came to be known as the "Jewel of Vietnam." *It's so beautiful. But, soon I will be body surfing at my favorite beaches back home.*

While awaiting departure at the transit facility, I ran into three soldiers I knew from training at Fort Ord. I hadn't heard from any of them for the entire year. We arrived in Vietnam on the same day, but each had been scattered across South Vietnam.

"Hey guys, great to see you! Looks like we all made it through in one piece."

Parsons, the only one of us with a soda in hand, raised the can in a toast; "My friends, here's to us for makin' it outta here!"

The rest of us raised our fists and cheered.

Larkin asked me, "Where's Uncle Sam sending you next?"

"After my three weeks leave I go to Fort Hood, Texas where I'll finish out my last five months. Don't know what I'll be doing there."

Parsons said, "I'm going back to Fort Ord, which is good news because I'm from Santa Rosa. I'll only be two hours away from home."

Martinez replied, "Lucky you! I'm goin' to Bragg. It's a long way from my wife and kid in Texas. I never been to North Carolina, but duty there's gotta be a cakewalk compared to Nam."

We shared stories about our year in the war and then wished each other good luck in the future.

June 2nd—it's time! It sure feels good to be clean as a whistle and smartly dressed in my Class-A uniform. A group of us eager soldiers arrived by bus to the airfield, and waited impatiently in line to board the big military jet soldiers called, "The Freedom Bird." *Boy, my heart is beating hard. I hope the VC doesn't decide to lob rockets or mortars onto the airfield. Not now, not now.* As I walked up the steps toward the door, I took a quick look back at Cam Ranh Bay—my last close up view of a country that had profoundly impacted my life. Taking a deep breath, I entered the cool, air-conditioned cabin. An attractive stewardess greeted me with a million dollar smile. It had been a year since I had seen a Caucasian woman—especially one with such angelic features. I wanted to kiss her on the lips and wrap my arms around her shapely physique. *Tame the tiger, Richert!* I just smiled and said hello. Another stewardess directed me to the less desirable middle seat, but my excitement level was so high I didn't feel squeezed between the two soldiers.

The four big engines fired up. The fellow in the window seat turned to me and stated eagerly, "As soon as the jet leaves the runway, everyone is going to cheer like crazy!"

Someone responded, "Yeah, for sure!"

The stewardess ran through the standard announcements about fastening seat belts and airplane safety, but no one paid much heed—it seemed so trivial after what we've been through. *I should go to the bathroom—no, not now—too late. I don't have to go that bad. I can hold it. It's just nerves.* Slowly, all too slowly, the silver bird began the long taxi ride to the runway. *Stop wringing your sweaty hands, Bob.* It was hard to remain still. Someone up front began singing the Simon and Garfunkel song, *Homeward Bound*, and others joined in the soft choir.

Finally, the engines roared at full throttle and off we went. The huge jet lifted off the runway like a dandelion fluff released by a gentle breeze. *We're airborne, we're outta here!* SILENCE! *Why isn't anyone cheering? Why am I not—?* Before I could finish the thought and with a flurry of waving arms and high fives, the men started clapping, yelling, and laughing. "We made it—see ya Vietnam—we're goin' home—I'm goin' home!" Why the delayed reaction? We hesitated because lingering doubts about our safety remained until we were clearly out of potential enemy firing range. The jet banked away from Vietnam and over the South China Sea. Now, most certainly away from danger, my heart rate finally began returning to normal.

The Freedom Bird began winging its way eastward for the long flight across the Pacific. After thirty minutes in the air, the celebration waned, and it became quiet on board. My feelings of elation gave way to relaxation. The pressure and tension of Vietnam began evaporating like rain puddles under a scorching desert sun. *This is the first time I've really relaxed since leaving Oakland a year ago. I feel almost weightless.* The big jet stopped briefly in Tokyo. Like most of my fellow soldiers, I slept during most of the all night flight from Japan to Fort Lewis, Washington.

It's still Tuesday, June 2nd here, but June 3rd in Vietnam—strange. The Freedom Bird had hours ago sped past the International Dateline, and now approached the coast of Washington. *I can almost smell the good ol' USA!* The jet touched down on a welcoming Fort Lewis runway and everyone disembarked in a frenzy. Several of us caught a shuttle to Seattle Airport. *Gotta go check in.* Around 10 am, I boarded a commercial jet headed for LA. This time the stewardess sat me at a window seat. One of a handful of GI's on the plane, I began to feel more like a civilian again. In addition to slurping down endless sodas with lots of ice, I spent most of the three-hour long flight looking down at the beautiful landscapes and coastlines of Washington, Oregon, and finally California. *Oh, those are the San Gabriel Mountains. I'm almost there.* The big bird banked over the mountain range and the vast LA basin unfolded before my widened eyes like a curtain on opening night of a play. *What a magnificent sight—not even hardly any smog.*

254

I planned to meet my dad, mom, and sister at the baggage claim area. My brother Jim couldn't join them because he was serving on active duty at George Air Force Base near Victorville, California. LAX is one of our nation's busiest airports, so I knew it would be a while before meeting my family. *Patience, Bob, patience.* Sure enough, the jet circled several times before receiving the go ahead to land. *Will I ever get there?*

Once on the ground, the Boeing 737 followed a procession of other arriving flights before parking at its designated gate. I looked out the window in hopes of seeing my waiting family inside the terminal, but no luck. After disembarking, I raced toward baggage claim. *There they are, there they are!* I waved frantically at Mom, Dad, and Joanne, whose broad smiles warmed my heart. We met and hugged for minutes. Trying to hold back tears, I said, "We're finally together again—it feels like it's been forever."

Joanne enjoyed sunbathing at the beach, so I immediately noticed her deeply bronzed face and arms. "You're so tan!"

"Look who's talking, dear brother."

I winked, "Touché."

Mom, as Moms tend to do, observed, "You look good, but you lost some weight."

Dad said, "We are very happy to have you home in one piece. I'm proud of you my son. It must have been rough over there."

"Yeah, but it's over. Now I just want to go home and get back to my normal life—at least for my three weeks of leave. None of you have changed, well, except Joanne. Your hair is blonde now. It looks good."

"Let's get the hell out of here so we can beat the traffic," Dad said.

During the half-hour drive to Long Beach, my family caught me up with various occurrences on the home front. I said, "So, Mom, you finally learned how to drive while I was gone. I'm glad I was over in Nam where it was safe!" Everyone laughed. We would have laughed at anything. Meanwhile, I enjoyed seeing the many familiar landmarks lining the 405 freeway. *Not much has changed and it all looks good. I'll never take this place for granted again.* As we pulled into the driveway, I said, "Dad, the yard looks great!" He wouldn't have it any other way. We always entered our modest three bedroom home through the kitchen door, and the first thing I noticed brought a wide grin. On the kitchen table sat Mom's made-from-scratch cherry pie. "Oh, Mom, you made my favorite. I can't wait to dig in to a huge piece!" I gave her a slobbery kiss. Leaning against the pie, a hand printed sign stated, *Welcome home son. We love you.* My eyes welled-up.

Mom said, Go take your stuff to your bedroom and relax for a while. I'm sure you're tired. We'll have dinner in about two hours."

"Thanks, Mom! I can't tell you how many times I looked forward to one of your wonderful dinners, especially all those days in the field where I lived on C-rations."

Dad interjected, "We're having nothing special, just some Spam and canned beans."

Mom gave him a gentle nudge and we all chuckled. "I'm making your favorite—pork roast, dumplings, mushroom gravy, and German red cabbage."

"Oh, boy, can't wait—yum!"

I toted my duffle bag to the bedroom. "Wow, it looks just like it did when I left!" I threw the canvas bag off to one side, removed my coat and tie, and took off my shoes and socks. Lying down on my comfy bed with my hands placed behind my head, I sighed, *it's good to be home. I'm finally home.*

CHAPTER 13

Healing Open Wounds

"We want the facts to fit the preconceptions. When they don't, it is easier to ignore the facts than to change the preconceptions."
Jessamyn West, American Writer, 1902 - 1984

Beginning with sending advisors during the mid-fifties, the US spent almost twenty years and enormous resources in an attempt to win over the hearts and minds of the South Vietnamese people and ensure the survival of their government. During the Johnson and Nixon administrations, military and intelligence assessments revealed that without substantial and sustained US support, the corrupt and unstable South Vietnamese government and its ineffectual army would collapse. Both administrations kept this information away from the public. Then in 1971, military analyst Daniel Ellsberg released to the press the top secret Pentagon Papers, which detailed the above information. Disturbingly, for many years prior to Ellsberg's exposure of the documents, both Johnson and Nixon knew that a continuing presence of US troops in Vietnam would, at best, result in a stalemate. Yet, both pressed forward with the war.

257

The Nixon administration's Vietnamization program was premised on the belief that once US forces gradually withdrew, but with our continuing logistical support and weaponry, the South Vietnamese government would resist the North and survive. It seems Vietnam policy under both administrations relied more upon hope than a realistic assessment of cold, hard facts. Unfortunately, the worst of the cold, hard facts is 58,220 young Americans paid the ultimate price for a war kept going mostly by wishful thinking.

The sobering failures of Vietnam undermined confidence among the American public in our nation's ability to effectively conduct future wars. In its aftermath, our military and political leaders had some soul searching to do. Many experts, critics, and others advised that before sending American troops into countries involved in civil strife, our leaders must assess all aspects of the circumstances carefully, accurately, and dispassionately, and determine if intervention is viable. I believed our future leaders, having learned the painful lessons of the Vietnam War, would steadfastly follow the above advice and avoid future *open wounds*.

"The Iraqi regime . . . possesses and produces chemical and biological weapons. It is seeking nuclear weapons. We know that the regime has produced thousands of tons of chemical agents, including mustard gas, sarin nerve gas, VX nerve gas."
President George W. Bush, October 7, 2002

"Five days or five months, but it certainly isn't going to last longer."
Secretary of Defense Donald Rumsfeld, commenting on how long he believes the Iraq War will last, November 15, 2002

"My belief is we will, in fact, be greeted as liberators."
Vice President Dick Cheney, *Meet the Press*, March 16, 2003

In 2003 and with the horror of 9/11 still festering in the minds of the American public, the George W. Bush administration embroiled the US in another war in which our soldiers became embedded within the civilian populace of a foreign country culturally and religiously different from our own. We all know how things turned out. How is it that they got so many things wrong? Was it naïveté, willful ignorance coupled with excessive zeal to go to war, failure to conduct adequate research, or a combination of the above? The Bush administration and its allies blamed their foreign policy blunder on faulty intelligence. However, before the war began, many in government and elsewhere had expressed skepticism about the veracity of much of the evidence.

I became disillusioned and angry upon learning that no weapons of mass destruction had been found. *How could they make such stupid mistakes? Didn't they learn anything from Vietnam? All those lives lost—and for what? Here we go again*

Healing Public Attitudes

"I hate war as only a soldier who has lived it can, only as one who has seen its brutality, its futility, its stupidity."
Dwight D. Eisenhower, leader of Allied Forces, WW II, 5-star general, American President, 1953 - 1961

During the late sixties most of the American public had become tired of the Vietnam War, to which no end seemed in sight. Unfortunately, a significant percentage of these disgruntled people vented their frustration, not just toward our country's leaders and the military industrial complex, but also the common soldiers, like me, who served.

During advanced individual training at Fort Ord, California, and before I left for Vietnam, we inductees were allowed to go off base on weekends. Some of us visited nearby Monterey, a popular tourist destination. Although we dressed in civilian clothes, our close cropped hair and clean shaven faces shouted—*military!* On several occasions, people out walking or driving glared at us, gave us the finger, uttered expletives and, yes, called us *baby killers.* I wanted to yell back, "Hey, don't blame me! I'm not here because I want to be. I'm against the war." However, fearing causing trouble and possibly facing disciplinary action by the army, I never retaliated. I sucked it up.

After the war, few of us placed *Vietnam Veteran* bumper stickers on our cars or appeared in public wearing hats or clothing proudly announcing our service. Large scale ticker-tape parades did not await us, and most politicians or communities didn't fall all over themselves to acknowledge *our heroes who served us honorably in the military*. People weren't interested in hearing horror stories about the war, and many Vietnam Veterans felt varying degrees of shame and guilt about their service. I did!

Happily, much has changed since those dark days. The Nixon administration abolished the draft on January 23rd, 1973—two months before all US forces were withdrawn from Vietnam. Since then, America has relied upon an all volunteer military. In addition, the overwhelming victory of our forces over those of Iraq during *Operation Desert Storm,* 1990-1, under the George H. W. Bush administration, greatly boosted American confidence in the ability of our military to conduct war efficiently and effectively. As a result, and because of lingering guilt about treatment of soldiers returning from Vietnam, most Americans began showing support and respect for our troops.

Even those who opposed US involvement in wars overseas, like the invasion of Iraq in 2002, expressed compassion and respect toward the soldiers who served. Nowadays, when people become aware I am a Vietnam Veteran, they often say, "Thank you for your service." Although this acknowledgement has arrived late, I am comforted that many in my generation have come to the realization that inflicting their contempt for the Vietnam War upon those of us who served, especially draftees, was misguided.

Soldier Open Wounds

"In war, there are no unwounded soldiers."
Jose Narosky, Argentinean writer

Once US troops left Vietnam, most Americans just wanted to forget about the war and move on. I, too, wanted to put the past behind and move forward with my life. Unfortunately, programs to help veterans cope with the psychological impact of combat were not readily available—not just in the immediate aftermath of the war, but for many years afterward. It wasn't until 1980 that the American Psychiatric Association added a condition they named *Post Traumatic Stress Disorder* to the third edition of the *Diagnostic and Statistical Manual of Mental Disorders*. However, PTSD did not become widely known among the general public until the Nineties, and treatment programs for Vietnam Veterans didn't become in widespread use until early in the next decade. In what I call *the war after the war*, most Vietnam Veterans tried to keep painful memories of their experiences buried deep in their guts. They shut off communication about the subject from family and friends. Many tried suppressing their PTSD symptoms by resorting to excessive drinking and drug use.

Jack

I knew Jack and his older brother Dale from high school. Both brothers were popular on campus, but Jack and I became good friends through our mutual hangout—the bowling lanes near my home. Jack and I decided to join the army together, and we shipped out to Vietnam in early June, 1969. The army assigned Jack to the 1st Cavalry Division in the southern part of the country, and I ended up with the 23rd Infantry up north. During the one year tour we exchanged letters, and on one occasion, spoke on the phone.

The southwestern portion of Vietnam shares a border with Cambodia. Throughout the sixties and out of respect for its sovereignty, US policy forbade our troops from entering the country. Well aware of this fact, the North Vietnamese Army routinely moved men and supplies along Cambodia's eastern edge, and used it as a staging area. According to military leaders, the inability of US forces to cross the border and suppress the NVA impeded our objectives and cost American lives. As a result, the Nixon Administration began bombing missions inside Cambodia in March, 1969. Then in late April, 1970, President Nixon announced American troops would also conduct missions there. The decision, broadcast one month before Jack and I left Vietnam, made headlines and caused heated debate at home.

Not long after we arrived home from Vietnam, Jack told me his unit had penetrated the Cambodian border weeks *before* the Nixon announcement. Jack's revelation didn't surprise me. During my time in the infantry I heard stories about the exasperation many of our military leaders felt over their inability to thwart NVA activities just a few miles across the untouchable land west of the Vietnam border— not just in Cambodia, but also in Laos. I speculate the temptation to cross over and kick some ass must have been irresistible to aggressive senior officers, as Jack's experience likely reflects. Of course, the brunt of the fighting always belongs to low ranking grunts, not decision makers in the rear.

Jack saw a lot of action during the two week long mission, and as if this wasn't bad enough, he contracted malaria. After treatment for the illness, he managed to make it through the rest of his Vietnam tour without physical injury.

A year after the war, Jack confided to me, "My unit got hit almost every day in Cambodia. Guys were dying left and right and I was so scared. Of all my time spent in Nam, those two weeks were the worst. It really messed with my head."

"Yeah, you saw a lot more shit than I did. How you doin' now?"

"I still can't shake the nightmares, I get mad a lot, and I have trouble sleeping."

I replied, "My nightmares come in waves. It sounds like your situation is bad. I've tried to move forward with my life, and leave Vietnam behind, maybe you should try."

Jack looked at me with sad eyes, and said, "I can't...I can't let it go."

Even before Jack opened up to me, I had noticed he wasn't the same happy, sociable person I knew before the war. As time went on, he became more and more reclusive and moody, and more heavily involved with drugs. Drugs became his psychological crutch, pain reliever, and memory suppressant. During the seventies, Jack entered the VA hospital at least twice for recurrent bouts of malaria and related complications, but as far as I know, never for psychological issues.

As the years went by, Jack continued to use drugs heavily and gradually withdrew from my social circle. Eventually we lost contact.

Fifteen years after returning home from the war, I heard he had been living with his mother while struggling to maintain a normal life. Jack suffered from health issues and had difficulty maintaining employment. He never learned to readjust to civilian life and died of a heart attack in 2000. He was 53.

Jack's story saddens me not only because he was my friend, but because his experience echoes those of many returning Vietnam Veterans. Countless numbers suffered from what many years later would be labeled PTSD, and many became heavily involved with drugs and alcohol. Without readily available professional help, the lingering psychological baggage of the war festered. A statistic often repeated is America lost 58,220 young men (including some women) in Vietnam. It's a sad fact that many former soldiers, like my friend Jack, are not counted among the statistics, and their names are not memorialized on any monuments.

"I can't stand the words *get over it.* All of us are under such pressure to put our problems in the past tense. Slow down. Don't allow others to hurry your healing. It is a process, one that may take years, occasionally even a lifetime—and that's okay."
Beau, Taplin, poet

Even today, many Vietnam Veterans still harbor intense negative feelings about their experiences in the war, which continue to gnaw at their guts like cancer. I heard many examples during my sessions of group therapy at the VA. The hardened feelings of these vets are not uniformly directed. Some are angry that, "Someone wouldn't allow us to win the war." Some despise the anti-war movement because they believe it undermined soldier morale and prolonged the conflict. Some resent having been drafted to serve in a war they believed was immoral and unjustified. Some are angry because they believe, "My friends died for nothing." Some are embittered about the negative effects of the war upon their subsequent lives. The list of *open wounds* goes on.

After relating a terrible story, one of the participants in group therapy said, "I lost three friends that day, and for what? That fucking war was a waste of these good men's lives."

I said, "I don't see it that way. Rather than focusing on the war as a whole, I choose to see this issue from the perspective of a grunt on the ground. Wasn't our main concern in Vietnam to look out for ourselves and each other?"

"Damn right!" one member said.

I continued, "Hell, the bottom line is we all wanted to survive, so we each did our part to contribute to the overall safety of the unit. That being my goal, had I died I don't believe it would have been for nothing. It would have been for the sake of my buddies. What's a more noble purpose than that?"

I saw several eyebrows rise, including those of the man who raised the issue as well as the therapist. A few of the participants said they had never thought about it that way. It seemed my message elicited a positive reaction. I felt proud that I spoke up that day.

Hanoi Jane

In July, 1972, actress and anti-war activist Jane Fonda visited Hanoi, the capital of North Vietnam. The communist regime represented her ideal of what revolutionaries are supposed to be— patriots fighting a just war to achieve their independence and freedom. Thus, she perceived the US and its allies as imperialist aggressors trying to impose their will upon an independent nation. She denounced US military policy in Vietnam on Hanoi radio, and posed for photographers while sitting on an anti-aircraft battery—big guns that had shot down American fighter jets. The photo made the front page of newspapers across the world. Jane Fonda's controversial trip infuriated a large swath of the American public. Some military and political leaders advocated she be prosecuted for treason.

I believe it was in the fall of 1972, only a few months after Ms. Fonda's infamous visit to North Vietnam, some of my friends informed me she would be speaking at California State University, Long Beach. I expressed reluctance to go because I still struggled at putting the war behind me. However, my curiosity got the better of me and I joined two friends and attended the outdoor event. I estimate the crowd at about 400 mostly students. Fonda reiterated the standard anti-war slogans I had heard elsewhere many times before, but I thought her inflammatory rhetoric went way over the top. For example, several times she called President Nixon a Fascist and accused our military leaders of crimes against humanity. I walked away disappointed. Rather than offering well-reasoned arguments, it was obvious Ms. Fonda sought to stir agitation among the crowd.

Many Vietnam Veterans are beyond angry with *Hanoi Jane*, as she came to be known. They hate her guts. They believe her public visibility at anti-war events and especially her visit to the North Vietnamese capital contributed to the loss of American lives. Many are resentful, not only because she skated prosecution for associating with and supporting the enemy, but also because her career became successful after the war.

Not surprisingly, Fonda's name came up a few times during my group therapy sessions at the VA. A few of the participants expressed grudging forgiveness, but most of them became livid. One member said, "I'd like to blow the bitch's brains out!" I understand this rage. Fighting against a slippery enemy in a war with no clear objective and no end in sight weighed heavily on the morale of US soldiers. For many, the last thing sagging soldier spirits needed was for some misguided civilian to visit Hanoi and offer support to the North Vietnamese regime.

I cannot find it in my heart to hate Jane Fonda. I think youthful naivety and idealism caused her to become swept away with revolutionary zeal. Do I feel empathy for her? No! She should never have visited North Vietnam.

"I hated the gooks. I will hate them as long as I live."
John McCain, American Presidential Candidate, 2000

From the comfort and security of American life, it is easy to play armchair quarterback and condemn Senator McCain for such odious words. However, who among us has walked a few inches much less a mile in his shoes? I cannot imagine the terrible ordeal he endured for five and a half years inside a North Vietnamese prison camp. It would tear the heart out of anyone.

During his advancing years, Senator McCain came to quell the hatred and find emotional solace. However, residual animosity directed toward a former enemy is by no means unique to former Senator McCain. Many WW II veterans who served in the Pacific theater still harbor hatred toward the *Japs*. Today, many Vietnam vets still hate the *gooks*, and numerous soldiers who served in the Mideast wars hate the *towel heads*. Many of these veterans want nothing to do with and are highly suspicious of people from these countries who came to America and now live in their communities. Ironically, many of these immigrants are refugees who were loyal to our cause and had aided our soldiers. I offer the following excerpt of a poem I wrote while taking a creative writing class at the VA hospital in 2013:

What does it take to hate?
It takes distance
Distance between the haters and those they hate
Haters create stereotypes
      Cardboard cutouts
      Cartoon caricatures
Haters become islands
Because it's hard to hate those close to your heart
It's hard to hate those you know

Healing my Open Wounds

Recall from Chapter 1, the transformer explosion near my studio in the spring of 2012 caused my symptoms of PTSD to rise to a level higher than at any time since I left Vietnam. After two months of suffering from nightmares and anxiety, I decided to seek help at the VA. In June, 2012, two psychiatrists independently diagnosed me with PTSD. The VA scheduled regular visits with a staff psychiatrist, and for over three years I participated in various group therapy programs.

December 14th, 2012 is a date I will never forget—my first orientation meeting for PTSD group therapy at the Long Beach, California, VA Hospital. I tried to contain my nervousness upon entering the room. *Am I going to embarrass myself by crying like a baby in front of the others? Would this session trigger more nightmares? Will I end up worse off than before?* 18 vets, most from the Vietnam era, sat around tables in a small, windowless, unadorned room. Some of them wore camouflage jackets and baseball caps with *Vietnam Veteran* embroidered across the front. Some sprouted long hair and beards, one or two looked homeless, and some looked like me—clean shaven with short hair.

Enter Dr. Huston, psychologist. Her large, round eyes and crinkled brow revealed a confident demeanor. Well chosen words reflected considerable experience at helping veterans cope with PTSD, and to move forward toward healing. She explained the various programs available, and how the process worked. I felt reassured. With affection and respect, I nicknamed her and the other therapists at the VA, *Exorcists.* Yes, it really seemed as if they helped veterans to release their demons.

All in all, I came away from the one-hour orientation feeling optimistic, but I also retained a sense of foreboding about revealing my dark secrets during later sessions. Throughout the day I couldn't help but regurgitate memories from the war. I felt nervous and restless. My anxiety remained at a high level well into the wee hours of the morning. After shifting about in bed for three hours and not catching a wink, I decided to open my computer and start writing down my chaotic thoughts. Although I subsequently made some minor grammatical changes, following is as real and immediate an example of PTSD as it gets.

December 14, 2013
Guts

His guts are splayed out in a thirty foot radius. No, I didn't measure the gore, but it's crystal clear in my memory after 40 plus years. It's about 2:00 AM. I had a sleeping pill, two glasses of wine and went to bed at 11 pm, but I am wide awake and feeling incredibly sober. I didn't have a nightmare as I couldn't get to sleep at all. I just started thinking about Nam and an incident came to mind. Damn, I'm shaking like a leaf! Why am I so anxious? I feel like I've just been through a firefight. It's hard to type and I keep correcting my mistakes, but I must get this down—keep the flow going—get it off my chest. Come on Bob, be strong, you gotta do this, you gotta get some sleep. It's the middle of the night.

Okay, what's my problem? I went to the VA today for my first PTSD group therapy orientation meeting. Dr. Huston says she is going to help us release our demons, and it will hurt until it heals, but I had no idea how much it hurts. It's been forty plus years, and now the demons regurgitate themselves again tonight. Why? They say it is common among men my age. They also say writing it out helps to heal. I sure hope so. Writing has made me stop crying. I want to call my friend Marion. She's a therapist, but it's late and I am so embarrassed, so I ramble on.

Whose guts you ask? He was a South Vietnamese soldier I didn't know, so why should I care? I'm told he got in a fight with a fellow soldier and the soldier threw a grenade at him. It exploded at his stomach and I saw the results. His body was laying face up and his head, arms, and legs looked fine, but his guts were spewed out in a thirty foot radius. I could see his spine even though he was lying face up. The scattered organs were fresh and looked alive, not like those of the shriveled cadavers I saw later in art school. To be honest, it was fascinating and incredibly horrible at the same time.

Why am I writing about this Vietnamese soldier when something even worse happened because of these two idiots? A piece of shrapnel from the ill-fated grenade struck an infant in the center of his chest and pierced his tiny heart. I saw his hysterical mother carrying him to the center of the compound. Her top was drenched in her baby's blood. I guess her child was about three years old. I watched as the last of the child's blood oozed out of the nickel sized hole in his chest, his lips turned blue, his eyes glazed over, and his life ebbed away.

Watching this little infant die under such ridiculous circumstances is the nightmare that haunts me, much more so than seeing the dead Vietnamese soldier. The question I ask myself is why am I conjuring the dead soldier tonight instead of that child?

I know why! I am seeing this dead soldier with his guts splayed out because he is me. My guts are being spewed out after so many years in denial—so many years pretending the war didn't affect me. Me, not me! I am happy, I have a great sense of humor, I come from an Ozzie and Harriet family, and I have lots of friends. I am too smart, well-balanced, and optimistic to let this shit get to me. Yeah, right. That's why I'm sitting here at two-thirty in the morning and shaking as I pound away at my keyboard, spewing my guts out.

It's 3:15 AM, and I feel better now. I will try and go to sleep. Tomorrow in a better state of mind I will look at these hard words and I may decide to delete them.

I hope I don't.

First thing after waking up, I opened my computer. I couldn't wait to see if the words I had written down during my highly agitated state only four hours earlier made any sense. Frankly, it surprised me that despite downing two glasses of wine, taking a sleeping pill, and suffering extreme anxiety, I somehow managed to lucidly express the spontaneous thoughts exploding inside my head during those early morning hours.

My nightmare in a wide-awake state felt like a huge rock pressing down on my chest, but transferring the experience into words on my computer helped to lift the weight. I decided not to hit the delete button because I hoped that sharing this vivid experience might help my family, friends, and others better understand what it is like to suffer from PTSD. The trauma of war does not leave the mind when a soldier leaves the battlefield.

Learning to live with PTSD

After arriving home from Vietnam, I wanted to disassociate myself from anything having to do with the war. I paid little attention to related news items, refused to join friends in protest, and avoided the subject in conversation. Instead of immediately enrolling in college, where political issues thrived, I decided to join the work force. I thought holding a job for a year or so would be my best pathway forward at readjusting to the normalcy of civilian life.

I worked at three different jobs, but in the background my passion for creativity beckoned for expression. After one year in the work force, I thought, *now is the time—I'm ready to go back to college.* I majored in scientific illustration and bio-medical art at California State University, Long Beach. With the benefit of hard earned maturity, I was able to focus on my studies and earn good grades. In addition to the GI Bill, for added income I worked part time at the bowling alley near my parent's home.

Life was good and relatively carefree during my college days. For the most part, I believed I was on the road to putting Vietnam in the rear view mirror. During the day I more or less succeeded in suppressing my bad memories and feelings of guilt and shame from the war, but at night they emerged in my nightmares, which came and went in unpredictable patterns. Until receiving therapy at the VA in 2012, for 32 years after leaving the army I was unaware of many less obvious signs that adversely affected aspects of my life—for example, hyper vigilance and excessive nervous energy. I thought, *this is just me being me.* Interestingly, one form of PTSD expressed itself in a way I never have imagined.

Nightclubs and discos rose to popularity during the seventies. Friends often asked me to join them for a night out, but usually I made up an excuse not to go. On those occasions when I joined them, I invariably left the club early. It wasn't because of shyness, my personality is outgoing. I wanted to meet girls, but not in this environment. I attributed the cause of my reticence to a dislike of discos and dancing. However, I also felt the same discomfort at bars and clubs without dance facilities. In the back of my mind I harbored a nagging fear that something bad was going to happen, and I couldn't shake the anxiety until outside in the open night air. I never gave much thought to the cause—I just chose to extricate myself from these uncomfortable situations.

I haven't frequented bars and nightclubs for well over twenty-five years, but to this day I still feel the same sense of apprehension when I am in an environment in which I perceive chaos may arise—at a sports event in which some fans become rowdy—among groups of raucous teenagers or young adults at the community pool where I live—in a crowded theatre—in the presence of persons who are loud, shrill, or overbearing. I hold on to the fear that somehow, like some contagious virus, the noisy activity will spin out of control and disrupt my peace and security.

Upon occasion I have angrily confronted neighbors about toning down their partying—parties in which people are merely laughing and having a good time. I even become overly agitated when someone nearby is talking loudly on a cell phone. I must restrain myself from shouting, "tone it down asshole!" In all of these types of situations, a lightning bolt of fear strikes my heart. *Something bad is going to happen—chaos is going to erupt.* I have never been able to rid myself of this anxiety.

I've always enjoyed going to the movies, and in years past I routinely purchased a soda to sip during the film. However, as age began enlarging my prostate, I found myself having to rush to the men's room just after *The End* appeared on screen. Often, I stepped up to the urinal or toilet having to go badly, but couldn't let it flow because of extreme feelings of nervousness caused by the mere fact that a line of men stood behind me. I felt vulnerable—so much so and despite the urgency to relieve myself, I often stepped away to find a less crowded and psychologically safer place to do my business. As you might imagine, I had my share of close calls. These days, I never purchase a soft drink before entering a theater. No urges toward movie's end means not having to deal with the ensuing discomfort and panic. Problem solved.

Therapy at the VA finally enabled me to make the connection between my seemingly irrational civilian fears and war induced PTSD. I discovered my feelings of anxiety and foreboding are similar to those I experienced in Vietnam when faced with danger—like becoming involved in a firefight. Why did I not make long ago what seems like an obvious connection? Is it because I didn't want to face the cause? I don't have a definitive answer to this question.

Now that I know why I experience excessive feelings of fear within certain situations, I am better able to cope. No, the anxiety has not faded away, but understanding the cause helps me place the episodes within context. These days if I must visit a crowded bathroom after a movie, it may take a while to calm my nerves and get started, but I manage to get the job done.

"It is easier to build strong children than to repair broken men."
Frederick Douglass: African-American social reformer, abolitionist, and statesman, 1818 - 1895.

Stories involving children are featured predominantly in my book. On the bright side, the many kids who hung around and played games with us soldiers along Highway 1 boosted my morale when I needed it most. On the dark side, the young man hiding in the bunker who succumbed to my grenade still invokes nightmares and deep-seated guilt and pain, and the infant I witnessed die from a piece of shrapnel that penetrated his heart is a vision of horror I will never forget. These and other incidents in Vietnam greatly impacted my future attitude and feelings toward children.

After arriving home from the war, I entered a society far different from my upbringing during the conservative fifties and early sixties. With its many attractions, life in coastal Southern California invites a freewheeling lifestyle. Most of the girls I dated used birth control. Liberation from the fear of unwanted pregnancy enabled them to enjoy sex solely for pleasure. Throughout the seventies I dated a variety of young women, but I never desired to enter into a serious relationship or have kids.

I attributed not wanting to have children to my youthful vigor and chosen vocation, art, which does not supply a reliable, steady income. After receiving therapy, I realized my hesitation ran deeper. My experiences in Vietnam concerning children forever crystallized in my mind their fragility. After therapy I came to understand that wartime memories involving injury and death to young people, along with related nightmares, caused me to feel reluctant, even paranoid, about taking responsibility for their safety. If could not bear the psychological burden of seeing harm done to children I didn't know, how could I possibly cope with harm coming to one of my own.

Children as Healers of Open Wounds

"Anyone who does anything to help a child in his life is a hero to me." Fred Rogers, former TV Host, Mr. Rogers Neighborhood

Despite my apprehension about fatherhood, one positive consequence of my wartime experiences is that I gained a heightened appreciation for the welfare of children. During the eighties and nineties, I rented a second floor apartment overlooking a preschool. Each weekday around 7:00 AM, the kids began playing in a large outdoor area. On most mornings, I took a moment to look out my window and observe the goings on. Some people might be annoyed by the noise, but hearing children laughing and playing brightened the beginning of my day.

Today I live in a condominium complex and during afternoons, youngsters often play in the courtyard between buildings. I find it reassuring to see the kids in my neighborhood playing within a safe environment. Knowing they are happy and secure provides a positive psychological counter-balance to my horrific memories and nightmares involving children harmed in Vietnam.

Beginning in the late seventies and for twenty years, I volunteered as an interpretive naturalist at local Southern California preserves. During this period I escorted hundreds of individuals, families and groups of school kids on nature walks. I derived great satisfaction at inspiring young, curious minds toward a heightened sense of wonder and appreciation for the outdoors. For example, seeing urban children's faces light up upon their first encounter with a wild fox or bird of prey is something special to behold.

In addition to my volunteer work as a naturalist, I occasionally visited elementary schools to give talks about my art. At the time, I specialized in realistic paintings depicting wildlife subjects. I always

273

opened the slide presentation by posing the following two questions; "Raise your hand if you like to draw and paint," and "Raise your hand if you love animals." All hands rose sky high in response to both. I felt accepted immediately. In addition to displaying some of my original artwork on easels, I showed slides depicting the creative process of bringing a painting to life, and included information about my bird and animal subjects. I followed up with an exercise in which they rendered a shorebird. The kids loved my presentations, and their enthusiasm, curiosity, and willingness to learn always won my heart.

Sharing my artistic talent with young people and creating paintings that bring joy to my collectors is not only mutually beneficial, but, as my therapists at the VA confirm, it's an effective form of therapy. These activities have helped to heal my open wounds.

Wolves and Dogs

I chose to end my book with the following stories because of their impact upon my emotional well-being and outlook on life—and because I think their messages are powerful.

R & R (Rest and Recuperation)

After serving four grueling months in the infantry, I ended up at 11th Brigade base camp to receive medical attention for staph infections that had spread over a wide area of skin on my right ankle, leg, and butt. After the doc treated my wounds, the company sergeant informed me an extra R & R to Thailand had fallen into his lap. The army provided every soldier serving in Vietnam with one, four day long R & R to his choice of seven tourist destinations outside of the country.

The sergeant said, "The doctor says a clean environment will allow time for your sores to heal properly. The flight leaves day after tomorrow at 0:700 hours. Do you want to take it?"

"Sergeant, will this R & R take the place of the one I already have coming?"

"No. This one's on us."

"Yes—I'll take it. Thanks sergeant!"

Thailand offers many fine tourist attractions, but most soldiers visited mainly to get drunk and laid. Prostitution constituted big business in Bangkok, and soldiers made lame jokes about the city's name. However, a more important motive compelled me to snatch up the opportunity. My brother, serving in the Air Force, was stationed at Udorn Airbase in Northern Thailand. I called Jim and asked if he could fly down to join me. Despite the short notice, he arranged to meet me in Bangkok on my last day. *I can't wait to see him—this is great!* Meanwhile, I looked forward to enjoying the sights, sounds, and creature comforts of the big city.

"We humans fear the beast within the wolf because we do not understand the beast within ourselves."
Gerald Hausman, author and storyteller

In order to set the stage for the story that follows, I divert from the narrative to relate an analogy: I compare a soldier's demeanor in a combat environment to that of a wild wolf, and the demeanor of a civilian to that of a domestic dog. Unlike their wild counterparts, your average household canine is not compelled to hunt for food, face threats from rival packs, live under harsh outdoor conditions, or have to cope with the resulting stress. Cared for and coddled through time, many of their wild instincts have become subdued. Similarly, most people no longer suffer the hardships and anxieties associated with survival in nature. Humans and their dogs have been tamed by the fruits of civilization.

One memorable day in the early nineties, I visited Wolf Haven, a rehabilitation center near Tacoma, Washington. The facility covers several acres, providing plenty of room for the formerly injured or orphaned wolves to roam. From behind a chain link fence, I spent several minutes photographing and sketching a splendid white male. The differences in attitude and behavior between this wild wolf and the average domestic dog became readily apparent. With razor sharp alertness, the wolf's head swiveled, his ears perked, his nose sniffed around, and his eyes darted about the surrounding area.

I felt privileged to observe at close range an animal so fine-tuned to almost every aspect of his environment. After a few minutes observing and sketching him, I came to a sudden realization—*whoa, his behavior is like mine was in Nam—hyper alert and constantly at the ready*. The day at Wolf Haven reminded me of the quantitative differences between my *wild* demeanor in the infantry and that of my relatively cushy life as a *domesticated* civilian.

Off to Bangkok

After four months enduring the grit and grind of the infantry, I couldn't wait to indulge in the luxuries and comforts beckoning in Bangkok. At the time I didn't give it a second thought, but the situation posed a difficult psychological challenge. Transitioning abruptly from the infantry to a modern city meant the highly stressed, hyper alert, potentially aggressive wild wolf must be tamed.

My flight arrived at Bangkok airport in the late morning, and a bus whisked me and other GI's into town. *It's so beautiful and modern— almost like being home. I'll never take concrete, glass, and paved roads for granted again.* The army had booked me four nights at a hotel located in the heart of the city. Upon entering, I stopped to take in the lobby. *Wow, this is nice, almost like the Hilton, and the air conditioning feels so cool.* After checking in I caught the elevator to my room, tossed my duffle bag into a corner, and looked around. *My goodness, a genuine bed with fresh sheets—this is heaven!* Although I washed up before leaving Vietnam, I couldn't wait to jump into the shower. *The bathroom is so clean and modern. Oh boy, hot and cold running water—and a fresh washcloth—and nice smelling soap!* For ten minutes I enjoyed the gentle flow of warm, sparkling water caressing my body like a masseuse with hundreds of miniature delicate fingers. Embedded grime from the field dissolved from my scalp and skin and spun down the drain. *Good riddance, Vietnam.*

After showering, I put on a snow white hotel robe and spread out on the bed to relax. *Oh, so comfy. I'll sleep like a rock tonight. But, I can't fall asleep now, there's too much to do.* After resting for a half hour, it was up and at 'em to eat lunch and enjoy the sites of the city. During R & R, we GI's wore civvies—civilian clothes. My clothing had been tucked away in my duffle bag since arriving in Nam, so soon after arriving at the hotel I had staff quickly clean and press some of the items. I put on comfortable slacks and a short-sleeved cotton shirt. *I feel great! It's like I'm not even in the army.*

Like most GI's visiting Bangkok, I hired a cab driver to serve as my personal guide for all four days. His fee was inexpensive and he managed to always be on call. Topping my afternoon agenda and inspired by my passion for art, I couldn't wait to visit the internationally famed Grand Palace. Since 1782, the complex served as the official residence of the kings of Siam. Siam became Thailand in 1939. Upon arrival, I noticed countless elaborately adorned spires reaching skyward from steeply sloping and colorful roofs. *This place is magnificent!*

The palace temple houses one of the country's most sacred relics, the 26 inch tall emerald Buddha, which is actually carved from jade. It is set high on an elaborate alter. I couldn't obtain a close up look, and the museum forbade photography of the object. *That's okay, so much more to see.* The opulent palace interiors, abundant in inlayed mother of pearl, ornate statues, and baroque adornments, most gilded in gold, dazzled my eyes. *Geez, this place rivals Versailles. To think a few days ago I was humping the bush. What a contrast.*

The tour of the Grand Palace satisfied my esthetic palette, but after sundown more intimate urges needed fulfillment. The nightclub I visited the first evening appeared similar to those in the states—modern and clean, with a spacious, well-stocked bar and attractive decor—except for one major difference. Young, attractive prostitutes and horny GI's fresh from Vietnam filled the place. *I guess there's no escaping the army entirely, but, my goodness, I can't believe there's so many cute girls—I feel like I'm in a candy store.*

Like the Vietnamese, the majority of Thailand's rural population subsided on agriculture and fishing, and the average family struggled to eke out a meager living. Prostitution afforded young women from the countryside the opportunity to rake in relatively large amounts of cash, which in turn, enabled them to help take care of extended family. Believing this, I could not look down upon these *working girls* just because of the nature of their profession.

My cabbie joined me temporarily inside the club. I asked him, "What's the business arrangement for obtaining a girl?"

"It ten dollar for one hour and fifty dollar for all night."

I replied, "Okay, I think one hour is all I want. So, who do I give the money to?"

"When you choose girl, I come get you and you pay me."

"Okay, I'll call you when I'm ready—in a couple of hours." He left.

It's likely my cabbie and the hotel received a cut. However, ten bucks went a long way in Thailand at the time. Meanwhile, I schmoozed with some of the GI's and downed a few beers to boost my confidence. The time arrived for me to take my pick from the plethora of prostitutes. I scanned the room and honed in on a petite beauty named Kim. Kim is a common name is Southeast Asia, but in her business it probably served as a convenient alias. My cab driver arrived and I paid him a crisp ten. Off my *date* and I rode to my hotel. As we talked along the way, I felt excited, but also nervous.

Kim, who spoke English better than the girls I encountered in Vietnam, asked, "Where you live in America?"

"I'm from California. Do you know where that is?"

Kim's eyes lit up; "I know—Beach Boys from there, no? I like Beach Boys music very much. You like?"

"Oh, yes! I live near the beach, and I go there all the time."

"You do surfing?"

"Not with a board—I like to body surf—just me and the waves. It's lots of fun!"

Kim knew which of my buttons to push. Talking about life at home dissolved my anxiety. The untamed wolf from the wild turned into a cuddly puppy of the city.

When the two of us arrived at my room, I felt unsure of myself. My pre-war episodes of intimacy with the opposite sex amounted to mostly kissing and petting, and I never before made love to a girl I had just met, much less one from a strange country far from home.

Through kind words and gestures, Kim made me feel comfortable. Soon she lay on the bed naked and motioned for me to join her. I just stood and stared at her beautiful, well-proportioned body. Her unblemished skin, smooth as a China doll, her breasts, small but perky, and her pleasing smile lured me forward. *Oh, my...*

Not to boast, but our intimate affair lasted longer than the standard two minute boom-boom encounter in Vietnam. Flippancy aside, this experience was about more than gratifying my carnal urges. It served a greater need by allowing me to release huge amounts of pent-up tension from the war. When the time arrived for Kim to leave, I escorted her to the door. I gave her a kiss and hug, and while slipping an extra three dollars into her hand, said softly and sincerely, "Thank you Kim. You are kind and beautiful."

"Thank you, Robert. You good man."

I lay down on the bed and relived the experience in my mind. It had been a long time since I felt so relaxed and satisfied, and I drifted into a deep sleep. The next morning I awakened feeling totally refreshed. *I haven't slept nearly this well for over four months. What a great night!*

After a second day of sightseeing, I went back to the nightclub to seek another romp. I asked about Kim, but learned she wasn't available. *Oh, well, plenty of other girls to pick from.* I decided to have a few drinks and relax for a few hours before choosing a girl. I socialized with other GI's, but eventually ended up at a table by myself. My mood shifted toward thoughts of having to go back to the bush after this brief, but wonderful respite. *Only two more days left, damn! And right after seeing my brother, I have to go back to the field. I don't know if I can handle this. I need another drink.*

I believed alcohol would smother my qualms. It didn't. Instead, I drank too much and became rowdy. The wild wolf reemerged. The anger, frustration, and pressure of four months in the infantry could not be suppressed by a nice hotel room, civilian clothes, a visit to the Grand Palace, and even the previous evening's pleasure. On my way to a nervous breakdown, I started cussing and carrying on like a drunken sailor in a sleazy backwater bar.

"I'm not going back to Nam. I don't want to die. Don't make me go back to that fuckin' hellhole. You can't make me..." In an anguished voice, I begged, "I wanna stay here. Bring me another drink. I wanna a girl to keep me warm and safe. Where's my girl?" This back and forth rant went on for several minutes.

Some GI's out of my view yelled, "Shut up, asshole!"

I probably would have become involved in a fight, but a couple of Thai nightclub employees came over to settle me down. I submitted to their polite, patient, yet firm manner. I'm sure these bouncer/psychologists had seen American soldiers like me unravel many times before, and they knew just how to handle such situations.

Although I didn't make the call, my cab driver conveniently showed up. Despite my state of intoxication, I demanded to select a date

Motioning to one of the girls, my cabbie said, "She very pretty—you take her!"

I complied, and the three of us walked to his cab—well, I staggered. During the ride to the hotel I gained better control of myself, but my date seemed indifferent. She hardly spoke or smiled, and did not exude warmth and kindness. *She's no Kim, that's for sure. Oh well, maybe it's 'cause I'm so drunk.* Upon exiting the cab, my date slipped and almost fell, and just as the two of us entered the hotel elevator, she fainted. "What the hell?" While keeping the door open I called for help and two hotel employees arrived. My cab driver soon showed up to assist. The girl regained consciousness, but appeared groggy.

My cabbie looked up at me and said, "I take her to doctor."

Feeling guilty, I replied, "I'm so sorry—"

"No worry, she be okay." My cabbie put his arm around the girl's waist in support, and escorted her out. Feeling embarrassed, confused, and no longer in the mood, I boarded the elevator, stumbled to my room, and crashed.

The next morning I felt awful, and it wasn't just because of a terrible hangover. Sitting on the bed with my hands on my face, I muttered, *what the hell did I do last night? Boy, was I a jerk. I'm so ashamed. Yesterday I was happy and feeling like a civilian again. What happened to me?* I didn't have an answer.

During breakfast I mulled over the previous night's debacle, and suddenly a bulb lit up in my head. *I'll bet the girl faked the fainting spell. She and the others just wanted to get rid of me because I was too drunk and acted like an idiot. But, why go to all this trouble? Why didn't the girl simply tell me at the outset she wasn't interested? Maybe because they figured I'd want another girl, or maybe it's because she and the others didn't want me to lose face—it's an Asian thing.*

The more I thought about it, the more the conspiracy made sense. It unfolded like a mini-play, and everyone involved, except me, knew their part. My cabbie had selected the girl, and the two of them cooked up a scenario in which, without having to overtly reject my advances, she could exit the situation while leaving my ego intact. *Brilliant!* Under my aching head I managed to force a smile; *they sure had my number.* No doubt I wasn't the first GI to fall victim to a feigned fainting spell.

I jump ahead of my story. Unfortunately, I arrived back in Vietnam with an embarrassing souvenir from Thailand—I caught the clap. *Damn! And I thought Kim was so cute and clean. Hell, she was probably with another guy just before meeting me—yuck!* It hurt like hell to urinate, so soon after arrival at Duc Pho base camp I sought medical attention. With appropriate discretion and the standard robotically delivered lecture about personal hygiene, using protection, and avoiding prostitutes, the army doctor treated my ailment.

"Brothers don't let each other wander in the dark alone." Jolene Perry, American writer

On my third night in Thailand, I decided to enjoy a quiet dinner alone and sightsee near the hotel. *After the humiliating experience last night, no way am I going out and end up in a drunken, rowdy rage the evening before meeting Jim.* Most importantly, I wanted a good night's sleep so I would feel in top form by morning. My plan worked. I slept well and awakened feeling thoroughly refreshed. Meeting my brother preoccupied my thoughts. So much so, I put my underwear on backwards. *Oops! Take it easy Bob—you'll be together soon enough.*

My cabbie arrived around 11 am, and we drove to pick up Jim at the Military Air Terminal. On the way, my heart raced like a cheetah and I couldn't stop wringing my hands. The anticipation of seeing my brother sent the wild wolf scurrying in full retreat with his tail between his legs. I entered the terminal and looked around. *There he is—I can't believe this is happening.* Waving like a man shipwrecked on a

281

deserted island who just noticed a passing boat, I yelled, "Jim, I'm over here!" We met and hugged.

Jim couldn't help but notice my gaunt appearance.

In a reserved voice lacking in sincerity, he said, "You've lost some weight, but look good brother—haven't changed much!"

I appreciated my brother's effort at diplomacy. Putting both hands on my concave, taught belly, I replied, "All that humping and living mostly on C's won't make you fat, that's for sure. But, you look real good, and we're both so tan."

During the cab ride downtown, Jim told me about his job, and how upon rare occasion, the base took rocket fire from local communist rebels aided and abetted by neighboring Laotians.

"I was never close to the action—it was no big deal. Not like the shit you've been through, brother."

I replied, "Yeah, the infantry sure is a bitch. But, I'm glad you are reasonably safe up there. Only one month left in Thailand, huh, short timer? I'm happy for you."

My cabbie drove us downtown and we lunched at a place known to serve American style food. We ordered a couple of cheeseburgers, a pile of fries, and ice cold soft drinks.

Jim said, "This food is good. The burger is better than the ones they make at the snack bar on my base. They must get their meat from water buffalo. This tastes like real beef."

"I guess 'cause there's so many GI's here, they cater to us. Plus, it's not hard to make a hamburger. I tried the Thai food and really like it, but you know how it is—we crave our favorite food from home.

Jim replied, "Yeah, I really miss pizza."

"Funny you say that because last night I had one—"

Jim interrupted, "They have a pizza place here?"

"Yeah, but the one I ate was awful. The sauce had no flavor, and the crust tasted like cardboard. I guess Thai and Italian cooking styles don't mix."

We laughed, and carried on with casual conversation.

I spoke little about the war because I didn't want to go down that road. Nor did I mention my embarrassing episode at the nightclub. I just wanted to be in the present and enjoy every precious moment spent with my brother. We reminisced about Mom's wonderful cooking, Dad's passion for his model airplane hobby, our sister Joanne's love of dancing and her frequent trips to the beach—and all the good stuff we both missed so dearly.

Before entering the service, Jim and I hung out at a neighborhood bowling alley. During our junior and high school years we hit the lanes every chance we could, and made extra money keeping score for evening leagues. Mom and Dad often joked that we practically lived there. I think my brother would agree these were some of the happiest days of our youth. Before Jim arrived in Bangkok, I inquired at the hotel concierge whether the city had a bowling alley. I expected a puzzled response like, "What's a bowling alley?"

Surprisingly, the clerk replied, "Yes. Very nice—not far."

Wow, this is great—Jim is going to love it!

After lunch Jim and I headed off to Bangkok's best lanes. Upon entering the modern building, we paused wide-eyed to take it all in.

Jim said, "Look—just like the bowling alleys back home, brother. It's amazing!"

"Yeah, and this place is bigger and nicer than our humble little sixteen lane house. Can you believe it? And we're in Thailand. Geez, being here with you almost makes me feel like I'm home. This is unreal."

Jim asked, "Loser pays for the games, okay?"

I snapped back, "Get your money out brother."

I lost the first game badly, so I needed an excuse; "Damn! I can't get a good grip on this lousy house ball. The finger holes are too big."

"Sure, blame it on the ball. You can't hit your ass at home, so why should it be any different here?"

I smiled while gently punching him in the arm.

Jim and I clowned on the lanes by imitating the inept styles of some fellow bowlers back home, inventing our own bizarre techniques, and distracting each other.

I said, "Everyone around us must think we are crazy."

Jim replied, "Who cares? Now watch this great form..."

We laughed until our sides ached. Although Jim hadn't seen much action at Udorn, I sensed that like me, the steam boiling inside the pressure cooker of being away from home and loved ones needed to escape.

Letter from my brother Jim to our parents - October 14, 1969
Bowling with Bob

We went bowling Sunday. I swear, we had such a riot—we laughed for hours. It was really great to see Bob again. I felt so bad seeing him having to go back while I only had 30 days left. He wants so bad to get home for Christmas—hates that Goddamn Vietnam!

I wanted our time together to last forever, but the hours zoomed by. My heart ached at having to part with my brother. At the cab stand in front of my hotel, we said our goodbyes and gave each other a bear hug. I didn't want to let go.

Jim offered parting words of encouragement he knew I would appreciate; "You better take care of yourself over there brother, 'cause once we get back home and start bowling again, I'm gonna kick your ass

"You wish!"

While watching the cab drive away, a smile came over my face and waterfalls of tears ran down my cheeks. I don't think Jim knew at the time how much our visit meant to the state of my emotional well-being. He could not know how the infantry had created the wild wolf in me. During our visit on that wonderful day, Vietnam seemed a million miles distant and home seemed only a bowling alley and bear hug away.

On the way back to face the war, feelings of uncertainty haunted my psyche. *Had I not met Jim my last day—who knows? Would I have spent another night causing a ruckus in a bar, or done something even worse? And what's going to happen to me when I get back to the field? Well, at least now I know when things go bad, I can always think about my time with Jim— one of the best days of my life. I hope that'll get me through.*

My spirits soared to the stratosphere during those precious moments we shared together in Thailand, and I felt a sense of closeness to Jim like never before.

284

Thank you dear brother...for saving me.

"Travel is fatal to prejudice, bigotry, and narrow-mindedness."
Mark Twain, American writer

Letter to my Family - April 9, 1970
A Changed Man

You will probably see some changes in me when I get home. Despite my bitterness and pessimism now, I think there are healthy changes. For the first time in my life, I have been exposed to all types of individuals and had to live with them under the worst of conditions. While here in Vietnam, I have gained insight and perspective that I never dreamed possible. But—it still wasn't worth the trip.

I wrote the above letter from the perimeter bunker on Arty Hill at the beginning of my guard shift three weeks before my scheduled departure from Vietnam. The beautiful pastoral view of villages and rice fields highlighted by the setting sun inspired me to reflect on my previous ten months. In June, 1969, I began a journey down a winding, dirty, and treacherous road toward greater experience, maturity, and wisdom. In retrospect, perhaps Vietnam *was* worth the trip.

Epiphany

On my way to group therapy for PTSD at the VA one day in 2013, I noticed a sign promoting a creative writing class designed for veterans and held weekly at the hospital. I signed up. Following is an expanded version of the first composition I wrote for the class. It was also the first time since leaving the army I had written anything about my year in Vietnam. Writing proved to be good therapy, and before I knew it, a few short essays sent me on a literary journey that became this book. I chose to end with my first ever essay because its message is one of hope.

285

"You know, sometimes I think there should be a rule of war saying you have to see someone up close and get to know 'em before its okay to shoot 'em."
Colonel Potter, the character portrayed by Harry Morgan in the television series MASH

Colonel Potter's comment reveals an ugly truth of war—demonization and dehumanization of the enemy is intended to ease a soldier's conscience when he is called upon to kill his fellow human beings.

I grew up in a suburban neighborhood with the many creature comforts average Americans take for granted, and all my friends and neighbors were white. I had never before visited another country, much less one as poor as Vietnam. The lifestyle and environment of the rice farmers and fishermen I encountered seemed worlds away from mine. They hand-built their crude huts, which we called hooches, from local materials, and lived without electricity or plumbing facilities.

Seeing villagers, even old ladies, defecating in rice paddies caused me to cringe in disgust. We Americans sat on furniture. The Vietnamese squatted on the ground—a degrading posture, I thought. Many chewed betel nut, which gradually turned their teeth black. Local tradition held that blackened teeth conveyed stature. I thought it disgusting. Although many of the Vietnamese girls of my age were physically attractive, their unrefined manner turned me off. Overall, I looked down on the Vietnamese people as primitive and inferior. Like my fellow soldiers, I called them *gooks* and *dinks*.

The primary mission of the infantry in Vietnam was to foot patrol through various sectors in search of enemy Viet Cong and the North Vietnamese Army. When visiting outlying areas, we grunts seldom knew whether village residents were loyal toward the South Vietnamese government and our forces, or the communist North. This uncertainty created a tense atmosphere for civilians and US soldiers alike. We entered villages with extreme caution, and treated the residents with suspicion and sometimes hostility. American soldiers often burned to the ground entire villages known or even suspected to harbor Viet Cong. Sometimes our forces destroyed

286

dwellings and killed civilians purely out of revenge—a result of festering rage resulting from previous battles in which friends had been injured or killed.

During November, 1969, I had been in country for six months of my one year tour. Our unit received orders to conduct a mission into the Central Highlands, where some of the worst battles between American forces and the NVA took place. A squadron of helicopters picked us up near the east coast and dropped us into a remote valley.

Numerous small villages dotted the vast rice growing terrain to the west, but we soldiers seldom encountered civilians or farms in the densely vegetated highlands. After trekking through the forest for three days, my platoon saw no signs of the enemy—or anyone, for that matter. While on patrol during our fourth day, we came upon a shallow, open valley, and noticed a handful of hooches along with a few acres of rice paddies. As we approached, I didn't sense danger.

I told a soldier near me, "I bet these Vietnamese haven't had much contact with either the NVA or American soldiers."

"Hope not," he replied.

It had rained daily during November, but most of the time it fell as a light mist. Not on this day. As we moved toward the village, it started coming down in torrents. *Jeez, this is the worst downpour I've ever been in. It's even hard to see.* In a panic of pounding rain, my soaked-through squad sought shelter anywhere it could be found. We made haste toward a nearby hut. All seven of us burst inside at once, and crowded together just inside its bamboo door. A Vietnamese man, his wife, and two small children glared at us in shock. What a sight we must have been—foreign soldiers standing almost a foot taller than the adults and draped with rifles, grenades, and bandoleers of ammo. However, once the initial surprise wore off, the man and his wife began smiling and nodding respectfully. Some of us reciprocated. I'm sure the couple understood we entered just to wait out the cloudburst.

Unlike some of his peers, squad leader Bryant didn't show contempt for the Vietnamese. He advised; "Guys, we burst in here unannounced and this couple has young kids, so let's cut them some slack. For now, just be polite, and when the rain lets up we'll leave."

After a few minutes, the couple offered us food.

287

I said to my fellow soldiers, "I can't believe this—these poor people want to feed us!"

My buddy Greg replied, "I don't think we should eat it 'cause we might get sick."

With hand gestures and smiles, we conveyed, *no thanks.*

The parents, an attractive couple in their late twenties, wore what we called *pajamas.* No, they weren't the typical American style bedtime clothing. Instead, this practical daytime attire consisting of a pair of black or cream colored silk pants and a long-sleeved, button-down silk shirt. Two or three pair probably filled out their wardrobe. The two children, between two to three years of age and wearing only shorts, huddled together in a crib-like box. Their straight, jet back hair, cut short at the sides with a crop like a small pony tail toward the top of their heads, typified that of the family's Buddhist heritage.

My thoughts drifted back a couple of months earlier when I witnessed a child about their age die from a single piece of shrapnel that had penetrated his chest and pierced his tiny heart. The incident caused me considerable distress. However, these two infants, so irresistibly cute and cuddly, warmed my heart. I doubt they felt the same way about me or the other men. Their big, brown eyes stared at us alien intruders with fear, but also childhood curiosity.

Having nothing better to do, I looked around the hooch interior, which appeared about the size of an average American living room. This small space served the entire indoor needs of the family—living room, bedroom, storage, but no kitchen. Most Vietnamese farmers cooked their meals outdoors. Several impeccably arranged implements and tools hung on the walls, and I noticed some appeared hand-crafted. The walls, table, and two-person cot-like bed were constructed from mostly cross-woven palm fronds supported by bamboo poles and bound by strips of fibrous plant material.

I whispered to machine gunner Ben, "The bed doesn't look comfortable, but it's well made."

He replied, "It beats sleeping on the ground like we do."

Everything in view appeared skillfully built and crafted—including the thick bamboo struts carefully fitted and tightly tied to support the walls and roof. Listening to the rain pummeling against the thatched roof, I said, "Hey guys, no leaks—can't say that about some

American homes." Overall, the interior appeared well organized, neat, and clean. This peasant farmer, perhaps with help from his wife and neighbors, had hand-built the hut, furnishings, and many of the implements.

Impressed by my surroundings, my mind soared home. My dad once labored at construction and learned to be handy with tools. He enjoyed working around the house and yard, and felt great pride in his accomplishments. I looked at the humble farmer and thought; *like dad, this man is proud of his home and family, and it shows. They manage to live in relative comfort in a wilderness area without the benefit of plumbing and electricity, or a nearby supermarket and hardware store. I sure as hell couldn't do it.* Inside, I saw none of the familiar decorative items found in my suburban home—no collectables, lamps, curtains, or artwork. Yet, and for the first time, I began to feel comfortable inside a Vietnamese dwelling.

After twenty minutes or so, the rain let up and it was time to leave—back to the war. After the squad exited, I paused to give thanks to our hosts. Smiling broadly, I waved approvingly with open hand toward the children and home interior. Hoping they understood the meaning, I gave the parents a thumb up and said, "Number one!"

Early upon my arrival in Vietnam, I learned that rice farmers endured a hard life in a harsh environment inside a war. They eked out a bare-bones living without basic modern conveniences. Sadly, during my previous six months in country, none of this ever hit home. Not until I entered this modest hooch and took the time and effort to observe and absorb its interior in detail did reality begin to sink in. *I have been in dozens of Vietnamese hooches. Why didn't I notice any of this before?* The question haunted me, but the answer became clear. Although I had *looked* into huts many times before, I had failed to *see*. Prejudice had blinded me.

As our platoon moved on, I became overcome with humility. I simultaneously felt guilt about the way I had previously thought about, talked about, and sometimes treated the Vietnamese people. At the time I couldn't have realized it, but I was on the road to fulfilling Colonel Potter's wish—I began to appreciate the Vietnamese people as equal *human beings*, not primitive, inferior *gooks*.

During those few minutes crammed inside the poor, but in many ways rich, family's homey hut, my eyes, heart, and mind opened up like a blossoming flower. I gained maturity and wisdom far beyond my twenty-two years.

If only more people, especially those living within cultures where religious, ethnic, and racial animosities fester, could experience an epiphany like mine. If only...

Made in the USA
Columbia, SC
18 May 2021

38110003R00181